Greenhouse Gardening as a Hobby

THE AUTHOR'S GREENHOUSE

Books by James Underwood Crockett

GREENHOUSE GARDENING AS A HOBBY
WINDOW SILL GARDENING

GREENHOUSE GARDENING

as a Hobby

James Underwood Crockett

DOUBLEDAY & COMPANY, INC.
GARDEN CITY, NEW YORK

To my mother,
who first taught me to love flowers,
and to my father,
who helped me build my first greenhouse,
this book is affectionately dedicated.

Contents

Contents

LIST OF ILLUSTRATIONS

PHOTOGRAPHS

LINE DRAWINGS

COLOR ILLUSTRATIONS

Greenhouse Gardening as a Hobby

WELCOME!

For years my wife has been living under idyllic conditions, according to her friends at least! Each guest, it seems, says, "Oh, Margaret, I wish my husband would buy me a greenhouse like yours!" Only then does the truth come out—the green-thumber of the family is the husband, and he spends his time with a greenhouse instead of a sports car or a motorboat. Nonetheless, a greenhouse, I have found, is a joy to the whole family, yes, even to a neighborhood boy, too, who shyly asks now and then if I could perhaps make up a little corsage for his current girl friend. Such a comment as "You grow Orchids too?" always gives the owner of a greenhouse a real boost even though he knows that with a greenhouse anyone can grow Orchids.

Welcome to that fortunate group of flower lovers who can garden all year long. If you have wondered if you can afford a greenhouse, do something besides wonder. Find out for yourself how inexpensive one really is to build, to maintain, and to heat. No lover of nature ever experienced a greater thrill than you will that first cold rainy day when you stand snug and warm amid your flowers, listening to the pelting of the storm outside.

Do you gain the impression that I am an enthusiastic greenhouse hobbyist? You will be, too, and to help you pilot a course through the rocks and shoals I have set down in plain language some of the things you will need to know. When you have mastered this basic training, your interests may lead you to more technical reading. For your guidance a bibliography is included which will give you an opportunity to pursue your hobby through such intriguing channels as advanced Orchid culture, the growing of rare plants, and commercial greenhouse practices.

One of the side effects of owning your own greenhouse is that you suddenly become a demigod. You are lord and master of sunshine and shadow; you become a doctor, a dietician, a rainmaker, and an exterminator. It never showers until you say the word; plants go hungry until you give them nourishment; bugs hold sway until you arrive with your armaments; sickly plants languish until you and your magic potions appear! All this semidivine business is just fine until you think the situation through; then the job becomes somewhat frightening! Luckily Mother Nature has not deserted you; you will find that the same laws that guide the world of growing things outdoors still apply within your glass garden, except that most of the natural disasters never occur.

Let's talk about leisure time in a greenhouse. The day you feel like gardening is the day you can do it; cold and snow, rain and darkness need not keep you from your flowers when you have the spare time and the inclination to be with them.

Controlling the weather is just a matter of setting a thermostat. Heat turns on and off to suit your wishes; ventilators rise and fall to the commands of another thermostat, closing when the weather is cool and opening when it becomes too warm for your plants. Automatic watering is practical for many plants and easily installed. Even the humidity of the atmosphere may be maintained in its proper balance through the use of a humidifier.

If you need further coaxing, just remember this: It is easily within your means to have a tropical paradise in your own home, complete with Orchids and Hibiscus, fragrant Jasmine and Gardenias, climbing Stephanotis and Passion-flowers, exotic jungle plants, even Palms. Pipe in some Hawaiian music and you'll think you're on the beach at Waikiki!

J.U.C.

Concord, Massachusetts

Greenhouse Gardening as a Hobby

CHAPTER I

SO YOU WANT A GREENHOUSE

Every person who ever grew a house plant has a secret longing to have a greenhouse where he is sure that he could grow plants so much better than he can on his window sill. His idea is a valid one, and, better still, having grown house plants, perhaps without realizing it he already knows many of the most essential things necessary to growing plants in a greenhouse. He particularly understands the need for light (the most limiting factor in growing plants in houses) and knows that a greenhouse offers him all the daylight of outdoor gardening with the warmth and comfort of indoor gardening.

It comes as no surprise to flower lovers to hear that horticulture is the most popular hobby in the United States and Canada and, without a doubt, in all the countries of western Europe as well, where the art of gardening has reached its most advanced forms. Yet, how many have stopped to consider that this marvelous hobby is available to most of us for only seven months of the year. A greenhouse changes all of that and lets us pursue our floral interests regardless of rain and cold, snow and darkness. We can enjoy gardening when we have the time to spend on it in spite of the inclemencies of the weather. Glass gardens offer us throughout the year the relaxation and pleasure we know in spring, summer, and fall. How often we find that an hour in the garden will loosen taut nerves and let us forget the tensions that have us tied in knots.

Most flower lovers garden at a distance. A hoe handle usually separates them from the miracle of germination and growth, but in a greenhouse most plants are grown at bench level. There is little stooping or bending necessary, and with the world of growing things at an intimate level one has a greater awareness of the beauty and wonder of the world around him. The redolence of warm fertile earth and the fragrance of living flowers give to indoor gardening a charm rarely known to those whose gardens are exclusively outside.

It used to be that home greenhouses were the privilege of the wealthy alone. That was back in the days when boilers had to be hand-fired and ventilators had to be watched constantly throughout each day and opened and closed manually time and again as the temperature fluctuated. No wonder only an estate owner could have a greenhouse, for he had to be wealthy enough to hire a man to take care of this greenhouse, in addition to buying it in the first place. It is our good fortune that automatic controls now have taken over the drudgery and in fact do the jobs better than they can be done by hand. Thermostats sense the slightest changes and command their electric servants to alter their settings accordingly.

The age of mass production has reached horticulture, making available fine-quality, low-cost greenhouses which any man can assemble. No longer does greenhouse construction require skilled artisans. Today's greenhouses can be put together with a few simple tools. All parts, including glass, come precut and are decidedly easier to fit together than the jigsaw puzzles which six-year-olds master.

Greenhouses and outdoor gardening are not separate undertakings; they supplement each other to a wonderful degree. All gardeners have special plants that they would like to protect over winter or that they would like to propagate. A greenhouse offers them that opportunity. When you have a greenhouse it is no trouble at all to start a bunch of seedlings in the springtime and have them at the flowering stage when the weather becomes warm enough to set them outside in the garden. How many gardeners wish that they could grow some exotic plants in their gardens, but know that it is impossible because there is no way to help the plants live through the winter. With a greenhouse one can grow them in tubs and take them inside the greenhouse during the inhospitable seasons of the year. In that way a northern gardener can enjoy the charms of such tropical plants as Bird-of-paradise, Hibiscus, Oleander, Camellia, and countless others, in addition to the plants he can grow outdoors throughout the year in his garden.

It is easy to gain the impression that greenhouses belong only in cold climates, but how misleading that idea is. Gardening is one of those all-engrossing interests which make each hobbyist an addict, who wants more no matter how much he already has. Today we find greenhouses in such semitropical settings as Miami, just as we find them in Minneapolis and Montreal. Where you live does not seem to matter. If you are an ardent gardener, you want a greenhouse.

Strangely enough, by far the greater part of those who would love to have a greenhouse have never even investigated the cost. They have a preconceived idea, originating no doubt from the fact that wealthy men used to be the only ones who could own greenhouses, that a greenhouse of their own simply would be beyond their means. If this book does nothing else, I hope that it dispels this fallacy. Greenhouses for the amateur gardener are very inexpensive both to build and to heat. They may be had in any size from that which will fit over a window to an elaborate structure of any dimension. Most home greenhouses average ten to twelve feet in width and fifteen to twenty feet in length and cost far less than such things as motorboats, which have rightly become a part of modern living. Greenhouse manufacturers have even taken the cue from other lines of business and now offer their products in such a way that they can be financed over a period of time so that one may enjoy his greenhouse while he is paying for it.

CHAPTER II

THE GREENHOUSE ITSELF

Choose the Right Greenhouse Style
Surely every gardener knows a greenhouse when he sees one, but even so he might be at a loss to describe the construction details of any but the most simple ones. Briefly, there are two main types of home greenhouses, the freestanding and the lean-to. The freestanding greenhouse is shaped more or less like a little house having sides, ends, and a roof which pitches away in two directions from a central ridge. Freestanding greenhouses may be attached to a building or not, since they can stand alone. A lean-to greenhouse is best described as being a "half greenhouse." It must be built against the wall of another building and so is always an attached affair. Figure 1 diagrams typical greenhouse profiles.

Whether or not you buy a freestanding or lean-to greenhouse depends upon several factors. You must decide which style will adapt itself best to the architecture of your house, for one thing. The space available and its relationship to your home grounds has a lot to do with the shape of the greenhouse you buy. You are well advised to consult greenhouse catalogues carefully and get the assistance of a trained greenhouse representative to give you sound advice. Once your greenhouse is built, even if it is not the way it should be, you will be loath to tear it down and rebuild it!

It is well to consider convenience. If your greenhouse is a lean-to or an attached freestanding one, you will always be able to enter it from your house even if the weather is not pleasant. A detached greenhouse sitting by itself is not always easy to reach and may be more difficult to heat.

Among prefabricated greenhouses there are several distinctive and attractive roof styles from which to choose. The simplest is shaped like a conventional house with straight sides and an even-pitched roof. A beautiful variation of this style is one in which the eave section joins the roof and sides in a lovely sweep of curved glass. Still another very popular style features a gambrel-like profile in which the side walls of glass are tipped in at a slight angle from the vertical and joined high up to a relatively short expanse of roof. This style of greenhouse also may be had with curved eaves, giving a graceful modern touch to the lines of the greenhouse.

The greenhouses mentioned thus far must be constructed on a solid foundation, a subject covered more fully later in this chapter. There is still another style of prefabricated greenhouse, however, in which the side walls are glass all the way to the ground. They are not recommended for severe climates, but for sections where winter temperatures rarely go below 10 degrees Fahrenheit.

Construction Materials

At this point it would be well to mention the materials used in the framing of modern greenhouses. As might be expected, the trend nowadays is toward more and more aluminum, though wooden greenhouses will always have their place. Those of us who built our greenhouses a decade or more ago made them of heart redwood or cypress. There are many greenhouses standing today that are fifty or more years old which are made of these durable woods, and they are still in service. However, and this is important, wooden greenhouses require periodic painting, which is both an expensive and time-consuming task. An aluminum greenhouse will last indefinitely and always be clean and beautiful. Also the various parts of the framework when made of aluminum can be stronger though of smaller dimensions; thus when the two types are compared, the aluminum one wins on the score of allowing more light to reach the plants since its smaller parts cast smaller shadows.

All of the greenhouses described so far are available in prefabricated form. The manufacturers include detailed assembly plans so that anyone can put them together by following simple directions. Each part is numbered, and when the job is done in its proper sequence, there is no mystery to it at all. These prefabricated greenhouses have several notable advantages over homemade greenhouses. First, all the parts are prefitted so that skilled labor is not necessary to construct them. Also, it should be pointed out that since the parts are standardized, it is a simple task to add on to an existing greenhouse of the same design. All of them come sectionalized so that one may buy as many or as few sections as he needs. Since they are mass produced, the unit cost is very low as compared to building a single greenhouse of similar materials. Of course, it goes without saying that all the parts of greenhouses are designed for greenhouse conditions. For example, all sash bars have built-in drip grooves to collect and carry off condensation so that it will not drip on and ruin plants.

Perhaps this would be a good time to mention the mistake of trying to make a greenhouse out of ordinary lumber such as one can buy at a local lumberyard. First of all, unless one uses heart redwood or cypress, the wood members will soon decay under the extreme moisture and humidity of a greenhouse. Even wood preservatives do not protect ordinary wood for long under these conditions. Next, it should be pointed out that unless small-dimension lumber is used, so much shade will be cast by the roof bars that light transmission will be seriously impaired. Then we come to the factor mentioned earlier regarding dripping from the roof bars. Roof bars have to have a means of collecting and carrying off the cold waters of condensation. Regular wooden greenhouse roof bars have drip grooves milled into their sides to handle this problem.

You Can Build Your Own Greenhouse

It is possible and in some cases practical for a person to build his own greenhouse. In the first place it should be pointed out that he should be, or should hire, a skilled carpenter for the job. The materials, however, may be purchased from greenhouse manufacturers, just as commercial greenhouse operators purchase theirs, and used to build one's own greenhouse. Such a greenhouse is not expensive to build, and if one is skilled, there is no reason why he should not build his own greenhouse. It would be wise, however, to have one's plans checked over by a representative of a greenhouse company before starting construction so that he can be sure that the design is one that is practical for plant growing. It is easy enough to say that one can build his own greenhouse, but he should know that greenhouses should be constructed in certain ways both to save money and to ensure that the greenhouse will be one adapted to plant growth. My statement regarding the question of building a greenhouse oneself or buying a prefabricated one is this: I am convinced that, all things considered, a person is able to buy a greenhouse for less money than he can build one of comparable quality, and I recommend that any person seriously considering getting a greenhouse buy a prefabricated one. They are engineered to grow plants; they are inexpensive; and they are attractive.

Greenhouse Foundations

It should be pointed out that greenhouse prices do not include foundations. Masonry foundations are built by the buyer to certain sizes ascertained from the greenhouse manufacturer. They should be constructed of concrete or cinder blocks, stone, brick, poured concrete, or some other material that will give them strength, and the footing upon which they rest should extend below the frost line in the soil so that they will not heave during the freezing and thawing of the soil. Foundations, especially in the case of an attached greenhouse, should blend with the foundations of your house and be built with the height of the greenhouse in mind. For example, if the top of your greenhouse is going to extend nine feet above the foundation, and you have a low house roof or some other obstruction, be sure to allow for it when you build your foundation. It would be embarrassing to have the peak of your greenhouse coincide with the middle of an upstairs window. In my own case, I sank the floor of my greenhouse two and one half feet into the soil so as to have my greenhouse roof come under the eaves of my house. With greenhouse benches two and one half feet high, from the outside looking in, plants appear to be growing right at soil level.

Orienting Your Greenhouse

How should a greenhouse be oriented in relationship to the sun? Perhaps that question has never occurred to you, but it must be taken into consideration by commercial greenhouse men who intend to make their living from the plants they grow in their greenhouses. The opinion of most experts in the field is that greenhouses should ideally run roughly east and west, a few degrees north of east and south of west being the best possible orientation. How does all this affect home greenhouses? First, it means that a south or southeast exposure is the best for a home greenhouse because it thereby can get the most benefit from the winter sunshine. An eastern exposure will do quite well because it will get the early morning sun. A western exposure is not so good because by the time the winter sun gets around to it, its rays are weak and the light is not very strong. In a western exposure a greenhouse usually is subjected to strong winter winds also, which make heating more costly. Manufacturers of home greenhouses say that if you have a location where plants can get at least three hours of sunlight a day, there are many plants you can grow, and that is surely true. I might even say that if the only exposure I had was one facing north, I would still have a greenhouse. In such a house the usual flowering plants would not thrive, but foliage plants would be beautiful, and African Violets, Tuberous-rooted Begonias, Achimenes, and many other plants, including some Orchids, could be made very happy.

Have an Outside Door!

In planning your greenhouse you should think through the whole subject carefully and get some expert on-the-spot advice from the representative of a greenhouse manufacturer. For one thing, it is imperative in my mind that an attached greenhouse have a door leading to the outside. If you have ever tried to carry soil, fertilizer, dirty flowerpots, and dripping plants through a living room to get them into and out of a greenhouse, you will know what I mean. A greenhouse should have an outside exit, and the door should swing outward so that potted plants can be grown in front of the door if you wish, and only a few need be moved if you want to squeeze in and out of the door. (I say *squeeze* here, for every person who ever has a greenhouse soon finds that it takes a shoehorn to get another plant into it.) You should plan to make your greenhouse as large as you can, then learn to live with it, for it can never be large enough to hold all the plants you will want to grow.

Some Like It Hot; Some Like It Cold

Relatively few beginners are aware that some greenhouse plants require different temperatures from others. A greenhouse is a place where all kinds of plants can grow, they think, but that is not true. It is well known that Daffodils grow outdoors in the chilly air of springtime and that Orchids come from the humid jungles of the tropics. It is not easy to reconcile the different needs of such dissimilar plants while growing them in the same greenhouse. One thing a person can do is this. Get several inexpensive thermometers and check them for accuracy, then distribute them throughout your greenhouse. You will soon find that certain places are definitely warmer or cooler than others, and you can place your plants with this in mind. A warm corner may harbor an Orchid while the exposed end of the greenhouse might be cool enough to keep a Daffodil reasonably happy.

The real way to settle this question is a very simple one. Build a glass partition in your greenhouse and keep one section at a warmer temperature than the other. Thermostatic control will take care of the problem of temperatures very easily. This suggestion is more than an ideal. Nothing will be more frustrating to you after you get your greenhouse than to find that there are many plants you cannot grow because they will not thrive in the temperatures that the rest of your plants need. The time to put in the partition and separate heating zones is when the greenhouse is being built. At that time the cost is relatively small, though it will cost you considerably more in money and inconvenience if the job is done later.

This suggestion has taken only a few words to make, but it is one which should be acted upon by every person who wants to have a home greenhouse. Plants differ tremendously in their temperature needs, and it is foolhardy to ignore this fact.

Site Location

It is well to consider how you intend to use your greenhouse so that you can locate it accordingly. Some gardeners like to have their greenhouse stand alone in the yard so that the plants will have the benefit of full light from all directions. It is also easier to fumigate a detached house, too, since there is no chance that fumes will invade a dwelling. On the other hand, the convenience of being able to step from the house right into the greenhouse without getting cold or wet has its advantages too. My own greenhouse is off my study, and in addition to the glazed door leading into it there is a large picture window overlooking the plants. Over the years it has proved to be a very happy arrangement. Another suggestion is to have sliding glass doors that open from a living room into a home greenhouse; such a setting can be attractive beyond words, bringing the glamour of the greenhouse right into the home.

An attached greenhouse also has the advantage that it is usually easier to heat and generally can be connected to the existing heating system of the home with little cost. A detached greenhouse can often be heated by extending a home heating system also, but it should be no farther than fifty feet from the house and will require extensive underground preparations to carry heat to it without undue loss.

Plastic Greenhouses

If you have done much investigating of greenhouses, you have discovered that plastics are sometimes being used to replace glass. The following discussion of the pros and cons of using plastics should help you make up your mind as to whether you want to use plastics or glass. In the beginning it should be asked why there should ever be a trend toward the use of plastics at all. The answer is simply that it costs less money to erect a plastic-covered greenhouse than it does one covered with glass; therefore, commercial greenhouse men have turned to plastic as a way to increase the size of their growing area at a minimum cost. It should be pointed out that under these circumstances appearance is not important, and, no doubt, that is the real answer to the whole question with regard to home greenhouses. Most of us want our home greenhouses to look nice, and it is difficult to achieve this with most flexible plastics.

In general there are two types of plastics, the flexible and the rigid types. The rigid plastic combines a plastic with fiber glass and is of the kind often used to cover patios or carports and is colorful and durable. Such material is sometimes used to glaze greenhouses devoted to the culture of Orchids, since they thrive in the less intense light conditions encountered in such structures. This type of plastic is an exception to the rule that plastics are cheaper than glass, for the cost of each is very much the same. For special purposes these greenhouses are excellent and highly recommended. It must be remembered that these plastics are not clear like glass, but have the value of diffusing light rays so that a greenhouse constructed of this material has a very uniform light condition throughout the entire structure.

There are many different kinds of flexible plastics, of which polyethylene is one of the most common. It is used by many growers, but it has to be replaced nearly three times a year since it does not stand up under heat. Such a material is not practical for a home greenhouse.

Polyvinyls are another "family" of plastics sometimes used in commercial floriculture. According to tests made by the George J. Ball Company, West Chicago, Illinois, who are specialists in commercial greenhouse products and seeds, the polyvinyls tend to attract dust and to darken rapidly.

The one type of flexible plastic which so far seems to hold the most promise is DuPont's Weatherable MYLAR. I have seen a greenhouse covered with this material after three full years' exposure to summer and winter weather, and it appeared to be still as good as new. It is clear and glossy and extremely tough, and a greenhouse can be covered with this material for about one third the cost of glass. As with all plastics it is difficult to keep all the sags and billows out of the material, but it seems to be the best on the market to date.

In conclusion, it is my opinion that the only plastic that has a place in home greenhouse construction is the rigid type and that for only limited usage, for though it lets in light, its structure is such that one cannot see through it as one sees through glass. A glass-covered greenhouse will last a lifetime and, especially when combined with an aluminum framework, gives a structure that will remain fully serviceable as well as beautiful.

Weatherizing Wood-frame Greenhouses

There is a unique method of cutting down on the maintenance of greenhouses which have sash bars made of wood. The usual method of glazing is to set the glass in a bed of putty or glazing compound and hold it in place with special glazing nails. Now one can buy aluminum "bar caps" which, set in a glazing compound, are screwed directly to the sash bars. Thus only glass and aluminum are exposed to the weather, and all outside maintenance is eliminated. This is a highly recommended procedure for both older greenhouses and new ones constructed with wooden sash bars.

Protection Against Glass Breakage

Hailstones! The very thought strikes terror into the hearts of greenhouse men, though they can insure against loss from this type of damage. Certain parts of the country rarely have hail-storms, and if they do occur they cause minor damage. Other places have hailstorms nearly every year; so the greenhouse oper-ators protect their glass by constructing a permanent wire-mesh covering over it. Roller shades, described in Chapter IV, make ideal hail covers which may be lowered when needed.

Pit Greenhouses

See Chapter XI, "Greenhouse Stretchers."

CHAPTER III

GREENHOUSE FURNISHINGS

Now that we have discussed greenhouses themselves, we have arrived a bit closer to the point where we can talk about plants, the ultimate purpose of having a greenhouse at all. Right now we must get an idea of some of the items we should have inside a greenhouse to make it a proper place in which to grow plants.

Greenhouse Benches

The most bulky and perhaps most important greenhouse "furniture" consists of the raised benches upon which most plants are grown. Those not familiar with greenhouses might well ask why in the world we need benches upon which to grow plants in greenhouses while outdoors we simply plant them in the ground. Such a question is certainly a valid one, for it brings into focus one of the really important factors concerning the growth of plants in greenhouses. Growing plants in raised benches gives a gardener perfect control of the soil and drainage conditions under which he grows his plants. Ground beds, especially in the winter months, are apt to be poorly drained and cold. A spell of dull cloudy weather affects plants adversely under the best of conditions, but when they are in ground beds there is little that a greenhouse grower can do to offset its influence. The convenience of being

Various bench arrangements possible in lean-to and free-standing greenhouses. Courtesy Aluminum Greenhouses, Inc., Cleveland, O.

LEAN-TO MODELS

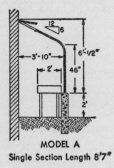

MODEL A
Single Section Length 8'7"

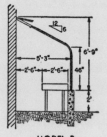

MODEL B
Single Section Length 8'7"

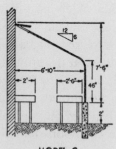

MODEL C
Single Section Length 8'7"

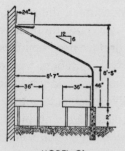

MODEL GL
Single Section Length 10'0"

FREE STANDING MODELS

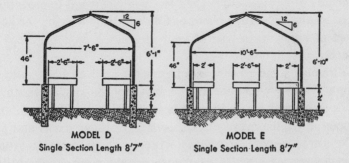

MODEL D
Single Section Length 8'7"

MODEL E
Single Section Length 8'7"

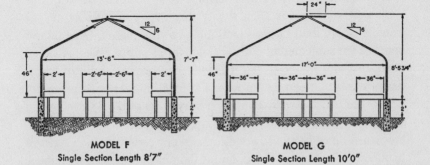

MODEL F
Single Section Length 8'7"

MODEL G
Single Section Length 10'0"

able to work at counter level without bending or stooping is not to be discounted either.

Greenhouse benches may be arranged in several ways, the idea being to utilize the growing area most effectively. Figure 1 shows various greenhouse bench arrangements, but you may want to make yours in a manner more suited to the use you intend to make of your greenhouse. For example, you may want an open area in the center in which to have a patio atmosphere, with plant benches on the sides only. Then too, you may want to grow fairly large specimens of such plants as Camellias and need all the headroom possible; so in part of your greenhouse you will need no benches at all.

Although some greenhouses have glass walls all the way to the ground, most greenhouses have a masonry foundation which extends somewhat above ground level. This raises the greenhouse proper above the average snow level in northern areas and provides a firm support for the glass structure above. Glass-to-ground greenhouses are usually recommended for more southerly latitudes. Raised benches more or less coincide in height with the top of foundation walls so that plants get the full benefit of light from all sides, yet the benches themselves are hidden from view by the foundation.

It goes without saying that benches must be constructed of durable materials and in such a way that they can support an extremely heavy load of moist soil and growing plants. Greenhouse benches are subjected to constant moisture so must be constructed of rot-resistant material. Ordinary wooden benches built of varieties of wood that can be purchased at local lumberyards are practically useless, for such lumber is very susceptible to decay and will disintegrate in a very short time. If you use wooden benches, they must be of heart redwood, cypress, or cedar. At one time all benches were made of wood, and if the proper varieties of lumber are used, they are very satisfactory.

Commercial greenhouses often have permanent heavy-duty benches made of concrete, but these are not practical for a hobby greenhouse, not only because of their bulk and weight, but also because special forms must be rented in order to cast them in sections on the job.

By far the best material for greenhouse benches is a composition "board" made of asbestos fiber and cement. It is practically indestructible and is used widely for both commercial and home greenhouses. Benches made of asbestos-cement board will last a lifetime, since they are impervious to decay, moisture, and insects. Greenhouse manufacturers supply these benches ready-cut to size and drilled to make assembly an easy process. It should be noted that it is possible to buy benches with asbestos-cement bottoms, flat or corrugated, with wooden sides (which may be stained), as well as with conventional sides of asbestos cement.

Bench fittings must be of heavy galvanized iron or some other rust-resistant metal, for constant moisture would soon rust out ordinary iron brackets and supports.

While benches hold the soil so that plants can grow, something must hold up the benches themselves! You will find that poured concrete piers spaced four to five feet apart, topped by galvanized iron pipes laid lengthwise of the bench, make ideal supports for the heavy loads encountered under greenhouse conditions. Some growers use concrete or cinder blocks rather than poured piers because they are more easily moved if it becomes necessary.

Drainage in plant benches is achieved by leaving holes through which excess water can run off. Wood-bottom benches are made of boards spaced about three quarters of an inch apart. When they are installed, a piece of burlap is usually laid down before soil is put in the benches so that the soil will not fall through the cracks. When the boards take up moisture, they swell so that the gaps become much narrower. Benches with corrugated asbestos-cement bottoms drain from the edges where the bottoms are attached to the sides. Such a system allows for dry storage space under each bench, something not possible under wooden benches.

A specialized type of bench used extensively for Orchid culture will be discussed in Chapter IX, "Anyone Can Grow Orchids."

Supports for Cut Flowers

Among the crops ordinarily grown in benches there are many which require supports as they grow, and for this purpose greenhouse manufacturers supply what is known as bench wiring frames. These galvanized metal frames are well braced on the ends of benches and are spaced along the length of benches at regular intervals. Wire is strung the length of benches and string is tied across benches to give support to tall-growing flowers. The wiring frames are made in such a way that the supports can be raised as the plants increase in height. Such crops as Carnations, Chrysanthemums, Snapdragons, and Stocks should be supported as they grow. I suggest that only a part of your bench area be fitted with wiring frames, for some bench-grown plants do not need them. Figure 2 shows construction details of a typical bench wiring frame.

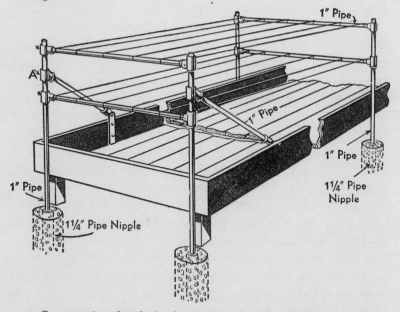

Construction details for bench wiring frame. Supports can be raised or lowered to suit needs of crops being grown. Courtesy National Greenhouse Co., Pana, Ill.

Cut-flower crops can also be supported by the use of wide-gapped wire mesh laid on the wire frames. This system does away with the necessity of tying cross strings.

It is possible, of course, to support plants with individual stakes of bamboo or wire, but the job is more easily done with less damage to the plants by the use of one of the above methods.

Extra Growing Space

Remember that you will never have enough room in your greenhouse for all the plants you would like to grow. No sooner do you fill all your bench space than you acquire another plant or two that you have always wanted. It is not long before you are forced to put in shelves, and you will find that they are fine investments. You will be wise to buy your shelves engineered to fit your growing area as well as to allow the maximum amount of light to reach the plants beneath. Many shelves are of plate glass, an ideal material for greenhouse shelving, combining ample strength with minimum shading.

One thing to watch for in growing plants on shelves is to choose plants which do not spread so far as to hit the cold glass, for their foliage will be injured. Not only will the plants suffer, but the dead leaves will cling to the glass in an unsightly manner. Trailing plants, as well as upright-growing ones, are ideal for shelves. Cacti make excellent subjects also, for they thrive in the bright atmosphere close to the glass.

Once you have the benches filled with flowers, the aisles crowded with larger plants in tubs, the walls adorned with plants on shelves, you have no other way to go but up. This introduces the subject of hanging pots. Greenhouse roof bars and ridge poles are strong enough to carry a considerable load of hanging plants, and they can easily be the most decorative plants in your greenhouse. In addition to regular hanging baskets you can buy metal pothangers which clasp ordinary flowerpots securely and can be hooked to a roof bar overhead.

Lovely plants for hanging containers are blue or white Browallias, lavender Trailing Lantanas, blue or white Italian Bellflowers, pink, white, or yellow Oxalis, colorful Nasturtiums, graceful green Sprengeri Ferns, and many varieties of Orchids, to name but a few.

There may well be places on the walls of your greenhouse too small to make a shelf practical, but large enough to hold a single plant. For such spots you can buy single pot-holding wall brackets that do an excellent job.

Working Tools

There is no doubt but that the ideal way to handle the problem of greenhouse tools is to do as commercial greenhouse men do and have a separate work building (known as a head house) attached to one end of the greenhouse, wherein all soil, fertilizer, tools, and supplies may be stored. Such an idea is clearly impractical for hobby greenhouse owners who grow their flowers for pleasure only and are interested in the attractiveness of their grounds, especially around the greenhouse.

Since we rule out the head-house idea, we must turn to the garage, cellar, tool house, or to the greenhouse itself as a work area. This problem is an individual one to be decided by each person, but I want to point out that, though a greenhouse may be full of plants, there is still a way to have a fine work area in it.

In the first place, there is a lot of space under benches where bins can be built to hold sand, soil, peat moss, pots, and fertilizer. Such bins should be constructed of rot-resistant lumber such as redwood and be of the type that tips open in the front as old-fashioned flour bins used to do. They should be raised somewhat off the floor to allow for the circulation of air under them and be provided with watertight covers. Galvanized cans with covers to fit are also serviceable containers and have the advantage of being portable.

An excellent work or potting bench of the drop-leaf style can be attached to the side of a bench convenient to the storage bins. Such a bench should have three raised sides, four to six inches high, to keep soil from spilling off during potting operations.

Tool storage is not a big problem in a greenhouse, for all tools are small. Trowels, hole markers, hand cultivators, sieves, and such tools are easily attached to the sides of a bench near the work area. I have found that a set of well-made children's or ladies' garden tools, consisting of a rake, hoe, and shovel, are very useful in a home greenhouse. The cheap ones are impractical, but the better-quality ones are very helpful, especially for working over soil in a bench or for mixing potting soil. The short handles are long enough to reach across the width of benches, but not so long as to be awkward to use.

Among the other tools you will need are a pair of scissors, a knife, a scoop for taking material from the under-bench bins, a watering can with small openings (called a fine rose—it makes a soft spray for watering seedlings), a hand sprayer, and some labels. I have found that a sieve made by tacking a piece of fine-mesh hardware cloth on a small frame makes an excellent device for sifting the small amounts of soil needed in a home greenhouse.

Although not properly a tool, a garden hose should be included in your greenhouse equipment. Also your greenhouse should be equipped with warm- and cold-water connections through a mixing faucet. Plants suffer noticeably during the cloudy dull months if they are watered with icy water. Plants such as African Violets must be given water which is warmer than the temperature of the greenhouse. Here again, though the message is a brief one, take it to heart and provide for both warm and cold water in your greenhouse.

Plant Containers

Not all greenhouse plants are grown in pots or benches. Such items as bedding plants or vegetable seedlings are usually grown in small flats, in plant bands in flats, or, better still, in expendable peat pots. Flats are wooden boxes usually eighteen inches long, twelve inches wide, and three inches deep, though they may be of other dimensions. Plant bands are rectangular pieces of rot-resistant material which are inserted in flats and filled with soil. A seedling is planted in each plant band, and since its roots are restricted to the band, it suffers very little upon transplanting to the open ground. Peat pots are the latest idea for handling small plants since pot and all are planted into the ground, the plant sending its roots right through the walls of the peat pot.

For countless generations gardeners have used clay flowerpots in which to grow their plants, but someone has dubbed this the "Age of Plastics," and surely one of the most successful applications of plastics has been the development of plastic flowerpots. They are extremely light in weight, do not break easily, and, best of all, plants thrive in them. Plastic pots do not lose moisture through their walls; so plants do not need to be watered as frequently as when clay pots are used. Clay pots will always be with us, and you can grow blue-ribbon flowers in them, but sometime try a few plastic pots and see how you like them.

When you try to grow a Camellia in your greenhouse, and I am sure you will, the time will soon come when you will find that it has outgrown your largest flowerpot. Then it is that you will have to shift to a plant tub of some sort. Ordinary wooden butter tubs, if treated with a wood preservative, will give about three years' service. Plant tubs made of redwood are much more decorative and will last for many years. Lately, plastic pots have been made up to twelve inches in diameter, which will hold all but the very largest of plants and will last indefinitely. A method of keeping tub plants small and yet thrifty will be discussed in Chapter V, "Down to Earth."

Have a Conservatorylike Atmosphere

Until now all the subjects discussed in this chapter have been of a utilitarian nature, but now we come to the human side of home greenhouses. A home greenhouse should be like another room in the house except that it should be a very special one. It has the elements of warmth and fragrance and a moist earthy atmosphere most of us associate with tropical gardens. A home greenhouse has the qualities of a conservatory, and it is nice to capitalize upon them.

Let us begin with the floor of your greenhouse. For the sake of your plants as well as for appearance do not put down a slab of concrete and call it a greenhouse floor. A concrete floor holds too much heat during the summer months, and it does not hold moisture and release it to the atmosphere to preserve life-giving humidity. Why not make a floor of old bricks set in a deep sand bed or laid in mortar? You can choose any one of many delightful patterns when you lay the bricks, and the job is within the scope of any loving husband. Best of all, it provides an ideal, clean, moisture-retaining floor combining elegance with utility. A floor of flagstone is lovely to look at too, but it should be set in sand, not mortar. Such floors as these are easily cleaned with the greenhouse hose, and if they are elevated an inch or two above the rest of the greenhouse floor which is under the benches, they will dry quickly.

While on the subject of floors, it is well to suggest that you provide a coco mat on which to wipe your feet before walking from the greenhouse into your house. Greenhouse floors are apt to have many of the elements found in gardens, including some mud.

CHAPTER IV

CLIMATE CONTROL

What is the first thing to come to your mind when you think about caring for a greenhouse? Is it not, "How will I heat it?" As a matter of fact, this is only one of the considerations which are involved in routine greenhouse operation. Heating is surely the most important one in the winter, but in the summer a greenhouse can become unbearably hot unless some method of cooling is provided. Likewise, there is the problem of ventilation, for it is well known that plants thrive on fresh air, and diseases thrive on stagnant air. Provision must be made to keep the atmospheric humidity high too, whether manually by using a garden hose or mechanically by the use of a humidifier. Certain greenhouse crops must be shaded and others lighted; some are adapted to automatic watering and even hydroponics, while others can go a week between waterings. This is the era of the air-conditioned greenhouse, and this subject as well as the others mentioned above will be discussed in this chapter. If you want to be a demigod, you will have to know how to control the climate in your greenhouse, or surely you will have a "brown thumb" instead of a "green" one.

How to Heat Your Greenhouse
The ideal way to heat your greenhouse is to extend your present heating system to it. This simple statement will answer the heating

problem for nearly all prospective home-greenhouse owners. Whether or not it will suit your needs will depend upon a study of your heating system by your own heating engineer, or one from the company from which you buy your greenhouse. You may be sure that if you can extend your household heating system, you will be able to save a great deal of money, for such an extension involves only the addition of another "heating zone" to your present system. This may be done if your home system is steam, hot water, or forced warm air. Some greenhouse manufacturers sell kits that can be used to extend hot-water or steam systems, but usually forced-warm-air systems require the services of a local dealer familiar with the particular system in your dwelling. In any case, now is a good time to caution you to use a thermostat suited to greenhouse operation. See your greenhouse dealer. Many household thermostats are not reliable under the extreme moisture conditions found in greenhouses.

If you cannot, or do not want to extend the heating system in your home, you are faced with the decision as to what type of separate system will best serve your needs. Here your choice is vast, for there are steam, hot-water, electric, and hot-air systems available, and your choice of fuel includes oil, natural gas, or electricity. It is important to know that only a vented gas or oil heater should be used in a greenhouse, and if gas is the fuel it must be natural gas, since *manufactured gas will kill plants*.

It is not within the province of this book to go through all the details of heater installation; each greenhouse problem is a special one dependent upon location, inside temperature desired, outside temperatures expected, protection from or exposure to cold winds, and similar factors, and the advice of a qualified person should be sought to give you the correct answer to your particular heating needs. Greenhouse manufacturers will gladly send you a form on which you may note the data they need to know in order to recommend a proper heating system. When your greenhouse man suggests a unit somewhat larger than appears to be sufficient for your needs, follow his advice, for a larger unit does not have to operate as continuously to heat your greenhouse, and, too, you may decide to add to the size of your glass house, and all you will need then will be some extra pipes.

It might be pointed out that there are today, in addition to the standard forced-hot-water systems formerly thought to be the only kind suitable for home greenhouses, some very fine forced-warm-air heaters. The question of dehumidification of the air has been found under controlled experiments to have been overstressed. If the air from such a heater should make the atmosphere dry, it is an easy matter to raise the humidity by wetting down the walks or by installing a humidifier, which will handle the problem automatically.

Where electric rates are low, electric heaters can be used for home greenhouses, and it is suggested that if they are used a fan should also be installed to circulate the heat throughout the greenhouse.

The Importance of Ventilation

It is easy to assume that all one needs to have in a greenhouse is a glass structure and a heating system, but there is more to the story than that. If a greenhouse is closed up tight and the sun shines on it, in a matter of a very short time the temperature rises to the point where plants can be cooked nearly as effectively as in a pressure cooker! There simply must be some way to let out the excess heat, and the problem is handled nowadays in one of two ways. One method is by the use of horizontal ventilation; ventilators are placed in the ends of a greenhouse, and the air is moved through the house horizontally by the means of an electric fan. This type of ventilation will be discussed in this chapter under the heading "Cooling and Air Conditioning." The second method, vertical ventilation, is the type most commonly seen and has been proven in use for many years. This system utilizes movable ventilators attached at the high point of greenhouse roofs, as well as wall ventilators in the side walls. In this system the air circulates in through the wall vents and out the roof vents by convection. Most home greenhouses are equipped with the vertical ventilation system, which is economical, effective, and as nearly foolproof as any ventilating method can be.

The actual ventilators used in vertical ventilation are, in effect, "windows" in the roof of the greenhouse. They may be opened and closed to maintain the desired temperature for the particular crop being grown. For many years all ventilators were opened and closed manually by the use of ventilating machines actuated by pulling ropes or chains. Such a system is relatively inexpensive to buy and will last a lifetime, but for the home greenhouse owner it has one all-important drawback: Someone must be around all of the time to open and close the vents. Perhaps the greatest thrill any commercial greenhouse man ever had came on the day that he installed automatic electric ventilators in his greenhouse. For once in his life he could be relatively carefree, at least as far as the ever-present task of tending ventilators was concerned. The installation of automatic ventilators should, in the writer's opinion, be considered of equal importance to the installation of a heating system. Especially in the spring and fall of the year there are great daily fluctuations of temperature, and sometimes there are cold windy days, but with a great deal of sunshine. The sun will heat the greenhouse more than adequately, and automatic ventilation will take care of the excess heat. Then there are those days when the sun plays hide-and-seek behind the clouds. These are the days when manually operated ventilators keep a person on the jump to open and close vents. Automatic ventilators open and close the vents dozens of times a day and maintain, by the use of their thermostat, more even temperatures than can be done manually.

Greenhouse manufacturers have their own makes of electric ventilators to sell, and they all do the job effectively. Do not make the mistake of thinking you can do without automatic ventilation. All you have to do is to forget to open the vents one day, and you will find that you have paid for the cost of automatic ventilation in the loss of your plants. It is a costly lesson. Also, automatic vents cost less money when they are purchased with the greenhouse than they do if they are purchased as separate items at a later date.

Wall ventilators are rarely operated automatically, but are opened and closed by hand for the reason that they are moved much less often than roof vents. Wall ventilators can be opened in the late spring, for example, and left open night and day for most of the summer. Because they would create cold drafts, they are rarely opened in cold weather. Enough air circulates through the greenhouse during much of the year by the use of the roof vents alone.

In connection with ventilating greenhouses it might be well to point out that the larger the greenhouse, the easier it is to maintain at a given temperature. A large greenhouse holds a large volume of air and changes temperatures relatively slowly, but a small house heats up and cools off rapidly. This is another argument for getting as large a home greenhouse as possible. You will find it easier to grow plants in a large house than in a small one.

Although all the discussion so far has centered on the actual process of ventilation for cooling greenhouses, it must be pointed out that ventilators serve another purpose of great value, for they allow the interchange of fresh air between the greenhouse and the outside. Without fresh air plants will not thrive. Even in cold weather during the days many commercial greenhouse operators "crack the ventilators," as they say, to let in fresh air. This circulation of fresh air also serves to carry off excess moisture, thereby helping to prevent certain diseases.

Cooling and Air Conditioning

While it has been pointed out in the section above that roof and wall ventilators cool conventional greenhouses, the topic of this section is that of modern horizontal cooling and air conditioning, whereby the actual movement of the air within the greenhouse is done by a type of electric fan. Many of the newer greenhouses utilizing this method of cooling do not have roof vents at all, being completely weather-tight as far as the roof is concerned, but have jalousie-type vents in side or end walls. All air enters at one end of the greenhouse and is expelled at the far end, or in

PLATE 1 An aluminum lean-to greenhouse with curved glass eaves blends gracefully into the garden landscape.

Courtesy Lord & Burnham, Irvington-on-Hudson, N.Y.

PLATE 2 Plants growing in this even-span aluminum greenhouse receive light from three directions. Note use of roller shades.

Courtesy Lord & Burnham, Irvington-on-Hudson, N.Y.

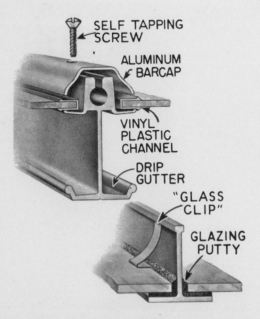

SELF TAPPING SCREW

ALUMINUM BARCAP

VINYL PLASTIC CHANNEL

DRIP GUTTER

"GLASS CLIP"

GLAZING PUTTY

PLATE 3 Construction details of modern aluminum greenhouses.

Courtesy Lord & Burnham, Irvington-on-Hudson, N.Y.

PLATE 4 Corrugated fiber-glass shading panels in soft green shield plants from the hot sun in this lean-to aluminum greenhouse.

Courtesy Aluminum Greenhouses, Inc., Cleveland, O.

PLATE 5 Installation of automatic ventilating motors.

Courtesy Lord & Burnham, Irvington-on-Hudson, N.Y.

PLATE 6 The garage to which this even-span greenhouse is attached serves as a convenient place to store potting soil and greenhouse supplies. Lath-type shade on the south side protects plants from summer sun.

Courtesy Lord & Burnham, Irvington-on-Hudson, N.Y.

other installations is drawn from side to side rather than from end to end.

The simplest form of air cooling by this method is accomplished by installing aspen-wood excelsior pads (aspen wood because it is absorbent and decay-resistant) in a section of the end of a greenhouse, and one or more large fans in a section of the opposite end of the greenhouse. The pads are kept moist by circulating water. Outside air being pulled through the moist pads loses much of its heat and takes up moisture, cooling greenhouses twenty or more degrees below outdoor temperatures. Such a system is relatively inexpensive to install and has meant a great deal to greenhouse owners, both in the cool and warm sections of the country. Many greenhouses used to be vacant during part of the summer months because they became too hot to grow good quality flowers. Nowadays excellent quality Carnations and Chrysanthemums, cool-weather crops, are being produced during the summer months as well as during the balance of the year. The ability to keep commercial greenhouses in production all through the year has been a boon to greenhouse owners.

As a refinement of the above process especially suited to home greenhouse installation, one may now purchase a compact unit which will do the entire process, but in a somewhat different manner. A boxlike unit, which is usually installed at ground level outside the greenhouse, consists of a fan mounted in the end of the unit facing the greenhouse, with the other three sides fitted with aspen-wood pads. The pads are kept moist by a recirculating pump located inside the unit. The cool moist air is blown into the greenhouse and expelled, in this case, through the roof ventilators which are left open about one inch. This is a wonderful answer to the problem of greenhouse cooling for the home greenhouse. Not only do crops grow far better under these conditions, but the cool atmosphere in the greenhouse is a pleasure in the summertime.

In addition to the method of cooling outlined above for conventional greenhouses, a similar system is sold for those greenhouses now being built without the usual ventilating facilities.

These may properly be called air-conditioned greenhouses, for they cannot operate any other way. These greenhouses usually have two jalousies, one above the other, which may be opened or closed shutter-fashion to control the flow of air. The movement of air is accomplished by means of an enclosed fan in front of the lower jalousie. The air is drawn into the greenhouse through the lower jalousie and expelled through the upper one. An automatic misting mechanism is available to attach to the fan. As outside air is drawn in, it travels through the mist, being cooled by evaporation. This cool air circulates through the greenhouse, effectively lowering inside temperatures to those of outdoors or lower. Any greenhouse that has all, or part, of its roof shaded will cool down lower than one without shading, but whether your greenhouse roof should be shaded depends not upon this fact, but upon the needs of the crop you are trying to grow. As an example, you would be able to grow Chrysanthemums several degrees cooler if you shaded the roof, but, since Chrysanthemums require sunshine, you have to accept the temperatures you are able to achieve without shading.

How to Shade Your Greenhouse

It is well known that some outdoor plants thrive in full sunshine while others prefer a shady location. So it is with greenhouse plants as well. Such plants as African Violets, Gloxinias, Tuberous-rooted Begonias, many foliage plants, and Orchids all need to be protected from the sun for at least part of the year. The phrase *part of the year* holds the key to shading, for in the summer months when the sunshine is bright all the above-mentioned plants and many others must be shaded from the sun, but when the dull days of winter come with their limited hours of sunlight, many of these plants grow much better if they have full sunlight, or at least a much lighter shade.

For years before modern greenhouse-shading methods were developed, many growers shaded their greenhouses by the simple expedient of throwing mud on the glass! Strangely enough, this method, though messy, was quite satisfactory. Some of the mud splattered on thinly and in other sections thickly; so there was a dappled shade similar to what one might find under a tree. In certain parts of the country this method is still used, especially in those sections with long dry summers, for a sudden rain can wash such shading material off in a very short while.

Mud is not the recommended material for shading the home greenhouse, for there are many other more effective and attractive ways to do the job. Another one of the older methods which is still in common usage commercially is the whiting-and-gasoline system. Gasoline and whiting are mixed together to the consistency of light cream and applied with a brush or sprayer. It is apt to be a messy operation also and is another shading method not suggested for use in home greenhouses.

There is available for greenhouse shading a special preparation sold by greenhouse manufacturers in either white or green coloring. This material comes in a paste form and is mixed with gasoline or benzine and easily applied with a paint roller or brush. This is the material to use if you want an inexpensive and long-lasting paint-on type of shade. If you want an inexpensive shade which will be temporary in nature, use a green or white shading powder available from your greenhouse dealer. This material should be mixed with water and applied in the same manner as the more long-lasting material. In any event, do not use whitewash or any shading compound containing lime, as they are harmful to aluminum.

There are four other commonly used methods of shading greenhouses, any one of which may be the answer you choose for your greenhouse. All of them have the advantage of being non-messy, a big consideration for a home greenhouse. The first and most commonly seen system is the "roller slat" one. Wooden slats, linked together with rust-resistant couplings, are made so that by the use of a simple rope and pulley rig they can be raised and lowered in a minute to admit full sunlight or protect plants from sunlight (or protect the glass from hail). These roller slats last for many years and are of the type usually seen on estate greenhouses, yet they are well within the price range of the home-greenhouse owner.

The second non-messy shading method you may use is a variation of the first one in that fiber glass or Saran cloth is used in the place of the wood slats. This is a good shading procedure, combining relatively long life with good appearance.

There are still two other fine, clean ways to shade your plants. One is by the use of green fiber-glass panels which clip to roof bars. The other utilizes aluminum laths, thin pieces of aluminum which fit firmly into slots cut in strips of wood or metal that are attached to the roof bars. The amount of shading can be varied easily and quickly by shifting the aluminum pieces from one slot to another, giving wider or narrower bands of sunlight between the bands of shade. The aluminum pieces look much like the sections used in venetian blinds and are bent in a slightly convex manner when inserted in the roof-bar strips.

There are occasions in greenhouse operations when shading is needed for only a short time and then in only a small area. Under such conditions it is very easy to tack up a piece of muslin inside the greenhouse to make a temporary shade, or even to cover cuttings or seed flats with pieces of newspaper for the day or two that shading is necessary.

How to Maintain the Proper Relative Humidity in Your Greenhouse

Relative humidity is the technical term for the amount of moisture that air will hold at any given temperature. If the humidity is 60 per cent, for instance, it means that the air contains 60 per cent of the possible moisture that it can contain for that temperature at that time. As temperature increases, so does its ability to hold water. Thus if greenhouse temperatures rise and no additional moisture is added to the atmosphere, the relative humidity falls. It is under these conditions that a greenhouse needs some method of adding additional water to the air. Conversely, if temperatures fall and the air becomes saturated with moisture (100 per cent relative humidity), then water will condense on the colder surfaces in the greenhouse. This accounts for the coating of frost often found on the inside of greenhouse glass on cold winter mornings.

Men have been growing plants in greenhouses for generations without any more elaborate humidifying equipment than watering cans and garden hoses, but that is no reason why your greenhouse should not be equipped with a modern method of maintaining proper humidity automatically. Plants grow better when there is considerable moisture in the air, and unless the walks are wet down often on hot, dry summer days, the relative humidity of a greenhouse quickly reaches the point of being of little value to plant growth.

It is not generally discussed in this day of gadgets, but plants themselves are the most efficient kind of humidifiers. They give off moisture to the air all the time, as any person knows whose job it is to water house plants. Leaves have innumerable "pores," more properly known as stomata, which allow for the interchange of air between the outside air and the inside structure of the leaves. It is through these stomata that plants give off moisture, after having taken it up from the soil through their roots. Thus the old story that plants grown in abundance in homes do better than plants grown singly has its truth in the fact that more plants create a more humid atmosphere to their mutual benefit.

A great many crops will grow perfectly well without any artificial means of humidification. The very facts that the soil is kept moist and there are plenty of plants growing, plus an occasional wetting down of walks and benches on hot days, will solve the humidification problem nicely.

Greenhouses that are equipped with an evaporative cooling system are supplied with sufficient atmospheric moisture not only from the fact that the air is drawn in through saturated pads, but because the lowered temperatures in such a house mean that a given amount of moisture in the air will give a higher relative humidity.

Where humid conditions are necessary, such as in Orchid culture, and cannot be supplied by wetting down of walks and other manual methods, it is a good idea to have some type of mechanical humidification system. Homemade systems, utilizing oil burner nozzles because of their exceedingly fine spray, can be used, but they must be tended from time to time. The best way to do this is to buy a small greenhouse humidifier and a humidistat to govern it. When the humidistat is set at the desired relative humidity, it will turn the humidifier on and off to meet its commands.

Automatic Watering

It is a mistake to have everything in the greenhouse self-controlled, for soon we would be so lazy that we would want a weeding machine, too, and would then miss half of the fun of gardening. Nevertheless, there are times when automatic watering is a real blessing, and this is especially true when commercial greenhouse operators have to pay high labor bills to men watering by hand. Home greenhouse growers can use many of the commercial methods and perhaps have better growth in their plants than if they water in the haphazard way sometimes necessary when one becomes too busy with some other project.

Automatic watering can be done by four different methods, at least one of which may be useful to you in your home greenhouse. Perhaps the simplest system of all, and the least expensive to use, is the *wick* method. In this method fiber-glass wicking, available at florist shops and garden centers, connects the plants with a reservoir of water an inch or two below the plants. By capillarity water rises through the wick into the soil and keeps the plants supplied with moisture until the water in the reservoir has been used up. This method works very well for pot plants growing in shallow pots. In practice, the wicking is thrust through the drainage hole in the bottom of a flowerpot, and the end unraveled and spread out somewhat in the bottom of the pot. Instead of the usual coarse drainage material in the bottom of the pot, fine soil is placed directly on top of the wicking, and then the plant is potted as usual. The close contact of the fine soil with the wicking allows the water to rise easily up into the rest of the soil in the pot. Under fast drying conditions it is sometimes necessary to add some extra water from the top of the pots, but this seldom is necessary. If you use the wick method, you will find that it is a real time-saver for the ever-present chore of watering. Of course, wicks must be wet initially for their full length before they are capable of carrying the column of water up to the plants. This system can be adapted so that a whole row of plants, for instance, can sit in a line above a section of eaves trough and draw their moisture from a common source.

The three other methods of automatic watering are considerably more expensive to install, since they require the presence of a solenoid valve and/or a tensiometer and electrical connections, as well as other items to be described below. (A tensiometer is an instrument which measures the amount of moisture in soil by capillary tension on a section of the instrument which is inserted into the soil. This capillary tension influences a column of mercury to give an indication of soil moisture.) Electrical devices can convert the tensiometer reading into commands to a solenoid valve, causing water valves to open and close in answer to the moisture needs of plants. Needless to say, such a system is very technical and expensive, and I do not recommend it for the hobby greenhouse owner whose chief interest is plants.

The system described above can be used to open water valves to spray water on the surface of the soil of a bench, in which case the water is distributed evenly through nozzles or tiny holes in pipes laid on top of the soil. The number of pipes needed depends upon the width of the bench.

The tensiometer-solenoid-valve system can also be used in connection with what is known as constant-level watering. In this method a *level, watertight* bench is needed. Coarse gravel topped by fine sand is laid on the bottom of the bench before soil is added. By the use of the instruments mentioned above, a constant inch of water is maintained in the gravel. This rises by capillarity to the soil above, keeping the plants constantly moist.

The fourth method also utilizes a watertight bench and is known as the injection system. This time the bench is covered with gravel and then sand as mentioned above, but a section of eaves trough, or similar material, is inverted and laid down the center of the bench. Water is "injected" via a hose or pipe into this central canal, which carries it the length of the bench. It flows horizontally through the sand and gravel layer and then upward via capillarity to the roots of the plants.

All of these methods are good in that the foliage of the plants is kept dry, an important factor in restricting the spread of various diseases especially in dull, cloudy weather. Whether they are important to a home-greenhouse hobbyist is questionable. As a practical means of watering plants, I suggest a garden hose and a mixing faucet connected to hot- and cold-water lines.

Greenhouse Lighting and Electrical Outlets

Part of the thrill of having a home greenhouse is to be able to show it to guests. During the wintertime when greenhouses are most appreciated, darkness comes early; so there should be some means of lighting your greenhouse. Ordinary incandescent lights will do the job very effectively, but the lamps themselves should be protected by the use of some outside globe because if you should happen to sprinkle water on a hot light bulb, it will probably pop.

In addition to the lights to show off your greenhouse, there is the possibility that you may sometime grow plants which would enjoy supplemental lighting. For this purpose it is well to have at least one watertight electrical outlet into which you can plug a light or two, or you might like the outlet for an electric fan, a humidifying unit, or a soil-heating cable.

You will surely need some electrical connections for your automatic ventilation and for your thermostats. Such wiring will be taken care of by the greenhouse contractor as the various items requiring electricity are installed.

Hydroponics or Soilless Culture

It should be stated that horticulture has had more than its share of fads, and immediately prior to World War II the cry was all for soilless culture. It would seem, to hear the wonders attributed to it, that hydroponics was the answer to all gardening problems and that garden soils should be done away with! As is so often the case, a lot of the claims turned out to be nonsense, but there was a core of truth in the story. During the war when green vegetables were unobtainable for troops in the western Pacific, lettuce and similar crops were grown by this hydroponic system. Water and nutrients were pumped into prepared beds of ground-up volcanic cinders; result, vegetables grown without soil.

This brings up the question often asked, "If you take away the soil, how are the plants able to stand up?" The answer is that some sort of inert material is used instead of soil as a place for the roots of the plants to range. This material may be gravel, perlite, sand, or even chicken wire!

The inert material is placed in a watertight bench which is flooded periodically with water containing minute quantities of the various elements known to be necessary for plant growth. In the hot days of summer the benches must be flooded and drained two or three times a day, and during the colder time of the year the cycle may be spread to every day or so, depending upon the water-holding capacity of the material in the benches. Since the benches must be drained as well as flooded, there has to be a storage area (usually under the benches) to hold the solution until the plants need it again, as well as a pump to move it from the storage tank to the bench. For a detailed treatment of the chemicals needed for the solution see *Florist Crop Production and Marketing* by Kenneth Post, late Professor of Floriculture and Ornamental Horticulture at Cornell University, Ithaca, New York.

Emergency Measures

It would be foolhardy to trust entirely to the constant performance of mechanical devices, for we know that, though they operate without malfunction for long periods of time, they can wear out. Then too, the various motors which power the oil burner, the circulator, and the ventilating equipment depend upon electricity. When the power goes off because of a storm or because of a blown fuse, there must be a way of knowing about it as soon as possible.

This valuable task, rarely needed, but indispensable, is performed by what is called a "minimum-maximum temperature alarm." This unit is housed in a circular metal box much like that of an alarm clock, and its face is calibrated so as to show temperatures from 20 to 100 degrees Fahrenheit. There are three hands on the dial; one records the temperature while the other two are movable and may be set at any place on the dial. In my greenhouse I set the lower dial for 40 degrees and the upper one for 90 degrees. The unit is energized by dry-cell batteries, and when the temperature hand touches either the low or high marker, an alarm bell in the house rings incessantly until shut off manually.

If the problem signified by the alarm is that the greenhouse has become too warm, then a door or ventilator can be opened by hand until repairs can be made, but if the trouble is too little heat, then something must be done quickly or plants will freeze. You should plan to have a small stand-by unit of some kind which does not require electricity to function. A portable kerosene heater will do the job for a small greenhouse until the heating system can be repaired. Such a unit can be purchased from mail-order houses if unavailable locally.

CHAPTER V

DOWN TO EARTH

Someone has pointed out that mankind exists on the top six inches of this planet, and to a great extent this is true, for most of the world's crops grow in this thin outer crust. It is here that nearly all of the organic matter in the world is concentrated in the form of decaying leaves, grass, and other materials of animal or vegetable origin. It is well known that farm lands or suburban gardens prosper alike when their soil is rich in organic matter. Nowhere is the need for organic matter more acute than in greenhouses where plants are grown in shallow benches. All the nourishment greenhouse plants receive must come from this small amount of soil. It may be more than coincidence that greenhouse benches usually have about six inches of soil depth. Roots can find all they need to support the plants well if this amount of soil is of the right texture and sufficiently supplied with nutrients.

What Is Soil?

The inorganic part of soil is made up of weathered rock particles ranging in size from the coarse pebbles of gravel through the gritty nature of sand on to the floury texture of silt and the stickiness of wet clay. Each of us must work with the type of soil that he has, but it is well to know what is considered to be an ideal greenhouse soil. For the record, greenhouse men as well as research workers have found that a sandy loam—that is, a soil midway in texture between sand and silt with about one fourth of its volume organic matter—is an ideal greenhouse soil for most crops. Certain crops require special soil mixtures, and these will be treated under the care of the individual plants in Chapter VIII. In addition there are experiments being carried on in which plants are being grown in man-made soils composed of various combinations of peat moss and sand. These projects are not to be recommended for the amateur, however. He is better advised to use a mixture which has been used successfully by tens of thousands of greenhouse growers for centuries.

What Is Organic Matter?

It has been mentioned that the ideal greenhouse soil contains one-fourth organic matter by volume. This organic material may be decayed leaves, peat moss, manure, partly decomposed sod, or any similar material of animal or vegetable origin. Generally speaking, organic material is not at its best for plant growth when it is in early stages of decay. The bacteria responsible for decay require nitrogen for their own growth, which they take, leaving soil deficient in this element. Thus if one is using organic matter only partly decayed, he should use a supplementary inorganic nitrogen fertilizer to tide his plants over until further nutrients become available as the decay process continues.

When organic matter decomposes to the point where it can no longer be identified as leaves or peat moss, for example, but has become a brown, soft, homogeneous material, it is known as humus. It is now that the organic matter does its best job, for its particles have become so small that they approach the elemental nature they must attain in order to be absorbed by plant roots.

Organic matter is a paradoxical material in that it lightens heavy soils and increases the water-holding capacity of light soils. Because of its dark color it warms up more easily under the influence of the sun, and because it lightens soil, it likewise improves drainage. All of these factors invite increased activity of beneficial soil bacteria, promoting more thrifty plant growth.

The Role of Organic Matter in Plant Growth

It is not the author's purpose to be technical in this book, but for a moment we should examine the underlying reason why we should have an abundance of organic matter in our soil. It would be simple enough to say, "Because plants grow better." That is the real reason, after all, but the principle behind it all is this: There is in the soil a considerable amount of extremely tiny particles which agronomists have named colloids. These tiny bits of matter have the ability to attract and hold the various chemicals needed for plant growth. This is where organic matter enters the picture, for as organic matter decays it forms a weak carbonic acid, which is able to replace the other chemicals held by the colloids, releasing them in ion form so that they can be assimilated by plant roots. If this diversion seems complicated, forget it, and go back to the original reason why we keep our soils well supplied with organic matter: We know from experience that plants prosper in such soils and languish in soils deficient in organic matter.

The Structure of Greenhouse Soils

Each person endeavoring to produce the finest soil for greenhouse use must strive for the twin goals of nutrient-supplying power and loose texture. Greenhouse soils tend to become compacted after watering month after month with a hose, and it is important to begin with a soil that is light enough in texture to resist this compacting action. Soil which becomes compacted also becomes low in oxygen, and, without soil oxygen, roots cannot thrive. One must not make the mistake of thinking that ordinary garden soil is good enough for a greenhouse. Unless it is fortified by the addition of organic matter in liberal amounts, the average good garden soil will become nearly as hard as concrete after being in a greenhouse a short time.

How to Prepare Greenhouse Soil

If you have just bought a greenhouse, you surely want to grow some plants in it as soon as possible. In that case, go to your favorite greenhouse and persuade the owner to sell you some

prepared greenhouse soil. This will get you started for the first
season, and from that time forward you can fix your own.

Greenhouse soil is known as composted soil and may be
prepared either by "field" composting or by the use of a compost
pile. For practical purposes, field composting is not suggested for
home greenhouses since it entails such projects as cover crops and
other field operations, but the compost-pile method is surely within
the province of many home-greenhouse owners. A compost pile
for the preparation of greenhouse soil is made by piling alternate
six- to eight-inch layers of sod and horse or cow manure in a
flat-topped pile. It should be flat on top so that it can catch and
hold moisture to help it decay. If you cannot buy natural manure
from a farm, use dehydrated cow manure, available from florists
and garden centers, and use it in layers one and one half inches
thick, the sod layers being the regular six to eight inches in thickness. In the preparation five pounds of superphosphate per one
hundred square feet of manure layer are added. The pile is
"broken down" by cutting through it from top to bottom with a
sharp spade about a month after it is built. One more turning
a month hence, plus an additional month of decaying, will make
it ready for greenhouse use. Such a soil has a wonderful earthy
fragrance, is soft to the touch, retentive of moisture yet well
drained, full of nutrients, and abounding in bacterial life for good
plant growth.

There is hardly a plant known to floriculture, with the exception
of Orchids, which will not thrive on a soil composted as described
above. You can use it for seed flats by screening out the lumps
and adding a bit of sand; you can use it straight for most pot
plants and bench-grown crops; and you can supplement its
organic content with peat moss for particular crops such as
Azaleas. In Chapter VIII, "Plants You Can Grow in Your
Greenhouse," there will be found special mention of soil requirements of plants if they differ from this basic mixture.

It is possible that you have neither the time, the space, nor the
inclination to prepare a composted greenhouse soil, but there is
still another way to do a good job. If you will mix seven parts of

loam with three parts of peat moss and two parts of sand, you will have what is known as *John Innes potting compost*, developed in 1939 at the John Innes Horticultural Institute in England. To such a mixture the originators suggested the addition of a fertilizer "base" made of materials difficult to buy in this country. For practical purposes, the addition of an inorganic fertilizer such as 5–8–7 will give very good results. The chief reason for the mention of the John Innes mixture here is to give an alternative to more difficult soil preparation methods.

The University of California has also developed its own group of soil mixes particularly suited to growing plants in containers, but they are used by many florists in greenhouse benches as well. Basically the U. C. Type Soil Mixes are made up of sand or peat moss or combinations of sand and peat moss. Such materials have very little nutrient value; so they must be supplemented with specific formulas adjusted to the individual mixture. The entire story in a 332-page manual is available from Agricultural Publications, 22 Giannini Hall, University of California, Berkeley 4, California, for one dollar. Such a system is very useful for certain commercial growers with all the continuing facilities this method requires, but it is rather impractical for the home grower with only a few square feet of bench space in which he would like to grow a variety of crops.

Soil Sterilization (More Correctly, Pasteurization)

In commercial floriculture it is a general practice to sterilize soil before planting most greenhouse crops. The value of sterilization lies in the fact that it kills weed seeds, insects, and soil-borne bacteria, and in some methods makes fertilizers more readily available to plants. In spite of these advantages, I am reluctant to advise the owner of a home greenhouse to sterilize his soil except under special circumstances. My own personal experience over the years has convinced me that it is not usually necessary; until a relatively few years ago there was no way to sterilize soil, and yet plants grew beautifully. (An exception to this broad statement is in relation to seeding. I have found that it is very useful to control damping-off fungi by the use of a soil disinfectant.)

The secret of growing plants without sterilization of the soil is to change the soil in the beds each year, returning the old soil to your garden. You will find that it will perk up that part of the garden, but it still is not satisfactory for a greenhouse crop. This is true because of a buildup of soil diseases and because an excess of fertilizer salts will have accumulated in the old soil. If you will make it a practice to change the soil in your greenhouse benches each season, you will find that you will be able to grow marvelous crops without the nuisance of sterilization.

There are four methods of soil sterilization. The one most often used in large greenhouses involves the injection of steam into tightly covered soil beds where temperatures are raised to 180 degrees or more and held for a thirty-minute period. Of course, such a system has little chance of being adapted to small home greenhouses.

The second method now holding the stage—and a very practical one—is sterilization by the use of chemicals. Formaldehyde has been used for over fifty years, but there are many new products which do a more effective job and do it in a more pleasant manner. The fumes from many of them are obnoxious and some are highly dangerous; some cannot be used in a greenhouse with living plants, and many require a waiting period of two weeks before plants can be safely put into the soil. In any event, it is imperative that the user follow directions to the letter. Do not try any short cuts or improvisations, but adhere to the method suggested by the manufacturer. These chemicals are sold under many trade names, some of which are Vapam, Terraclor, Larvacide, and Dowfume, and are made of such substances as methyl bromide, chloropicrin, ethylene dibromide, and formaldehyde.

Those soil disinfectants which are so wonderful in controlling damping-off include Captan, Ferbam, Thiram, Nabam, Semesan, and Pano-Drench as well as many others. If you have ever grown a lusty-looking flat of seedlings and then one morning found that they had all rotted off at the soil surface, you are acquainted with the ravages of damping-off. With the use of these materials all your seedlings will be protected.

The third soil sterilization method is achieved by the use of electricity. Such a system is especially useful when relatively small amounts of soil need to be sterilized, since it involves a boxlike unit, which, though new to the market, ought to find a ready sale among home-greenhouse owners. One of the really fine points of soil treatment by this method is that the soil can be used immediately, the only waiting period being for the soil to cool.

The last soil sterilization method I shall discuss is surely a home method, for it involves the oven of your kitchen stove. Small quantities of soil put in the oven and held at 180 degrees for thirty minutes will be found to be ideal for starting seeds, not only because disease organisms will have been destroyed, but because all weed seeds will have been killed too.

Potting Procedures

When should a plant be potted or repotted? This is a question which must be answered before we talk about how to do the actual operation. Cuttings must be potted when they have developed a good set of roots; seedlings should be potted when they start to show their third or fourth true leaves (not seed leaves); and older plants should be repotted when (1) their roots fill the soil ball of the pot in which they are growing, (2) when the soil in which they are growing has become exhausted of nutrients, or (3) when plants show weak growth due to insufficient drainage.

The first step in potting plants is to see that the pots you intend to use are clean. Any dried-on dirt or incrustations of fertilizer will come off easily if the pots are soaked in a pail of warm water. A stiff brush and a quick rinse will then do wonders for a pot which has been used before. If you have clay pots in which you know sick plants have previously grown, bake the pots in your oven for thirty minutes; then after they cool, let them soak up clean water in a pail before using them.

Prepare for the proper drainage in the flowerpot by putting

a layer of pebbles, cinders, or broken pots into the bottom of the pot, covering the drainage hole. Over this place a bit of Sphagnum moss or some coarse soil; then add your potting mix to such a depth that the crown of the new plant will be at a point about one-half inch below the rim of the pot. Fill in around the old soil ball and tap the pot on the bench to settle the soil. You may want to firm it somewhat with your fingers, too, but do not compact it too much. Be sure to leave a space at the top of the pot about one-half inch in depth in which to hold water when you water the plants.

How to Keep Large-growing Plants Small

When you first get your greenhouse, you might think that there would be no reason to keep large-growing plants small. After all, the Camellia you just bought is only a foot tall, and you want it to be a giant! The trouble is that in a very short time the Camellia *will be a giant,* and you will have to chop it down if you cannot find some way to keep its growth within bounds.

It is interesting to know that this problem was solved for us many centuries ago by the Japanese. Surely you have seen some of their miniature Bonsai trees growing in shallow containers, plants which in many instances are hundreds of years old. In your greenhouse you do not have to grow Bonsai trees, but you can use some of the principles whose application has kept the Bonsai trees small. In the first place, remember that all pruning is a dwarfing process, since it robs plants of the leaves they need to produce and store food for new growth. It is possible to keep your Camellia, for example, very small simply by cutting it back judiciously. Do not let it get big before you start pruning; make your cuts as soon as the plant has nearly reached the size you have set for it. Thereafter keep at it, removing branches which want to grow too tall. As a result you will force more flower buds to develop on lower branches.

No matter how often you prune, your Camellia, though kept small, will sooner or later exhaust the food value from the soil of the container in which it is growing. Then you have to repot it, but you do not have to repot it into a larger pot! This may come as a genuine surprise to some gardeners. When you knock it out of its pot, you will find that the roots fill the whole container with a solid mass. Get out your garden hose and begin to wash away some of the soil from around the roots, and after they are exposed, cut some of them off. Soon you will find that you can put the plant back into the same pot and fill in around it with a good supply of fresh soil. Treat the plant gently for a month or so by shading it from the strongest rays of the sun and by keeping the soil somewhat on the dry side. Such a soil condition will allow new root growth to develop quickly.

There is no reason that you cannot keep large-growing plants happy, though small, for an indefinite number of years. In my greenhouse, for example, are two Chinese Hibiscus now twelve years old, but only two and one half feet tall. Outdoors in a more temperate climate they would have been ten or more feet high years ago. These small plants blossom with full-sized flowers throughout the year.

Before we get to the subject of fertilizers in the next chapter, it would be well to point out that pot plants are usually not placed on top of soil in benches, but on a layer of more porous material an inch or so deep in the bottom of the bench. The depth of the porous material should be such that the tops of the pots are about even with the tops of the benches. This porous material, which may be gravel, crushed rock, perlite, or other loose material, serves more than one purpose. It allows for perfect drainage, and, best of all, it discourages plant roots from growing through the drainage holes. When plants are set on soil, the roots soon sneak through the drainage holes of the pots and draw their nourishment from below. It is exasperating to have a plant "root in," and the porous bench layer will prevent most of this type of trouble.

CHAPTER VI

FERTILIZERS
AND THEIR FUNCTIONS

In a general discussion of fertilizers it can be said that there are two basic kinds available to flower growers: the organic type, of which manure and bone meal are examples, and the inorganic type, of which nitrate of soda and muriate of potash are common examples. In greenhouses we sometimes find one type of more value than another and should choose the type most suited to our needs. If we were potting up a large plant in a tub in which we knew it would stay for a matter of years, we would surely use a fertilizer high in organic value. On the other hand, if we should be growing a crop which from seed to picking would take only a few months, a quicker-acting inorganic fertilizer would be used, if not in the initial soil preparation, then surely to spur the plants into quick growth.

Before organic fertilizers, such as manure, cottonseed meal, or bone meal, can be utilized by plants, they must be converted into the basic elements of which they are composed. This process is carried on by decay bacteria and is a progressive one. Therefore, though some value is apparent from organic fertilizers right away, their real usefulness lies in the fact that they release nutrients over a long period of time, a very good reason why they have been the first choice of good gardeners for generations.

Inorganic fertilizers are wholly, or partly, soluble in water, and for that reason are quickly available to plants. The solubility of fertilizers, however, has its drawbacks, for every time water is applied to the soil some of the fertilizer is washed out of it and lost. It is also important to know that inorganic fertilizers are concentrated and can easily be applied too generously. Whenever you use an inorganic fertilizer, be careful to read the directions fully and follow them.

What Is a "Complete Fertilizer"?

Beginning gardeners are often confused when they are sold a "complete fertilizer" and find that it contains only three elements: nitrogen, phosphorus, and potash. Somewhere they have heard that plants require a whole multitude of chemicals such as iron, sulphur, copper, manganese, zinc, silicon, boron, and magnesium, and the idea of a complete fertilizer's having only three chemicals raises a question in their minds. Actually, all plants must have nitrogen, phosphorus, and potash, and since many of the other elements, sometimes called minor or trace elements, are already in soil to some extent, they are not considered a part of the analysis of an ordinary fertilizer. There is a trend, however, for the manufacturers of fertilizers to add some of the less-common chemicals to their mixtures. It is an indication that the findings of the experiment-station plant scientists are beginning to be heard. It has been proven beyond a doubt that the trace elements must be present for best plant growth, though the reason why and the way in which they induce better growth is not always known.

It is likewise upsetting to the new gardener who knows his grade-school arithmetic to read the symbols on a bag of fertilizer and be told that the 5–8–7 means that there are five pounds of nitrogen, eight pounds of phosphorus, and seven pounds of potash, and yet the bag weighs one hundred pounds. No matter how he figures it, he can come up with only twenty pounds of plant food, and he knows that he has paid for a one-hundred-pound bag of it. There is no catch to the story, but there is a simple explanation: Pure chemicals are so concentrated that, were they applied to crops in an undiluted form, they would burn them up almost like fire. Thus they are mixed with some sort of filler. This material may be of organic nature, such as ground-up peanut hulls, or it may be sand or some other inert substance. In any rate, the 5–8–7 is still so concentrated that it can burn plants, too, and must be used sparingly. It would be a good idea if every once in a while each gardener should touch a bit of a chemical fertilizer to the tip of his tongue and feel how it stings. It would give him a better picture of why fertilizer must be applied with caution.

The Relationship of Nitrogen to Plant Growth

It has been said that we sometimes notice things when they are gone rather than when they are with us, and this is an apt description of the appearance of plants when certain chemicals are not available to them. When nitrogen is lacking, plants display a uniformly pale-green color. Growth is weak and spindly, and plants tell the most inexperienced observer that they are unhappy. Nitrogen promotes dark-green color and fast growth, and though both of these factors are ideal goals for lawn fertilizers, they may not be entirely what is desired in greenhouse crops, where flowers are the desired product. Too much nitrogen stimulates lush, weak vegetative growth, often at the expense of flower production, and, in addition, plants which have too much nitrogen are more susceptible to disease and take longer to mature.

Nitrogen is an important component of good greenhouse fertilizers, however, but its role is only a part of the entire picture. It must be used in combination with other nutrients in a balanced ratio so that each element may do its part toward promoting thrifty, floriferous plants. Common sources of nitrogen are nitrate of soda, manure, urea, bone meal, cottonseed meal, calcium nitrate, dried blood, ammonium nitrate, and ammonium sulphate.

The Role of Phosphorus

You will remember that in the preparation of the composted greenhouse soil a liberal amount of superphosphate was added as the pile was built. This is because manure, the chief source of nutrients in the compost, is very low in phosphorus. Phosphorus is known to induce stockiness in plants and to hasten maturity, as well as to promote the production of buds and flowers. Whereas nitrogen leaches quickly from the greenhouse soil because of watering operations, phosphorus is relatively stable and is most effective when it is thoroughly mixed with the soil prior to planting. The most common source of phosphorus is superphosphate, but some is available from bone meal, though so slowly as to be of limited value for quick-growing greenhouse crops.

Why Potash Is One of the "Big Three"

One of the oldest recorded fertilizers known to gardeners is wood ashes. Observers of nature have always noted with awe the tremendous new growth that springs up in a woodland in the wake of a forest fire. The potash in wood ashes is responsible for much of this vigor, and though we usually buy the potash for our gardens nowadays, we would do well to save the wood ashes from our fireplaces too. Potash particularly stimulates root growth; it also helps in the formation of starch, sugar, and other substances in plant cells, as well as helps plants resist cold weather. Wood ashes which have not been wet contain about 5 per cent potash; muriate of potash contains 60 per cent; sulphate of potash 50 per cent; and potassium nitrate 44 per cent, as well as 13 per cent nitrogen.

Practical Soil Testing and Its Value

Gardening without soil testing is like driving without a road map: You may know where you want to go, but you don't know how to get there. Every year millions of gardeners apply fertilizer or lime to their gardens without any regard to the needs of the plants. They do their gardening by faith and hope, and the wonder is that their results are as good as they are. Of course, since they do not know what is deficient in their soils, they simply apply some of everything in the hope that they will somehow hit the target. There is no question but that this philosophy of gardening is a wasteful one, and there are times when it is a dangerous one as well. There are optimum conditions for plant growth, and as we have stated earlier, it is easy to be too generous with fertilizer.

Acid or Alkaline?

The most common soil test is called the *p*H test. It is a method of testing the relative acidity or alkalinity of soils and is based on a scale numbered from one to fourteen, calibrated to record the hydrogen-ion concentration of soils. Soils are said to be neutral when the scale reads 7.0 and means that the soil is neither acid nor alkaline. Below 7.0 soils are said to be acid and above 7.0 are said to be alkaline. Greenhouse and garden flowers and vegetables have been classified as to their *p*H needs and recorded in booklets available with soil-test kits. When plants are said to prefer acid soil, it is meant that they do best when the *p*H reading is from 4.5 to 5.5. Most other plants do nicely when the range is from 5.5 to a bit over 7.0. Very few plants can grow below 4.0 or above 8.0, and, practically speaking, none of these are cultivated plants.

When one has determined the present *p*H reading of his soil, he can change it to any other reading that he desires by adding lime (to make it more alkaline) or aluminum sulphate or sulphur (to make it more acid). The amounts of these materials to add will be determined by the results of your soil tests and are prescribed in the booklet accompanying your soil-test kit. Most soils in areas receiving thirty or more inches of rain each year are acid, and soils in dry areas are apt to be alkaline in reaction.

Testing for Nitrogen, Phosphorus, and Potash

Now that you know how to test for soil *p*H, you are ready to test for the amounts of nitrogen, phosphorus, and potash that your soil requires. These tests are as simple to perform as the *p*H test, and the recommendations of the chart in your booklet should be followed to get maximum results from your soil.

The Sudbury Soil Testing Kit uses color charts to help the gardener determine the percentage of each plant food that is needed in the fertilizer mixture when it is applied at the rate of

5 pounds per 100 square feet. The tests may show, for example, that the fertilizer should contain 10 per cent nitrogen, 20 per cent phosphorus, and 12 per cent potash. A 100-pound bag of fertilizer analyzing 10–20–12 applied at the rate of 5 pounds per 100 square feet would be ideal. Of course, a fertilizer that tested 5–10–6 could be used equally well, but at the rate of 10 pounds per 100 square feet. The exact formula you need may not be available, but at least you can find one close enough to your requirements to suit your needs . . . if not perfectly, then surely better than the "guess" method.

CHAPTER VII

WHERE PLANTS COME FROM

Hybrids and Mutants; Colchicine and Gibberellin

One of the most enduring laws of the universe is that all its inhab-itants, flora and fauna, must reproduce their kind or die. The miracle of ever-renewing life has fascinated mankind since the beginning of time. Through all the years those who have grown plants of any description have done their best to pry into the secrets of nature so as to learn how to reproduce certain plants which have displayed outstanding characteristics. The task is a never-ending one as plant scientists today continue to produce larger and more beautiful flowers, more delicious fruit, or more prolific grain.

It must be recognized that flowers are the means by which plants are able to make seeds to perpetuate themselves. Normally, the wild species are those best adapted to take care of themselves in competition with other plants in nature, but often man finds the wild blossoms are of small size, sparse petalage, or colors which do not please his eye. Thus they have been altered, not only by selection, but by cross-pollination with other varieties. Many of the hybrid flowers today, as well as most of the double-flowering plants, would soon die if they had to compete with their wild cousins in woodlands and meadows. Having produced these lovely things, we know that we must also protect them or they will perish.

It is easy enough to say that we shall save the seeds of our best plants and thereby get superior seedlings, but all plants do not reproduce themselves exactly in their offspring. If you have ever noticed the Petunias which spring up in your garden from self-sown seeds, you have seen how few of them resemble their lovely parents. All too often the seedlings are pale and washed-out in appearance and are usually lavender or magenta as were their original ancestors which came from the plains of Argentina. Thus it is that we say plants revert unless a controlled breeding program is carried on. Yet we accept without a question the fact that when we buy a package of pink Petunias of a certain shade all of the plants will be exactly as we ordered. Somewhere men have been able to do a better job than the bees!

It is true that many plants can be grown from seed and that the seedlings will exhibit a remarkable uniformity; such plants are said to "breed true." Others, as with many hybrids, will come true for one generation only; succeeding generations will be a mixture of all sorts of colors reflecting their multihued genetic background. So-called F1 hybrids—that is, first-generation hybrids—are usually hand-pollinated and produce very vigorous offspring which all look alike on the outside but which are all mixed up genetically. Plant breeding is a very specialized field of horticulture based upon discoveries first made by an Austrian monk, Gregor Johann Mendel, a century ago.

There are records dating back to about one hundred years before Mendel's time which describe men's efforts to improve their crops by selection of desirable seedlings, and, no doubt, this practice goes back many centuries prior to this time. However, all this type of work was limited to the "one-in-a-million" chance that some particular plant would be found that would be superior to all others. As living examples of this type of selection, the Baldwin apple, a favorite today, was discovered growing wild in a pasture in Wilmington, Massachusetts, one hundred years ago; the McIntosh apple was likewise found growing in a field in Ontario, Canada, while the Wealthy apple came from a seedling on a farm in Minnesota.

Now the seeds from these apples will not bring forth more Baldwin, McIntosh, and Wealthy apple trees because they do not breed true. In order to get more of these trees, they must be propagated vegetatively. This process of vegetative propagation by the means of cuttings, grafting, budding, layering, or division must be practiced for a great many plants grown both indoors and out. For example, named varieties of African Violets must be increased by the means of leaf cuttings. When seedlings are sown, they show an immense variation. Some kinds of plants such as seedless grapes must be propagated vegetatively simply because they produce no seeds.

Although this chapter will describe various methods of plant propagation, when you get to Chapter VIII, "Plants You Can Grow in Your Greenhouse," you will find the various methods of increasing each of the specific plants included in its cultural notes.

Still another way in which new varieties of plants have evolved is by what is known as mutation, sometimes called sporting. In these instances certain branches of trees, for example, for some unknown reason produce flowers or fruit unlike that of the rest of the plant. Mutations can be better than, or inferior to, the parent plant and, of course, must be increased by vegetative means.

It is a common occurrence for African Violets to display mutation. Although it would seem that all plants propagated from leaves of a parent plant would be like the parent, nature rules otherwise. Two leaf cuttings of the African Violet *Prince Charles,* a double-flowering dark-purple variety, produced on my window sill one plant that is like its parent and another double-flowering plant with lavender and white flowers.

Mutation is often induced in plant-breeding programs so as to give plant breeders an opportunity to select from a host of mutants which normally might have taken many years to occur in nature, if indeed they occurred at all. Mutation is brought about by the alteration of the chromosomes within the cells by radiation or by the use of the drug colchicine, which is derived from the roots of the Autumn Crocus.

Another substance now being used to regulate plant growth is gibberellin. It has the capacity to stimulate plants into gigantic growth and to shorten the length of time ordinarily required between seeding and blossoming, as well as the ability to break the dormancy of many seeds and buds. Whether it will have a place in plant breeding is not yet established. This material, as well as colchicine, is available from seed-catalogue houses and can form the basis for an intriguing series of experiments which may be conducted by any person interested in gardening.

Growing Plants from Seeds or Spores

Of all the ways to produce new plants, the sowing of seeds or spores (which are the "seeds" of Ferns) is the easiest method. No doubt, you have already grown thousands of plants this way in your garden; so you will find no difficulty in growing them in your greenhouse. The fact of the matter is that they will grow better and easier in a greenhouse. Seed sowing involves soil preparation in such a way that the soil particles are fine enough for the little seedlings to push through when they sprout. Many greenhouse plants grown in benches, such as Stocks and Calendulas, are often sown directly in the benches where they are to grow and thinned out to six or eight inches apart. The finer seeds, nevertheless, are usually started under conditions more apt to give a better stand of seedlings.

The standard seeding mixture is composed of one part each of sharp sand, loam, and peat moss or leaf mold. All of the soil in the flat or flowerpot in which the seeds are to be sown should not be sifted. Coarser soil should be put in the bottom to facilitate drainage, but the upper layers should be sifted. A small wooden frame eight or ten inches square with a piece of one-eighth-inch-mesh hardware cloth makes an easy-to-make sifter, or you may get a hand sifter from the dime store. Make sure that the surface of the soil in the pot or flat is level and firm and about one-half inch from the top of the container. The seeds should be sown thinly, either broadcast or in drills (small rows), and covered over with more sifted soil, but not more than twice the thickness of the diameter of the seeds. It is very easy to bury seeds too deeply. Remember that they are very small and the soil is very heavy.

After seed is sown it must be watered. Here it is that I suggest that you mix one of the soil disinfectants, such as Pano-Drench or Semesan, with the water and apply it to the surface of the soil. It must be done very gently so as not to wash the seeds out of the soil. A bulb syringe with a fine spray does the job nicely. The disinfectant will control damping-off fungi, which are present in all nonsterilized soils. (Of course, you can easily sterilize small quantities of soil for seed flats by putting it in your oven at 180 degrees for thirty minutes and thus kill weed seeds and Fern and Moss spores as well. This practice is especially recommended for those seeds which take a long time to sprout, for it is discouraging to have a green scum form on top of the soil long before your seedlings are expected to sprout.)

With the advent of plastics it has become easy for the most inept amateur to produce a fine stand of seedlings. It used to be that seed flats had to be watered time and again before the seeds would sprout, especially in hot weather. Now, if the seed flats are slipped into clear plastic bags or covered with sheets of clear plastic large enough to tuck under the bottoms of the flats, the initial watering will be found to be sufficient to enable the seeds to sprout. Once the seeds have sprouted, the plastic should be removed and the plants watered in the normal way.

Of course, this sealed-in method of seed sowing has been practiced for a long while by careful gardeners sowing very tiny seeds. An ordinary large-mouth bottle, laid on its side, can be partly filled with soil, the seed planted and watered, and the cover screwed on. Seeds that are very tiny, such as African Violet seeds, are ideally planted in this way. It is a real thrill to watch the tiny seedlings grow in their own protected environment.

It is imperative that seeds planted by any of the sealed methods be placed so that they will get light, but they *must not be put in the sun!* In a matter of a few minutes the sun would raise temperatures so high as to kill all seedlings. Thus even the newer and more certain methods of raising seedlings have their limitations. Sunloving plants must be moved to a very light place and their cover removed as soon as they sprout, or they will become too tall and spindly. Others, such as African Violets and Begonias, which normally grow in subdued light, do not need to be moved but may be allowed to grow in a protected location.

You will be pleased with the results of sowing tiny seeds on a brick. This idea is not as odd as it sounds, and it works this way: Take an ordinary clean brick and sift on it some of the soil mixture for seedlings. Bake it in your oven at 180 degrees for thirty minutes; then set the brick in a covered plastic or glass dish and fill in around the brick with water. It will immediately absorb water and carry it up into the layer of fine soil. Sow your seeds on this fine soil, cover the dish, and wait for them to sprout.

It should be mentioned that when planting tiny seeds under these sealed-in conditions, it is not necessary to cover them with soil. There is so much natural moisture in the atmosphere of the container, coupled with the fact that the seeds fall into small crevices in the soil, that they will do better if not covered.

In the beginning of this section it was noted that spores and seeds can be grown in the same way. Spores serve the same purpose for Ferns and Mosses as seeds do for other plants. They are usually found on the underneath side of Fern fronds. If you dust a mature frond on a sheet of white paper, you will be able to catch untold numbers of tiny spores by which you can multiply your Ferns.

How to Increase Plants Vegetatively
CUTTINGS

One of the most notable ways in which plants of the world differ from animals lies in the fact that tiny pieces of plants can be rooted and grown into mature specimens similar in all respects to the plants from which they came. This remarkable facility has been capitalized upon by men to increase those plants which they find especially useful or beautiful, but which cannot reproduce them-

selves exactly from seeds. This field of horticulture has seen remarkable advances with the perfection of various root-inducing
substances. As recently as twenty years ago, for example, it was
very difficult to root Azaleas, but with the preparations now being
used, growers expect nearly every cutting to send out roots and
grow into a healthy plant. Such materials are based on the use of
indolebutyric and naphthalene acetic acids and are sold as powders
under such trade names as Rootone and Hormodin.

There are several types of cuttings, their names based on the
portion of the plant used, such as stem cuttings, leaf cuttings,
leaf-bud cuttings, and root cuttings. Each of these will be described in the paragraphs that follow.

Stem cuttings, or "slips," as they are sometimes called, are the
most common way to increase plants vegetatively. Every gardener
has at one time or another rooted stem cuttings. The process simply involves the taking of a section of the stem of a plant and
inducing it to root by placing it in sand, sand and peat moss,
vermiculite, or even water. Once the cutting is rooted, it is potted
up in soil and becomes a small plant. Some plants root very easily
in a week or so while others require months to form roots. These
slow-to-root species are treated nowadays by dipping the mois-
tened end of the cutting into a rooting powder, such as Rootone or
Hormodin, shaking off the excess powder, and inserting the cutting
in the rooting medium.

Stem cuttings may be used for many greenhouse plants (see
next chapter) as well as various evergreens and garden shrubs.
A variation of the stem cutting is used to propagate such plants
as Dieffenbachia and Hawaiian Ti (*Cordyline terminalis*). In pro-
ducing new plants of these species, the stem is cut into sections
a few inches long and laid flat on the rooting medium (sand or
sand and peat moss). The sections are partly covered with the
sand, or sand and peat moss, mixture, and in a short time young
plants will spring out from the sides of the stems. They can be
cut off and potted up to make new plants.

Just as surely as most gardeners are familiar with stem cuttings, so are most of them familiar with *leaf cuttings* as well. All of us have rooted African Violet leaves at one time or another, and this is a perfect example of how leaf cuttings work. Mature leaves of such plants as African Violet, Gloxinia, Hoya, Streptocarpus, Peperomia, and Christmas Begonia root readily if inserted into moist sand or a sand and peat moss mixture. Tiny plants and roots form at the tip of the stem, which is under the rooting medium. When the plants become large enough to handle, they are potted into a regular potting soil.

Leaf-bud cuttings are a means of increasing a small stock of plants quickly and are made in the same manner as regular cuttings, except that each cutting consists of a single leaf with a portion of the stem attached instead of an entire stem. The bud which lies in the axil of the leaf where it joins the stem grows and becomes the new plant. The usefulness of this method of propagation is apparent when a rare plant is concerned, for theoretically every leaf could be used to start a new plant. When stem cuttings are used, the number of new plants possible is limited by the number of stems. Most plants which can be grown from stem cuttings will also grow from leaf-bud cuttings, but they take a bit longer to grow into a given size because they have to start from a single bud, rather than a stem several inches long.

There are interesting variations in the production of plants from their leaves. Certain plants normally produce plantlets on the margin or the ends of their leaves, are said to be viviparous, and are analogous to animals which give forth living young. A common example of this type of plant is known as Air Plant (*Kalanchoe* or *Bryophyllum pinnatum*). If a leaf of Air Plant is taken from the plant and hung up on a curtain, it will produce a whole family of young Air Plants around its margin.

Many good gardeners are familiar with *root cuttings* of plants without realizing it. After all, when we plant Irish potatoes in our gardens, we divide up the tubers; surely this is a type of root cutting. Many ornamental plants can be increased in this way. Such plants as Gaillardia, Oriental Poppy, Bleeding Heart, Garden Phlox, Japanese Anemone, and Bouvardia will grow easily if sections of their roots an inch or so long are placed in a moist sandy medium. The roots to choose are the main roots, not the tiny feeder roots.

You will find it very convenient to reserve a section of a greenhouse bench for the purpose of rooting cuttings. It does not have to be more than a foot long, running the width of the bench. Separate it from the rest of the bench with a wooden partition so that its rooting medium will not mix with the bench soil adjacent to it. You should provide some sort of a shade for the bench. A shelter made of glass sides and a glass top will do wonders toward conserving humidity and hastening rooting. The rooting medium usually chosen is sharp sand, but plants will root in other mediums as well. Some plants prefer a mixture of sand and peat moss, and many growers have had excellent results using such sterile mediums as vermiculite or perlite. In any event, it is a good idea to soak the medium occasionally with Semesan or Pano-Drench to control damping-off fungi, which can attack cuttings just as they do seedlings. The alternative to the treatment of disinfecting the rooting medium is to change it at least once a season.

BULBS, TUBERS, CORMS, AND RHIZOMES

Many times amateur gardeners will extend themselves financially to buy a single tuber of a new variety of Dahlia, for example, and wish that they could afford to have a dozen of them instead. With a greenhouse this is entirely possible, for the tuber can be started into growth when the weather is still cold outside, and as the new shoots come up, they can be cut off and rooted to make an indefinite number of new plants. Then as the plants are harvested in the autumn, each tuber can be divided to make even more new plants.

Lilies are other expensive items in the garden budget, and it is nice to know that one can take a few scales off the bulbs, place them in moist sand, and in a few months have a whole stock of tiny new bulbs. When planted in the garden, they will eventually become large enough to blossom. Many Lilies also produce tiny bulbils in the axils of each leaf on the stem. These little bulbs can be harvested and grown in light soil in a greenhouse, gaining a season or more of growth.

The bulbs of such plants as Cyclamens, Tuberous-rooted Begonias, and Gloxinias can be divided with a sharp knife, and each section will produce a new plant. The division should be done just as the bulbs show new growth, and, of course, each section must have its own bud. The raw cuts should be dusted with sulphur and dried somewhat before planting in a light sandy soil.

Although Gladiolus are ordinarily grown as garden plants, you may want to try a few in your greenhouse for the novelty of it. The tiny bulblets or, more technically, cormels which form at the base of the mature bulb are used to increase Gladiolus varieties. It takes two or three seasons of outdoor growing for the cormels to develop into blossoming-sized corms.

Fancy-leaf Caladiums will surely be among the plants you grow in your greenhouse. They grow from rhizomes quite similar to those of German Iris and can be divided easily so that there is at least one "eye" to each section.

GRAFTING AND BUDDING

You may not think of *grafting* as having a place in the home greenhouse because it is so often thought of in connection with fruit trees. Yet, did you know that many varieties of Cacti can be grafted together? The Christmas Cactus (since it has a pendulous type of growth) is often grafted on an upright form of Cactus so that it will grow into a weeping-tree form, truly beautiful when its arching stems are laden with bright blossoms during the dull months of the year. There are many kinds of grafts which may be made, but the simplest kind for the beginner is done by inserting a section of stem of the variety wanted for the top of the plant into a split made in the plant already growing. The union is tied and in most instances covered with a material to keep out the air, and soon the two plants become one. Since the growing part of the bark of any plant is the inner cambium layer, this layer of both parts of the plants to be joined must coincide as much as possible. Although there are exceptions, most plants must be closely related species in order that they may be grafted successfully.

Budding is a similar operation in that a single bud of the desired variety is inserted under an incision in the bark of the plant which is already growing. When the bud begins to develop, the top of the stock plant is gradually pruned away, forcing all of the energy of the plant into the bud, which soon becomes the top of the new plant. Roses and peaches are two common plants usually propagated by budding.

DIVISION

The art of dividing plants is a simple one and consists of the separation of roots or the cutting of tubers so that each section has roots and buds. Most greenhouse plants are grown either from seed or from cuttings, but *division* is occasionally necessary as in the culture of some species of Orchids.

RUNNERS

As soon as the word *runner* is mentioned, the next word to come to the minds of most gardeners is *strawberry*, for this is a classic example of a plant ordinarily multiplied by this method. In greenhouses such a plant as the Strawberry Geranium (*Saxifraga sarmentosa*), sometimes called Strawberry Begonia, sends out runners on which full-fledged little plants grow. These may be potted up individually and grown into full size, at which time they, in turn, will send out more runners. Another common type of greenhouse plant propagated by runners is the Boston Fern (*Nephrolepis exaltata bostoniensis*).

AIR LAYERING

Outdoors, layering usually consists of covering a section of a plant's basal stems or part of its branches so that in time roots will form and new plants can be procured in this manner. In greenhouses, however, layering is usually thought of in the sense of *air layering*. An example of this type of propagation is as follows: Suppose that one has an India Rubber Plant (*Ficus elastica*) or other type of greenhouse shrub which has grown out of bounds or become leggy. The problem is to get another plant from it which will be smaller and more compact in growth. A section of the tip of a branch perhaps a foot long is selected; an upward cut is notched about two thirds of the way through the branch, and a pebble or matchstick is inserted to hold the cut open. The open cut is dusted with a rooting powder then wrapped in a ball of moist Sphagnum moss, which in turn is sealed with a piece of plastic so as to hold in the moisture of the moss. Soon roots will be seen growing through the moss inside the plastic covering. At this time the lower stem is cut off, the plastic removed, and the moss ball planted in a pot of soil. There you have it, a brand new plant.

CHAPTER VIII

PLANTS YOU CAN GROW IN YOUR GREENHOUSE

Out of the thousands of plants which, by some stretch of the imagination, could be grown in greenhouses, how does one decide which ones to include in such a chapter as this? Somehow one must have a balance upon which to weigh the good and poor points of all sorts of plants and make a decision based upon his judgment of the relative value of many factors involved. As an example, I feel that unless a plant is available from a reliable source and can be purchased with the reasonable expectation that it will arrive in a healthy condition, it would be foolish to recommend it to the amateur gardener who has a hobby greenhouse. Likewise, if a plant is so finicky that it requires conditions not normally attainable by the average greenhouse hobbyist, it is surely no favor to him to suggest that he try to grow it. There are plants which can be grown which yield relatively little return for the space and attention they require. These plants should be mentioned, but their faults should be made evident.

In writing this chapter I have tried above all else to be practical. Also, since there is no merit in verbosity, the cultural notes will be found to be brief. Unless a plant requires a special soil condition, it will be assumed that it will thrive in the "greenhouse soil" described in Chapter V, "Down to Earth." It is the writer's opinion that there is no justification to the cult which claims that each and every plant must have its own special soil mixture. Look outdoors at any field and forest and see for yourself the multitudes of plants growing side by side in ordinary field and woodland soils. While it is true that bog plants do not grow on hillsides, there are, nevertheless, innumerable plants which will thrive in any given location, especially if it is as salubrious as the soil mixture which has been suggested as the ideal greenhouse soil. Where special soil conditions will make the culture of a plant easier, you will find notes to that effect.

The kinds of insects and diseases which are apt to bother plants in home greenhouses are quite limited, and their control is a relatively simple one. All problems of this nature are grouped together in Chapter X, "Battle of the Bugs."

In an effort to make this book as practical as possible, the entire list of plants was not simply thrown together in one pile for the reader to sort out. Instead, though there is bound to be some overlapping, plants are grouped according to their botanical relationship to each other, according to their habit of growth, or according to the way in which they are most commonly grown, with cross references where appropriate. The twelve categories are as follows: *Pot Plants* (this includes also some plants normally used as cut flowers, but easier to grow in pots than in benches); *Cut Flowers* (those types usually grown in benches specifically to be cut for flower arrangements); *Bulbs* (this group includes all sorts of bulbous plants and plants with thickened rootstalks); *Vines, Climbers, and Trailers* (this section includes certain weak-stemmed shrubs best grown on some sort of support); *Hanging Basket Plants* (these are some of the most enjoyable of greenhouse plants); *Tub Plants* (larger plants and shrubs that require larger-than-ordinary containers in which to grow); *Succulent Plants, Including Cacti* (plants which are especially easy to grow on high shelves with an abundance of sunlight); *Bromeliads* (charming plants which are easy to grow, yet rarely seen); *Ferns; Gesneriads* (plants that are related to African Violets); *Bedding Plants;* and *Perennials*.

SECTION 1. POT PLANTS

ABUTILON, Flowering-maple

Flowering-maples get their name from the fact that their leaves are Maplelike in appearance, not because they are Maples. They are members of the Mallow family and have trumpet-shaped blossoms similar to partly opened Hollyhocks. The flowers are borne on slender stems, which droop from the leaf axils, and may be yellow, red, pink, or white in color. There are many fine hybrids available, all of which have a common ancestry in species native to tropical South America. Many varieties have variegated leaves, which add to the attractiveness of the plants.

Flowering-maples enjoy warm temperatures, with a 60-degree minimum, and bright sunshine. Ordinary greenhouse soil will suit their needs adequately.

New plants can be started easily from cuttings taken in fall or spring and rooted in sand. Plants grown from seeds, because of their hybrid background, will display a considerable variation in leaf markings and growth habits, as well as flower coloration. Some varieties of Flowering-maple make fine hanging basket plants.

ACALYPHA HISPIDA, Chenille Plant

The common name, Chenille Plant, is surely a descriptive one for Acalypha, for its blossoms are extremely tiny and are crowded on tassel-like inflorescences of reddish purple. This plant, which comes to us from the jungles of the East Indies, requires a warm greenhouse, with minimum temperatures of 60 degrees, and little fertilizer.

Start new plants from cuttings in fall or spring, using sand as a rooting medium.

ACALYPHA WILKESIANA, Copper Leaf

This plant is a cousin of the Chenille Plant and requires the same culture. Its beauty lies in its brilliantly colored leaves of coppery green, often mottled with yellow or orange.

ACHIMENES, see *Gesneriads*, Section 10.

AFRICAN VIOLET, see SAINTPAULIA,
Gesneriads, Section 10.

AGLAONEMA, Chinese Water Evergreen

For the darkest corner of a warm, shady greenhouse choose the Chinese Water Evergreen. Its common name signifies its choice of a growing location, for it will do well in either plain water or very moist soil. As befits a member of the Aroid family, its watery-white blossoms are similar in shape to those of a Calla-lily, but so small as to be relatively insignificant. Its usefulness lies in the attractiveness of its dark green, sometimes mottled, leaves.

Chinese Water Evergreens are available from florists who value them for their ability to withstand adversity in the dry atmosphere and often dark places their customers sometimes want to grow plants.

As one might expect from plants native to the Malayan region, they grow best with a minimum temperature of 65 degrees and considerable shade. Root segments laid on moist sand will send out new plants.

ALOCASIA, see *Bulbs*, Section 3.

ALTERNANTHERA

Brazil is the native habitat of Alternantheras, prized in the hey-day of carpet bedding for their brilliantly colored leaves and their ability to withstand shearing. They have leaves of red, green, yellow, or blotched pink, according to the variety. They like bright sunshine and are easily rooted in sand at any time of the year.

AMARYLLIS, see *Bulbs*, Section 3.

ANTHURIUM, Anthurium, Tail Flower

Anthuriums are extremely interesting and colorful plants for the warm, shady greenhouse and should be grown at a minimun temperature of 65 degrees. The leaves are leathery, glossy, and spear-shaped, and as each leaf unfolds it reveals a blossom of surpassing beauty. The flowers are heart-shaped, scarlet to white in color, with a single straight or curly spadix (similar to the central part of the Calla-lily flower) rising from the apex of each flower.

Rather than in soil, Anthuriums are potted in Osmunda fiber or fir bark, items discussed in detail in Chapter IX, "Anyone Can Grow Orchids." As the plants grow the main stems increase in length and send out many stout roots. The stems should be wrapped in Sphagnum moss and kept moist to facilitate growth.

New plants are easily started from offshoots from the main stem. Cut them from the main stem with a few roots attached and pot them up in Osmunda fiber or fir bark.

As cut flowers Anthuriums are extremely long-lasting, staying beautiful for two or three weeks. If left on the plants, however, the flowers stay colorful for several weeks. They grow well in a warm, shaded greenhouse in company with Orchids.

ARDISIA CRISPA, Ardisia

The Ardisia is an evergreen shrub from tropical Asia often grown for its bright red berries, which hang in great clusters below its shiny foliage. The berries ripen in the autumn and persist for an entire year; thus it is sometimes offered in florist shops as an unusual long-lasting Christmas gift plant.

Ardisias should be grown in a shady greenhouse at a 60-degree minimum temperature. New plants may be grown from seeds or from cuttings taken in late spring. They prefer a light sandy soil and relatively little fertilizer.

ARTILLERY PLANT, See PILEA MICROPHYLLA, this section.

ASPARAGUS PLUMOSUS, Asparagus-fern

This is the common Asparagus-fern found in florist shops. It makes a soft-textured foliage plant for the shady, warm greenhouse and has a tendency to climb. Give it ordinary soil and regular feedings, and it will grow for years in the same flowerpot. Asparagus-fern should have a minimun temperature of 60 degrees, since it comes from the warm sections of central Africa. Plants may be divided or grown from seeds.

ASPARAGUS SPRENGERI, see *Hanging Basket Plants,*
Section 5, culture as above.

ASPIDISTRA ELATIOR, Cast Iron Plant

You do not need a greenhouse to grow the Cast Iron Plant.
It used to be a favorite "parlor plant" in the Victorian days and
is sometimes seen nowadays in barbershop windows. Its tough,
leathery leaves are usually 1½ feet long. The plants are increased
by division of the roots. Any soil and temperature above freezing
will be tolerated by this plant, but it will do best if grown in a
shady greenhouse with a minimum temperature of 60 degrees.
The Cast Iron Plant comes from the southern part of China and
lives up to its name by having no important disease or insect
problems.

AZALEA

Few flower lovers would dispute you if you maintained that
Azaleas are the finest of all pot plants. Surely there are many
other plants with grand qualities, but Azaleas continue to hold
their popularity decade after decade.

There are three types of Azaleas commonly grown in greenhouses, though under glass there is no reason why one cannot
grow many other kinds if he wishes to do so. The reason that
Kurume, Indica, and Rutherfordiana Azaleas are the ones usually
grown is that they can be depended upon to produce a large crop
of flowers each year. Kurume Azaleas have relatively small flowers, but they are borne in such profusion as to cover the bushes
so that few, if any, leaves are visible. Indica Azaleas have much
larger flowers, somewhat comparable to open Roses. All the blossoms do not open at the same time; so their beauty-life is extended
to several weeks when grown in a cool greenhouse. Rutherfordiana
Azaleas, as well as even more recent hybrids, have resulted from
a blending of the free-flowering habits of the Kurume with the
large flowers of the Indicas. The results have been spectacular,
plant breeders having not only achieved their goal of good flower
size and floriferousness, but also attained a bonus of unusual
colors not found in the parent species.

Greenhouse Azaleas may be white, any shade of pink, red, purplish red, brick red, cerise, or salmon. Yellow-flowered Azaleas are among the hardy garden species not usually grown in greenhouses except for forcing at flower-show time.

The propagation of Azaleas is not usually attempted by the hobby greenhouse owner, not because he cannot root the cuttings, but because it is easier to buy plants already sizable enough to be colorful in his greenhouse.

Azaleas which are seen in flower shops in the East at Christmas have been given at least four weeks of cold storage before being brought into warm greenhouses to blossom. Such manipulation is not possible for most amateurs; so they are advised to buy early plants from their florists, getting them just as the buds begin to open. Azaleas grown in warm climates usually will blossom as early as Christmas without this special treatment if brought into a greenhouse in the fall. Azaleas grown in cool climates will start to blossom in January. It takes about six weeks of 60-degree minimum temperature for Azaleas to blossom after having been brought into the greenhouse. In cold sections of the country it is easy to protect Azaleas in a deep cold frame (see Chapter XI, "Greenhouse Stretchers") and bring them into a greenhouse as they are needed.

When Azaleas need to be repotted, use peat moss alone or with some sand mixed with it, rather than soil. Azaleas grow beautifully in pure peat moss, which provides not only the moisture-holding capacity the plants need, but also insures an acid medium. Azaleas do best with a pH reading of 4.5 to 5.5.

Two common troubles possible with Azaleas are *chlorosis* and *leaf drop*. Chlorosis is apparent when the leaves become pale green with dark green veins. This can be remedied by watering your plants with a solution made of one ounce of iron sulphate dissolved in two gallons of water. Leaf drop is caused by allowing the plants to become too dry, or by not giving them enough light.

BEGONIA REX, Rex Begonia
There are many varieties of Rex Begonias, differing somewhat

in the shape and color of their leaves, but requiring the same cultural conditions. Most Rex Begonias have large leaves often marked with areas having a peculiar metallic sheen. The underneath sides of the leaves, as well as the long leaf stalks, are usually somewhat hairy or shaggy in appearance. Most varieties have pink blossoms, which are borne during late winter and early spring.

Rex Begonias come from the warm, moist forests of Assam, thus they do best when given similar conditions in a greenhouse. They should have a minimum night temperature of 60 degrees, and they must have partial shade in order to do well.

Rex Begonias are easily propagated by division or by a unique method of leaf cutting. A mature leaf should have several of its main veins cut and then be pinned securely on top of a bed of moist sand. In a week or so new plants will grow at each point where the veins were severed.

BEGONIA SEMPERFLORENS, Wax Begonia

Few other plants are as well named botanically as the Wax Begonia, for it lives up to its name *semperflorens* by flowering constantly throughout the year. There are varieties of this Brazilian plant with pink, red, or white flowers, both single and double. There is a touch of yellow in each flower too, for the stamens are bright yellow and add a lively note to the color effect.

Wax Begonias are relatively short plants, rarely getting over ten inches tall, thus are ideally suited for pot culture. Some varieties have brilliantly colored leaves in reddish tones. They will grow in partial shade or full sun. In the sun the flower and leaf colors become intensified.

Wax Begonias do best at a 60-degree minimum temperature and should have a soil high in organic matter. Use one part peat moss and two parts composted soil for best results.

They may be propagated from stem cuttings rooted in sand, from division of old plants, or from seed. The seed is extremely fine and must be handled carefully. (See Chapter VII.)

The interesting old-fashioned Calla Begonia is a variety of Wax

Begonia whose new growth is so lacking in chlorophyll that the new leaves as they unroll look like miniature Calla-lilies.

You will find that your plants will do best if you keep them young by starting new plants from cuttings or seed and discarding old woody plants.

BEGONIA SOCOTRANA, Christmas Begonia

Christmas Begonias are among the most delightful of fall- and winter-flowering plants for a cool greenhouse. When in blossom the entire plants are so covered with pink blossoms that few leaves can be seen. Several varieties of Christmas Begonias have been developed, such as Lad^v Mac, Marjorie Gibbs, and Melior, all very similar. The original plants came from the island of Socotra, in the Indian Ocean.

Christmas Begonias are propagated from leaf cuttings taken in late autumn or winter, or from stem cuttings taken in summer. Root them in sand.

They do well with a 60-degree minimum temperature and must have partial shade from early spring until early autumn.

Do grow a few plants of Christmas Begonia in your greenhouse. You will be very pleased with them. Also grow some of the Bardse or Holland Begonias if you can get them. They have quite large semidouble flowers and require similar growing conditions.

BEGONIA, TUBEROUS-ROOTED, see *Bulbs*, Section 3.

BELOPERONE GUTTATA, Shrimp Plant

The Shrimp Plant is a well-named herb from Mexico whose coppery-yellow inflorescences hang from the ends of the stems like so many crustaceans. The plants like bright light in a warm or cool greenhouse and should be allowed to dry somewhat between waterings. Propagation is by cuttings.

BOUVARDIA HUMBOLDTII
and B. TERNIFOLIA, Bouvardia

These two varieties of Bouvardia are desirable greenhouse plants grown for their clusters of pink, red, or white flowers. The red and pink flowers are derived from *B. ternifolia,* and the white ones, which are extremely fragrant, from *B. humboldtii*. Both varieties, in wild forms, are native to Central America, where they become shrubby plants four to six feet tall.

Both varieties can be propagated by stem cuttings taken in midwinter, and, in addition, *B. ternifolia* can be grown from root cuttings.

Bouvardias like a soil high in organic matter, an abundance of moisture, a minimum temperature of 60 degrees, and full sun. They must have a soil that is nearly neutral or slightly alkaline, with a *p*H of 6.0 to 7.5.

BROMELIADS, see *Bromeliads,* Section 8.

BROWALLIA, see *Hanging Basket Plants,* Section 5.

CALADIUM, see *Bulbs,* Section 3.

CALCEOLARIA CRENATIFLORA, Calceolaria,
Slipperwort, Lady's Pocketbook
(Also sometimes listed botanically
as *C. hybrida* or *C. herbeohybrida*)

Calceolarias come to us from South America, the wild species being native to sections of Peru and Chile. They are definitely subjects for a cool greenhouse and must be grown with a night temperature of 60 degrees or lower. They do best when night temperatures are 45 to 50 degrees.

The pouchlike flowers of Calceolarias have delighted flower lovers for generations. The inflated flowers are usually some shade of yellow, orange, golden brown, or bronze and are marked with purple or brown spots.

Seeds, which are extremely small, should be sown during August or September, and the plants will blossom from March to May. Care must be taken to protect the plants from direct sunlight except in the darkest winter months. Since Calceolarias have soft pubescent leaves, watering should be done carefully so that they will not become soaked, for such a condition favors the development of crown rot.

CALCEOLARIA INTEGRIFOLIA,
sometimes called *C. rugosa,* Shrubby Calceolaria.

This species has smaller flowers in shades of pink, yellow, and red. Culture is the same as above, except propagation is from cuttings taken in midsummer.

CAPSICUM FRUTESCENS, Ornamental Pepper

Ornamental Peppers, popular pot plants of the autumn and Christmas seasons, are grown for their bright red, purple, or cream-colored fruit, usually held high above rich green foliage. There are many varieties with fruits of diverse shapes and sizes, but all are grown in the same manner.

Seed should be planted in a greenhouse in midsummer, and the plants grown at a minimum temperature of 65 degrees. They grow rapidly and should be potted into four- or five-inch pots directly from the seedbed. Keep them on the dry side so that they will not become too large.

Blossoms are small and white and look like tomato blossoms, for these plants are closely related to tomatoes, potatoes, etc. The fruit develop quickly and hold their color for months.

Ornamental Peppers are native to the tropics and in that part of the world become woody perennials, though we treat them as annuals in greenhouse culture. The fruit is edible, but very hot.

CHRYSANTHEMUM FRUTESCENS, Marguerite, Paris Daisy

Marguerites are often grown as bench plants in commercial greenhouses, but we suggest that they be grown as pot plants in home greenhouses so as to restrain their growth somewhat and to make them easy to move if necessary. Marguerites are native to the Canary Islands and may be either white or yellow in color. They blossom constantly from February to September and are always welcome as long-lasting, short-stemmed cut flowers.

Start new plants in midsummer by rooting cuttings in sand. Ordinary greenhouse soil suits their needs, and they will blossom at temperatures ranging from 50 to 60 degrees. They should have full sunlight. Some growers get extra blossoms by giving their Marguerites artificial light during the short days of the year.

PLATE 7 Home greenhouses are not limited to cold climates! This beautiful one is in Alabama.

Courtesy National Greenhouse Co., Pana, Ill. Photo Watson McAlexander, Birmingham, Ala.

PLATE 8 Pleasant interior of rigid plastic greenhouse used as sun room. Orchids grow on shelves at each side.

Courtesy National Greenhouse Co., Pana, Ill.

PLATE 9 This freestanding aluminum greenhouse affords plants the maximum amount of light for good growth.

Courtesy Lord & Burnham, Irvington-on-Hudson, N.Y.

PLATE 10 A Camellia fancier's greenhouse. Notice that most of the shrubs are being grown in long-lasting redwood tubs.

Courtesy National Greenhouse Co., Pana, Ill. Photo Watson McAlexander, Birmingham, Ala.

PLATE 11 Commercial application of flexible plastic greenhouse used in growing Orchids. Note fans used to draw cool, moist air through house.

Courtesy Neil McDade, Rivermont Orchids, Signal Mountain, Tenn.

PLATE 12 Renewing benches in author's greenhouse. Heart redwood lumber will last for many years. Pot plants will be grown in area covered with wire mesh and pebbles.

PLATE 13 Snapdragons at various stages of growth, illustrating the use of wires and cross strings as supports for the plants as they mature. Author's photo at Miller's Greenhouse, Kulpmont, Pa.

PLATE 14 The author's greenhouse in midwinter. It is summertime beyond the glass!

CISSUS, see *Hanging Basket Plants,* Section 5.

CODIAEUM VARIEGATUM, Croton

Crotons are native to the islands of the South Pacific and the East Indies. In order to do well, they require a minimum temperature of 65 degrees and abundant moisture. Croton foliage may be green, yellow, white, or red in an amazing mixture of stripes, blotches, or patches, and it is not uncommon to find nearly all of these colors on one plant. In addition, there are various leaf shapes, some of which are curiously twisted or curled. Flowers are inconspicuous.

Crotons are propagated by stem or leaf cuttings or by air layering. They will tolerate full sun if they are given enough moisture, but they do equally well under a light shade in the summer months.

COLEUS BLUMEI, Coleus

As long as gardeners enjoy plants with colorful foliage, Coleus will continue to hold a place in their hearts. Coleus are native to Java and are extremely sensitive to cold, so should be grown at a minimum temperature of 60 degrees. They will tolerate almost any soil and need little fertilizer, since a high nutrient level would cause them to grow too luxuriantly.

Coleus are easily rooted in sand or water, but a home-greenhouse owner is apt to find more pleasure in growing Coleus from seed. Sow the seed in early spring and see the wide variety of colors your plants display. Watch for the slow-growing seedlings, for they are usually the most colorful. They make fine bedding plants for outdoor gardens in sun or partial shade. Particularly nice plants can be saved over from year to year by taking cuttings from them before frost and carrying them over winter in the greenhouse.

CORDYLINE TERMINALIS, Ti, Hawaiian Ti

You are probably familiar with the red, purple, pink, or cream-colored striped foliage of the Ti plant because it is often used by florists in colorful flower arrangements. In nature the Ti plant grows somewhat like a miniature Palm, with a tuft of brilliant foliage atop a slender stalk. Tiny white flowers, though rarely seen in greenhouses, are borne in huge terminal clusters, giving this plant its specific name, *terminalis.*

It is possible to buy Hawaiian Ti "logs," which are merely segments of the stalks, and it is from them that new plants are produced. Lay the logs on a bed of moist sand, and in a few weeks' time new plants will grow from adventitious buds hidden beneath the bark of the logs. Cut them off and pot them individually.

Ti plants must have a minimum temperature of 60 degrees. They will grow in sun or shade.

CRASSULA ARGENTEA, Jade Plant

A common occupant of barber shop and Chinese-laundry windows, the Jade Plant is one of the most accommodating of pot plants. It will grow in nearly any soil and seemingly has only one requirement, and that is that it should not be given too much water.

Jade Plants have very thick silvery-green, oval-shaped leaves, and, though rarely seen on small plants, lovely clusters of dainty pinkish-white flowers appear on mature specimens. There is also a variety with green and white foliage.

Jade Plants will grow in warm or cool greenhouses in full sun.

CROSSANDRA UNDULAEFOLIA, known also
as *C. infundibuliformis,* Crossandra

It is too bad that such an attractive plant as the Crossandra should have such an unpronounceable botanic name! Crossandras are evergreen plants native to India and Ceylon, where they grow to be as much as three feet tall and blossom continuously. The type grown as greenhouse plants, however, is a dwarf strain developed in Europe from the original species and rarely grows more than a foot tall. Its leaves are similar to those of Gardenias, rich green and glossy, and its stems are topped with brilliant salmon- or orange-colored flower spikes held high above the leaves.

Crossandras should be grown at a minimum temperature of 70 degrees with high humidity and are ideally suited for a warm greenhouse. They enjoy humusy soil, high in leaf mold, and do best in filtered light.

Crossandras may be grown from seeds or cuttings. Seeds germinate irregularly, with most of them starting within a month of the time they are planted. Cuttings should be rooted in a close atmosphere to keep them from wilting.

CYCLAMEN INDICUM, Cyclamen

Few, if any, plants for the cool greenhouse give more satisfaction than a group of well-grown Cyclamens. Grown at temperatures of 50 to 55 degrees, plants stay in blossom for six months or longer, giving a continuing display of color during the winter season. Flowers may be white, pink, lavender, or almost any shade of red. Some types have petals edged in colors different from the rest of the flowers while others have frilled or ruffled petals. There are even double-flowering varieties. Although not usually thought of as cut flowers, Cyclamen flowers make delightful, low, long-lasting bouquets.

Cyclamens come to us from the Near East and are sometimes called Persian Violets. It is interesting to know that the Arabs grind the seeds and use them as a fish poison.

It takes a minimum of twelve to fifteen months to produce a crop of Cyclamens from seed. The seeds are usually planted late in October and are grown through the first winter in the greenhouse. With the coming of mild weather, they are transferred to shaded cold frames outdoors, where cooler temperatures will prevail. In September they are shifted into larger pots and brought into a cool, bright greenhouse for final forcing into blossom. It is our opinion that home-greenhouse owners would do much better to buy several plants early in the fall from a florist, rather than to try to duplicate all the steps necessary to grow healthy plants themselves.

Commercial florists have favorite potting mixtures for Cyclamens, but all are high in humus. A mixture containing one part well-rotted cow manure, two parts peat moss or leaf mold, and two parts soil, combined with a dusting of superphosphate, is a typical mixture.

Problems: It might be stated that Cyclamens have only one major pest, the Cyclamen mite, but it can be controlled by regular spraying with Kelthane. Good professional growers find the time to spray their plants once a week, year round. This is one of the best reasons for buying Cyclamens of blossoming size, since it is hard for home-greenhouse owners to take the time and effort to spray plants thoroughly when they need it.

CYPERUS ALTERNIFOLIUS, Umbrella Plant

The Umbrella Plant is a bog plant suited for culture on the edge of a greenhouse pool. Stems grow two to four feet tall and are crowned by drooping clusters of leaves, giving rise to the plant's common name. Any soil will suit the Umbrella Plant as long as it is moist enough. It is interesting to know that this plant is closely related to Papyrus, *Cyperus papyrus,* from which the early Egyptians made paper. Papyrus grows in a similar manner to Umbrella Plant, except that it becomes six to eight feet tall, too large for most home greenhouses.

CYTISUS CANARIENSIS, Genista

Golden yellow flowers are always a delight in the spring greenhouse, and no plant gives them more abundantly than well-grown Genistas. These plants are members of the Pea family, sometimes known as Brooms, and come to us from the Canary Islands. They must be grown at cool temperatures and will not blossom unless they can be kept below 60 degrees for four to four and a half months, the time necessary to initiate buds and have them open. Plants may be kept outdoors during the summer, sheared lightly in September, and brought into the cool greenhouse. They will blossom in February and March when their bright flowers are especially welcome.

They enjoy a sandy soil high in phosphorus and potash, but low in nitrogen. New plants root readily in sand in the spring if kept about 70 degrees. Leaf and flower drop are common if the plants are not given enough water, or the temperatures are too high.

DIEFFENBACHIA, Dumb Cane

Among the most striking of foliage plants are the Dieffenbachias, resplendent in their softly mottled garb, truly suggesting a feeling of the tropics by their lush, exotic growth. The jungles of Central and South America are the native habitat of Dieffenbachias, which means that they like to grow in a moist, warm atmosphere, protected from the direct rays of the sun. A shaded greenhouse kept about 70 degrees is ideal for their culture.

As they become old, Dieffenbachias shed their lower leaves and look somewhat like miniature Palms. If compact plants are wanted, it is a simple matter to cut off the tops and root them in moist sand and peat moss. The stems, too, if laid partly buried in moist sand and peat moss will send out shoots, all of which may be cut off and potted to make new plants. Pot Dieffenbachias in a mixture composed of one part well-rotted cow manure, one part leaf mold, one part sand, and one part soil.

The common name, Dumb Cane, comes from the fact that the juice of the plant, when applied to one's tongue, will produce temporary speechlessness.

DRACAENA

There are many kinds of Dracaenas grown as greenhouse or house plants, most of which show their kinship to the Lily family by sending out crowns of Lilylike foliage, variously striped with shades of green, yellow, or white depending upon the variety. They have a tendency to become Palmlike by dropping their lower leaves, retaining only those at the top of the plant. An exception to the rule is *Dracaena Godseffiana,* which bears its leaves in whorls of three, dark green in color, speckled with light spots like specks of gold.

Most Dracaenas come from Africa and do best when grown in moist soil in a warm, humid, shaded location. They are tough plants and will tolerate poor conditions, thus are often grown as house plants.

Propagation is by air layering, or by laying stems in moist sand and peat moss and removing the sprouts as they appear, potting them into a soil rich in humus.

ERICA MELANTHERA, Heath

Heath is often sold as Heather, but true Heather is known botanically as *Calluna* and is rarely grown as a pot plant. Although Heath is native to South Africa, it is known to us as "Scotch Heather" when we buy it in flower shops during the winter months. Large fields of it are grown south of San Francisco, where it thrives in the damp atmosphere of the fogs rolling in from the ocean. Its rosy bell-like blossoms literally cover the stems, making it an extremely attractive plant. In order to do well in a greenhouse, it must be grown in a temperature of 40 to 50 degrees.

Acid soil, at least one-fourth peat moss, is essential for good growth. Should Heath develop chlorosis (yellowing of the foliage from alkaline conditions), water with a solution of one ounce of iron sulphate to two gallons of water.

EUPHORBIA PULCHERRIMA, Poinsettia

No one needs to be introduced to Poinsettias; few realize, however, that they are native to Mexico and were introduced to horticultural circles little more than a century ago. They are now grown as outdoor shrubs in the tropics around the world, in addition to their role as America's most popular Christmas pot plants. There are single- and double-flowering forms and varieties with white or pink flowers in addition to the familiar red ones.

Poinsettias require specialized culture noted very briefly in the paragraphs that follow. Let us assume that one has a flowering Poinsettia at Christmas time. It should be grown in a warm, bright greenhouse with a night temperature of 60 degrees. After flowering, the plant may be allowed to grow vegetatively, though it will not blossom until the following December. Flower buds are formed in the northern hemisphere from October 10 to 20, day length being the factor that determines flower-bud formation. If a

plant is allowed to grow all year long, it probably will be too large
to be useful as a house plant the second year; thus home greenhouse growers should treat their plants in the way that commercial
growers do. They take cuttings of their large plants during the
summer months and thus offer short, sturdy new plants at Christmas time.

Poinsettia cuttings root readily in sand if treated with a rooting
hormone and shaded lightly to reduce wilting. They must be
syringed often until new roots form. Pot them up in the greenhouse soil mentioned in Chapter V and feed them with a complete
fertilizer every two weeks until they blossom.

Since they depend upon day length to initiate flower buds, be
careful not to expose them to artificial light during the critical
October 10 to 20 period, or they may fail to blossom. Poinsettia
blossoms, by the way, are tiny and not showy; what we think of as
blossoms are really modified leaves.

FATSHEDERA LIZEI, Fatshedera

This unusual foliage plant is a bigeneric hybrid between English Ivy and Fatsia, a Japanese shrub. It has leaves shaped much
like those of English Ivy, but they are much more robust and very
glossy. The plants will cling to a support and send out stem roots
as they grow. They should have a cool greenhouse, bright light,
and moist, but not sodden, soil. Propagation is by cuttings or air
layering.

FATSIA JAPONICA, Fatsia

Fatsias are evergreen shrubs from Japan, grown as foliage
plants for their exceedingly attractive palmately lobed leaves. They
like a cool greenhouse with filtered light and moist soil. Propagate
new plants from seeds, cuttings, or air layering.

FICUS ELASTICA, India Rubber Plant and
FICUS PANDURATA, Fiddle-leaf Fig

These two related plants, whose culture is similar, will be
treated together. Both come from jungles; the India Rubber Plant
from India and Malaya, and the Fiddle-leaf Fig from Africa. Their

leaves are large and handsome, and both have been popular house plants for many years. They do best in warm greenhouses and can stand partial shade. Given plenty of moisture and warmth, they soon try to grow through the greenhouse roof! Propagation is by air layering.

FITTONIA VERSCHAFFELTII, Fittonia

Fittonias are native to Peru and are widely grown because of the distinctive veination of their leaves. The species *F. verschaffeltii* has bright green leaves with silvery white veins, while the variety *F. verschaffeltii argyoneura* has dark green leaves with red veins. Fittonias creep along the ground, thus are used sometimes as trailing plants, being allowed to grow over the edges of the pots. They need abundant moisture in a warm shaded greenhouse. Cuttings are easily rooted in sand.

FUCHSIA, Fuchsia, Lady's-eardrops

The lovely plants we know as Fuchsias are hybrids of species native to the American tropics or New Zealand. There are many recent hybrids with colors far different from the original "fuchsia" shade. Beautiful pale pinks and rich reds, as well as clear whites and wonderful color combinations, have given Fuchsias a real boost in popularity since grandmother's day.

Fuchsias will grow in full sun or light shade in a cool greenhouse. They may be trained to a single stem in a tree form, or be allowed to develop naturally with many stems. Trailing varieties are especially beautiful in hanging baskets. Old plants blossom more freely if they are cut back somewhat to induce branching.

Cuttings root easily in sand, or one may experiment with seedlings to see what new colors he can raise.

GENISTA, see CYTISUS, this section.

GERANIUM, see PELARGONIUM, this section.

HELIOTROPIUM ARBORESCENS, Heliotrope

Your greenhouse surely should not be without the fragrance of old-fashioned Heliotrope, an easy-to-grow plant from Peru. Blossoms are lavender or white in color, depending upon the variety, and are borne in large clusters at the ends of the stems. The plants may be trained into treelike shapes, or they may be grown with many stems and allowed to trail over the sides of the pots.

Heliotropes prefer a rich soil and grow best with a minimum night temperature of 60 degrees. Cuttings root easily in sand. In addition to their use as greenhouse subjects, Heliotropes make excellent summer bedding plants.

HYDRANGEA MACROPHYLLA, Hydrangea

Any discussion of Hydrangea culture should be prefaced by the remark that many men spend most of their lives growing Hydrangeas, and even they have times when they are sure they do not know all the answers. In other words, they are not easy to grow. Briefly, their requirements are these: a fairly long summer growing season with abundant moisture and an acid soil, a period of at least six weeks in the autumn with the leaves on the plants when the temperatures are below 65 degrees so that flower buds may form, and another minimum of six weeks without leaves when temperatures should range from just above freezing to 40 degrees, during which time the plants rest. After that time they may be brought into a greenhouse and forced into flower. The temperature of the greenhouse may range from cool to warm, and the only effect it will have will be to make the plants mature slowly or rapidly.

Blue or lavender flowers are normal for most Hydrangea varieties grown in acid soil (pH 5.5). When blue color must be intensified, water plants with a solution of four ounces of aluminum sulphate to a gallon of water. Before watering, poke holes in the soil around the plant with a sharp stick or wire so as to damage some of the roots. This will enable the plant to absorb the aluminum more easily. Aluminum is the element responsible for the blue color.

Pink flowers are produced when the normal aluminum in the soil is unavailable to the plants because of neutral or alkaline soil conditions. If you want pink flowers, treat the plants to one tablespoon of hydrated lime per plant during late summer.

White-flowering varieties of Hydrangeas do not change color regardless of the soil conditions.

Remember that flowers will be produced only from fat terminal buds; so do not prune back your plants except in early summer before the buds are formed.

You may hear Hydrangeas called "French Hydrangeas." The reason is that, though the plants came originally from China and Japan, many of our varieties were hybridized by growers in Europe, though growers in this country are responsible for most of the better types we have today.

New plants are produced from terminal or leaf-bud cuttings easily rooted in sand in the spring.

IMPATIENS, Touch-me-not

Touch-me-nots are old-fashioned flowers, well loved by our grandmothers because they always had blossoms on them. There are many kinds with scarlet, pink, white, or purple flowers, resulting from the crossing of two species from eastern Africa, *I. sultanii* and *I. holstii*.

They like a warm greenhouse and will blossom under poor light conditions. New plants may be had easily by rooting cuttings in sand. You might try planting seed, too, just to see what different colors you might get.

IRESINE, Blood-leaf

Although Iresines are ordinarily used as outdoor bedding plants for the bright red of their foliage, they are likewise useful in the greenhouse to provide a touch of color, especially valuable when flowers are scarce.

Iresines come from South America, where they become as much as six feet tall. Here we use them in smaller sizes and propagate new plants from cuttings when the older ones become ungainly.

They do best in full sun with plenty of moisture.

KALANCHOE, Kalanchoe

Kalanchoes are representative of one of two similar plant families which come to us from South Africa and southern Asia, the other being Bryophyllums (see *Succulents,* Section 7). They are characterized by thick, fleshy leaves which in some instances are viviparous; that is, they have the ability to form tiny living plants on the margins of the leaves. The most common Kalanchoe in florist circles is *K. Blossfeldiana,* variety Tom Thumb. This little plant rarely grows over six to eight inches tall and is crowned in the winter months with clusters of four-petaled brick-red flowers. It is easily propagated by stem or leaf-petiole cuttings, but better plants are grown from seeds sown in March each year.

Kalanchoes normally flower in January, but by giving them short-day treatment as discussed under Chrysanthemum culture, one may have them in flower in December.

There are at least twenty kinds of Kalanchoes or Bryophyllums available to the home-greenhouse grower, most of which take the type of culture suggested for Succulents later in this chapter.

LANTANA CAMARA, Lantana

Lantanas are low-growing shrubs native to tropical America, widely grown in small sizes for their prolific blossoming tendencies. Flowers come in flat-topped clusters and may be white, yellow, pink, orange, or red. Yellow flowers have a way of changing through the other colors as they mature. Lantanas will grow in almost any soil and will flower continuously if given warm temperatures, food, and ample moisture. Cuttings root easily in moist sand. Small plants are easier to handle than large ones; so the usual practice is to start new plants when the old ones get too straggly or too large.

LANTANA MONTEVIDENSIS,
see *Hanging Basket Plants,* Section 5.

MARANTA LEUCONEURA KERCHOVEANA,
Maranta, Prayer Plant

There are several species of Marantas available to the home-greenhouse grower, but the one mentioned above is most commonly seen. Its leaves are oval in shape, about six inches long, bright green with two rows of chocolate to dark green blotches.

The plant gets its common name from the fact that the leaves fold together at night the way hands are folded in prayer.

Prayer Plants occasionally blossom, sending out slender spikes of tiny white, lavender-striped flowers.

Give Prayer Plants filtered light, moist soil, and humid conditions in a warm greenhouse. New plants may be had from division or from cuttings.

MIMOSA PUDICA, Sensitive Plant

Every home greenhouse should have a Sensitive Plant for the thrill it will give young visitors. This member of the Pea family has featherlike compound leaves which fold together at the slightest touch, whence comes its common name. Its flowers are like tiny lavender powder puffs. Grow it from seed in full sun in a warm greenhouse.

NEPHTHYTIS and SYNGONIUM

There seems to be much botanical confusion in the Nephthytis and Syngonium families, and, since they look alike to most of us and enjoy the same culture, we shall combine them here. Nephthytis comes from Africa and Syngonium from the jungles of Central America, but both have lovely usually arrowhead-shaped leaves variously colored with shades of green and white in selected horticultural varieties. Such names as Green Gold, Trileaf Wonder, and Imperial White are descriptive of the varieties they represent.

These plants are climbing vines which send out roots from along their stems as they climb and, for that reason, are often grown on some sort of a support, such as a tall piece of Tree Fern. They will grow in ordinary soil, but it should be kept moist. The temperature should be warm (60 degrees at night), and they must be given protection from direct sun. Filtered sunlight is ideal for their culture. New plants are easily grown from stem cuttings.

PANDANUS, Screw-pine

There are a great many species of Screw-pines native to Africa, the East Indies, and Polynesia, but only a few of them are of sufficiently compact growth to serve as house or small greenhouse plants. The long tapering leaves of Screw-pines are usually edged with sharp spines, and the structure of mature stems is twisted, giving rise to the common name. Older specimens lose their lower foliage, retaining only crowns of long wavy leaves, making the plants look much more like Palms than Pines.

Screw-pines like a warm greenhouse, rather poor soil, and filtered light. Start new plants from basal offshoots of old plants.

Two common species are *P. veitchii,* which has green and white striped leaves, and *P. sanderi* with yellow and green striped foliage.

PARSLEY

While Parsley is not usually grown as an ornamental, by all means dig a few plants from your garden each fall and give them a cool, bright spot in the greenhouse. It is nice to have a ready source of flavoring and garnishes; at least the women of the family think so.

PELARGONIUM HORTORUM, Geranium

Flower lovers never fail to study pictures of far-off lands to see what kinds of plants are being grown. How often it is that the most brilliant, or perhaps the only, plant in a picture is a Geranium! It is amazing to see that these natives of South Africa are now found in every part of the world. Although there are hundreds of different kinds of Geraniums, the one that is grown most frequently is the common red, white, or pink one that we all know. It is sometimes called the Fish, or Zonal Geranium, but to most of us the name Geranium means but one plant. When we speak of other Geraniums, we call them by their full names, such as Lady Washington Geranium, Ivy Geranium, or Scented Geranium.

Geraniums have a peculiar fascination for many flower lovers, and it is easy to collect a hundred or more different kinds. One of the nice things about them is that they all do well in a cool greenhouse at temperatures from 45 to 60 degrees. Another item of encouragement is this: Though Geraniums do not flower freely during the winter months when grown as house plants because they do not receive sufficient light, the brightness of a greenhouse ensures flowering throughout the dullest days of winter.

Geraniums do well in ordinary greenhouse soil with a pH of 6.5 to 7.0, but it must be well drained. Their nutrient needs are not high; a 5–10–5 fertilizer applied sparingly every month or two is sufficient. In a home greenhouse it is often to the owner's advantage to keep them from growing too rapidly.

All Geraniums root readily from stem cuttings placed in sand or vermiculite. Plants should be pinched back as they grow so as to make them form as many stems as possible, therefore, more flowers.

P. DOMESTICUM, Lady Washington, Fancy, or Show Geranium

These lovely plants, whose flower faces have been likened to those of Pansies, have one definite need which must be met. They will set flower buds only when temperatures are below 60 degrees. This limits them, except for winter months, to certain areas on the east and west coasts and in parts of Canada. Flower buds will open in about three months after the below-60-degree temperatures are initiated.

P. PELTATUM, Ivy Geranium

The culture of this plant is the same as the others, but its uses may be somewhat different. It makes an outstanding hanging basket plant and may also be used as a ground cover during the summer months outdoors.

PELARGONIUM (Species), Scented Geraniums

There are over two hundred kinds of scented Geraniums grown for their fragrances and for their unusual foliages. Among them one finds such favorites as the Lemon, Apple, Nutmeg, Cinnamon, and Rose Geraniums. Flowers of these types are usually single and lavender or white in color.

PEPEROMIA

Botanists tell us that there are at least five hundred different kinds of Peperomias to be found in the jungles of Central and South America, far more than most of us can use! However, more than fifty kinds are available to anyone interested. Peperomias in general are shade-loving plants which enjoy a warm greenhouse. They will grow in ordinary soil kept somewhat on the dry side especially during the dull days of winter. They are easily multiplied by cuttings of stems or leaves. Flowers are minute things, usually white in color, so tightly clasped to the stem that the whole structure often has the appearance of a mouse's tail.

P. CAPERATA, Emerald Ripple

Emerald Ripple is a dwarf-growing Peperomia whose very dark green leaves are crimped lengthwise in "permanent pleats." It rarely grows over six inches tall.

P. MINIMA

This tiniest of Peperomias has leaves no larger than the head of a corsage pin, reddish beneath, with red veins showing through the top of the pale green leaves. Mature plants grow about three to four inches tall.

P. OBTUSIFOLIA

This Peperomia is very common and is often used in dish gardens along with its green-and-white-leafed form, *variegata*. The leaves are two to three inches long, oval in shape, and waxy in appearance. It will tolerate poor light conditions.

P. SANDERSII, Watermelon Begonia

Of course, this plant is neither a Watermelon nor a Begonia, but the silvery bands which radiate from the center of each leaf do make the leaves look like miniature Watermelons. We have no idea of the derivation of the *Begonia* part of the name.

PILEA (See common names of varieties listed below.)

Although most of us rarely hear the name Pilea, we are well acquainted with at least one member of the family, the Artillery Plant, long a greenhouse favorite. Pileas are rather low-growing jungle plants which enjoy warm greenhouses, filtered light, humusy soil, and abundant moisture. Three of the six or eight varieties available are listed below. (Botanists say that there are 150 species native to the Central and South American tropics.)

P. CADIEREI, Aluminum Plant

The Aluminum Plant has strange leaves with deeply depressed veins, the sections between the veins being raised and blotched as though lightly and unevenly brushed with aluminum paint. It comes from Vietnam.

P. INVOLUCRATA, Panamiga

Panamiga has a leaf formation somewhat similar to that of the Aluminum Plant, best described as quilted. The leaves vary in color from deep green to coppery bronze, depending upon the amount of light they receive, and have an over-all fuzzy aspect from the multitude of tiny hairs that cover the leaves. Panamigas blossom freely, with tight clusters of creamy-rose flowers nestled close to the leaves.

P. MICROPHYLLA, Artillery Plant

For many years the Artillery Plant was the only Pilea available to plant lovers. It is easily recognized by its bright green stems and succulent leaves usually less than one-fourth inch across, borne so profusely as to cover the plants like tiny shingles. Its common name comes from the fact that the plant sheds its pollen in explosive puffs, especially when set in a sunny location.

PIQUERIA TRINERVIA (*Stevia serrata*), Stevia

Light airy-white blossoms are difficult to find among winter greenhouse flowers, but during the month of December the need is met by Stevia, whose tiny fragrant white flowers are welcome additions to winter bouquets. Stevias may be grown from seeds or cuttings, but the better strains are cutting-grown. Make the cuttings in March and grow the plants in an outside cold frame through the summer months in ordinary soil that is not too fertile. Pinch back tips during the summer to induce branching. Since Stevia comes from Central America, it is sensitive to frost and must be brought inside before cold weather. Set the pots in the coolest part of your greenhouse in bright sun. They will start to blossom early in December.

PLUMBAGO, Plumbago, Leadwort

Plumbagos have long been greenhouse favorites as well as garden plants in warm climates around the world. Rarely do the plants grow in a compact manner, but are more apt to be straggly in appearance. This drawback seems not to have dimmed their popularity, for their lovely clusters of clear blue, white, pink, or red Phloxlike flowers more than offset their poor growth habits. Since they are prone to trail or clamber, they have long been grown as hanging basket plants as well as regular pot plants, for in this manner the long stems can add to the attractiveness of the baskets.

Grow Plumbagos in a moderate greenhouse in full sun and keep the soil beneath them moist. They can easily be increased from cuttings. After winter flowering, the plants can be cut back and planted outdoors where they will blossom all summer.

P. CAPENSIS has azure blue flowers; its variety *alba* has white ones. It comes from South Africa and is the type most commonly found in greenhouses.

P. ROSEA comes from southern Asia. Its flowers are pink, and its variety *indica* has scarlet blossoms.

PODOCARPUS, Podocarpus, "Japanese Yew"

We hasten to say that the name "Japanese Yew," sometimes applied to Podocarpus, is apt to be misleading, for it is the correct name for an entirely different, though closely related, plant, *Taxus cuspidata*. Podocarpus have very slender evergreen Yewlike leaves, often three to four inches long. In mild climates the plants are used in gardens and in cold climates as unusual foliage plants. Although they prefer full sun, Podocarpus will tolerate shade to a remarkable degree. They will grow in any greenhouse, preferring a cool one. The common variety found is the low-growing *P. macrophylla Maki,* which comes from Japan. *P. macrophylla* is used in the Orient as a forest tree. Podocarpus will stand shearing, which will not only keep their growth within bounds, but will also make them become more bushy specimens.

PRIMULA, Primrose

Somehow the very sight of a Primrose makes one think of springtime; thus it is imperative that each home-greenhouse gardener have a few of these delightful flowers in his greenhouse to herald the coming of the spring outdoors.

The following notes apply to Primroses in general. Specific information for each commonly grown type is given below under each species heading.

Primrose seed should be sown in a mixture of one part sand, one part soil, and one part leaf mold (not peat moss) and, since it is very fine, should be barely covered, or better still, simply pressed onto the surface of the soil. Older plants like a rich loam well supplied with leaf mold. It is important to keep the plants supplied with moisture, but care must be taken in watering not to keep the crowns of the plants so wet that they rot. During the hot time of the year Primroses must have protection from the sun. Those grown outdoors do best in a cool, shady, moist cold frame during the summer. Greenhouse temperatures that suit Primroses range from 40 to 50 degrees; thus they are ideal for cool greenhouse culture.

P. MALACOIDES, Fairy or Baby Primrose

No Primroses will give you more pleasure than will some of the newer strains of the Fairy Primrose. The colors are lovely clear pinks in many shades, plus glistening white, and the flowers are borne in whorls or tiers, one set above another like fairy castle towers. Sow seeds of Fairy Primroses from June to September to flower from January through March.

P. OBCONICA, Obconica Primrose

Obconica Primroses are the ones most often seen in flower shops and have flowers in shades of pink, rose, and white in huge clusters, each separate blossom being as large as a fifty-cent piece, if not larger. Plant Obconica seeds in the greenhouse from January to March to blossom the following winter. Plant them in October to flower in late spring. There are many lovely strains to choose from, some with fringed blossoms, all extremely beautiful. No mention of Obconicas would be complete without stating that some persons are allergic to them and develop a rash similar to that from Poison Ivy. Handle them with care and enjoy them, for despite this drawback they remain the most popular greenhouse Primrose grown today.

P. POLYANTHA, Polyantha Primrose

This is the Primrose usually seen in gardens in the spring in all its glory of yellow, bronze, purple, and red shades. It is interesting to know that it is also a nice greenhouse plant. Pot up outdoor-grown plants in late summer and keep them in a cold frame, bringing them into the greenhouse at intervals for a succession of bloom. Seeds may be sown outdoors in the spring, and the plants will be large enough by fall to make a good showing in the cool greenhouse. After flowering, the plants can be returned to the garden.

Other Primrose species you should try include *sinensis, kewensis, vulgaris, japonica,* and *denticulata cashmeriana.*

SANSEVIERIA, Bowstring Hemp, Snake Plant

We have heard that Sansevierias are among the favorite plants upon which elephants browse in the wilds of Africa. In horticultural circles they are sometimes looked down upon simply because anyone can make them grow. Surely they will stand neglect and tolerate shade and lack of moisture better than most plants, but well-grown specimens are very attractive and, in fact, are apt to put forth the rarely seen clusters of dainty white flowers. Sansevierias are usually grown as foliage plants, however, and their long slender leaves are variously striped or marbled with yellow or darker shades of green.

There are about twenty wild species of Sansevierias available in addition to the commonly grown *S. trifasciata* and its numerous varieties and sports.

Sansevierias grow best in a warm greenhouse at a 65-degree minimum with partial shade. They are propagated from divisions of the rhizomes or from leaf cuttings made by cutting leaves into two- to four-inch sections and inserting them in sand. It is interesting to note that the variegated *S. Laurenti* produces only green-leafed plants when propagated from cuttings and must be grown from division in order to maintain the desired color markings.

SANTOLINA CHAMAECYPARISSUS, Lavender Cotton

For the sake of variety among your pot plants you might like to grow a plant or two of Lavender Cotton, whose soft, aromatic gray-green foliage is so unlike that of most plants. The plants are dwarf growing and very compact and are often used in gardens as border plants or in design plantings in public gardens. They should have full sun in a cool greenhouse and may be propagated easily from cuttings. Lavender Cotton is not related to true Cotton; it comes from the countries bordering the Mediterranean and has clusters of small yellow flowers.

SCHEFFLERA ACTINOPHYLLA, Australian Umbrella Tree

Although Scheffleras are more often grown as large house plants, you may want one of them in your greenhouse to give it an exotic touch. The plants become very large, but small specimens with their glistening, digitately compound leaves are extremely attractive. They need a warm greenhouse with filtered light and should be allowed to dry out somewhat between waterings. Plants are easily raised from seeds, but the average person would do better to buy one or two small plants from his florist.

SCHIZANTHUS, Butterfly-flower, Poor-man's-orchid

Without a doubt the very name Schizanthus has discouraged many a person from growing this lovely flower from Chile, yet once one has seen its glorious colors and the profusion of its blooms, it becomes an indispensable part of one's gardening each year. In one seed catalog a strain of Schizanthus is described as follows: "This is the brightest mixture of rose and appleblossom pink, salmon, crimson, deep violet, purple, and many indescribable variations. All are heavily veined in gold."

After such an intriguing description you will surely want to try Schizanthus. Sow seeds any time from August until late in January. The early sowings will give large plants, the later ones smaller plants. If kept somewhat on the dry side, early plantings will begin to flower during March, and later plantings will continue the flowering season until late spring. It is important to pinch back Schizanthus at least once to encourage branching. They like a cool greenhouse (45 to 50 degrees) and full sunshine.

SELAGINELLA

If you have ever seen a bright green Fernlike plant creeping along the ground under a greenhouse bench, then you have probably seen a Selaginella. They are particularly useful for that purpose, since they help to maintain a high humidity by keeping the ground shaded and by transpiring moisture to the atmosphere. Although they may be propagated from spores, the usual manner is to plant sections of stems, which root quickly in any kind of soil. They do best in a warm shady greenhouse, since they come from the forest floor of tropical Africa.

SENECIO CRUENTUS, Cineraria

We are indebted to the Canary Islands for many lovely horticultural plants, but surely none more colorful than Cinerarias. Every color except yellow may be found in a well-balanced mixture of modern Cinerarias. The Daisylike flowers themselves are borne in such huge closely packed clusters as to nearly hide the foliage from view. Each petal seems to have been cut from velvet, making the plants seem to be more expensive than they really are.

One thing that Cinerarias must have is a cool greenhouse. Night temperatures must stay below 60 degrees, or the plants will not blossom. Seeds are usually sown from August until October, thus giving flowering plants from February to April. They should have some light protection from the sun until late fall, and since they wilt very easily, care must be taken to see that they have water regularly. Be sure to grow a dwarf strain for best results in a home greenhouse. Repot as they increase in size so that they never become pot-bound.

SOLANUM PSEUDO-CAPSICUM,
Jerusalem or Cleveland Cherry

Jerusalem Cherries are easy-to-grow plants notable for their orange or scarlet berries, which ripen late in the fall on attractive little bushy plants usually about one foot tall. Sow the seeds in midwinter and when they get large enough pot them up in four-inch pots. During the summer plant them, pots and all, in the garden and let them stay there until September. At that time they should be repotted into larger pots and brought into the greenhouse. Although they are perennials in their native Madeira Islands, they do better if treated as annuals in the home greenhouse.

SPATHIPHYLLUM

Spathiphyllums are rather unusual foliage plants which bear a somewhat superficial resemblance to Calla-lilies. The thin but tough lance-shaped leaves are dark green and shiny and are borne on slender basal stems, as are the long-lasting white flowers, which look very much like small Callas. The flowers last a long while and eventually turn green as they mature.

Since Spathiphyllums come mostly from the warm jungles of Central and South America, they enjoy filtered light and high moisture in a warm greenhouse. Propagation is by division of the rootstalks.

Although there are a dozen or more species available, the one most commonly grown is *S. clevelandii*.

SYNGONIUM, see *Nephthytis,* this section.

SECTION 2. CUT FLOWERS

As you already know from having read previous chapters of this book, most cut flowers are grown in raised benches containing about six inches of soil. Such benches provide ideal growing conditions for plants, giving them ample soil in which to grow, excellent drainage, and access to light even during the dull days of midwinter. Since plants grown in greenhouses are protected from the wind and extremes of heat and cold that outdoor flowers encounter, they are apt to be more succulent in growth; thus support is often given bench plants in order that stems may grow erect without tipping or lodging against their neighbors. Some of the plants listed in this section are occasionally grown as pot plants just as some of the plants in Section 1 are sometimes grown in benches. The convenience of the home-greenhouse owner may dictate a transposition of plants from one section to the other, but the way in which they are listed here is the usual way in which they are grown in this country.

ANTIRRHINUM MAJUS, Snapdragon

No other note about Snapdragons for home-greenhouse use is more important than this word of caution regarding seeds. If you want to have Snaps blossom in the wintertime, you must plant varieties bred for that particular season of flowering. If you want them to flower in the spring, you should use spring-flowering varieties. These are obtainable from seed companies and are the same varieties used by commercial florists. Garden-type Snaps will not usually blossom during the winter, but simply make enormous vegetative growth and can be a real disappointment to the uninitiated.

Except for the double-flowering greenhouse Snaps, which must be propagated from cuttings, all Snaps are grown from seed sown at various times of the year so as to extend the season of bloom. Snapdragon seeds are very tiny and should be sown lightly on top of the seedbed and should not be covered. A thin layer of milled Sphagnum moss or fine vermiculite spread on top of the soil makes an ideal seedbed. Germinate the seeds in a dark place at 60 degrees and bring them into the light as soon as they show above the soil. They must be kept moist, especially when they are small. Snaps to blossom from late autumn through midwinter should be sown early in July while those to flower in the spring should be sown from October to February.

Snapdragons should be transplanted from the seed flat to the bench when they are very small and spaced about seven to eight inches apart in each direction. Spring crops can be grown somewhat closer. Let the plants get about eight inches tall; then pinch them back to three sets of leaves so that they will branch. Such a pinch should result in at least four sturdy spikes of flowers to each plant. After the first flowers have been picked, a second crop will develop. This is best encouraged by cutting all of the stems of each plant to about six inches in height. In this way sturdy rather than willowy new stems will develop. The direct benching of seedlings mentioned above may not be practical under some circumstances because another crop may still be occupying the bench space. In that case, transplant the seedlings to individual pots and shift them to the bench when space is available.

Night temperatures should be close to 48 to 50 degrees for Snapdragons. Soil should be kept uniformly moist, but not soaking wet. In watering try not to wet the foliage because it will encourage the development and spread of such unwanted guests as rust and anthracnose.

CALENDULA OFFICINALIS, Calendula, Pot Marigold

If you think that Calendulas make fine garden flowers, wait until you have grown them in your greenhouse. It is possible to get these beautiful cream, yellow, or orange Daisylike flowers as much as four inches across. They make wonderful long-lasting flowers either left on the plants or cut for bouquets. Their name comes from the Latin *calends,* the same root word which gives us calendar, referring to the fact that the plants have such a long blossoming period. They are native to the Mediterranean region.

Calendulas must have a cool greenhouse, 40 to 50 degrees being an ideal night temperature. Since they enjoy cool temperatures, many florists plant the seeds in cold frames during August and September because they can be kept cooler there than in greenhouses at that time of year. When the plants become large enough to transplant, they are moved into greenhouse benches and spaced eight to twelve inches apart in each direction.

If they are given ample moisture and full sun, the plants will develop quickly. The terminal bud should be pinched out. This sacrifice will enable side branches to grow, thus giving many more flowers throughout the winter months. Flowering season from August and September plantings will continue from November until May. In order to get the largest flowers, disbud each stem so that only one flower will develop. If more but smaller flowers are wanted, simply let them grow normally. Single flowers from double-flowering varieties result when Calendulas are grown at too high temperatures.

When the plants get large, it is advisable to water them cautiously to prevent basal rot from starting under the thick foliage. Keep them on the dry side. Since Calendulas in a greenhouse become quite large, it is a good idea to supply a support of wire and strings to keep the stems from falling all over each other.

CALLISTEPHUS CHINENSIS, China Aster

China Asters are normally grown as summer cut flowers except under special circumstances where day length can be regulated to suit their needs. Although this is feasible for the commercial greenhouse operator, it is of doubtful value to the home-greenhouse owner, since the lighting schedule would upset other plants being grown in the same area. The notes given below are for information only and are to be used by the person planning to grow Asters during the "off" season. The seeds of Asters destined to blossom in January, February, and March should be planted from July to September, and from the first of September on the plants need to be given additional light from sunset to 10 P.M. until they are nearly two feet tall. The usual practice is to use 60-watt bulbs in reflectors spaced five feet apart along each bench.

Greenhouse-grown Asters are planted eight to ten inches apart in each direction and are grown in a night temperature of 50 degrees.

In the light of the difficulties of flowering Asters in home greenhouses, it is suggested that Aster culture be confined to the growing of seedlings in the spring so that they will be large enough to blossom at an early date in the summer garden.

CHEIRANTHUS, Wallflower

Wallflowers are examples of plants rarely grown commercially yet ideally suited to home-greenhouse culture. Flowers may be brilliant orange, mahogany red, brown, yellow, or violet, and very fragrant. They do best in full sun in a cool greenhouse kept at 45 to 50 degrees. Most of the types available are perennials and are best grown from seeds outdoors during the summer, potted in early autumn, and kept in a cold frame from which they can be brought into the greenhouse from time to time to give an extended winter-flowering season. There is a tendency among some of the modern strains to act as annuals, however, and the plant sold as *C. allioni*, really *Erysimum asperum*, will blossom from January to May from seeds sown from June to September. This type does best if planted four inches apart each way in shallow flats and not watered too heavily.

C. cheiri is the perennial type usually grown for its fragrant yellow, orange, or brown flowers. For variety try *C. kewensis* with its golden yellow or purple-violet flowers. There are double as well as single types of Wallflowers, some of which must be propagated from cuttings.

CHRYSANTHEMUM CARINATUM
and C. CORONARIUM, Annual Chrysanthemum

Annual Chrysanthemums differ from their more familiar perennial cousins not only in their nativity, being from the Mediterranean region rather than the Orient, but also in the manner of growth and blossom characteristics. Their foliage is apt to be thick and succulent; thus care must be taken not to give them too much water during the dull days of winter. The blossoms which appear in April and May from October and November plantings may be cream, yellow, red, or white in color, each flower showing an inner concentric ring of a color different from that of the rest of the flower.

CHRYSANTHEMUM MORIFOLIUM, Chrysanthemum

Now we come to some of the most wonderful and worth-while plants known to greenhouse gardeners, Chrysanthemums. There are all kinds of flowers to be had from tiny button varieties and single Daisylike types all the way through the pompons to the gigantic "mums" as big as footballs. All of them require a similar greenhouse environment, but the manner in which they are trained varies with the type of flower.

Chrysanthemums grow best in a soil rich in peat moss. If 25

per cent of the bench soil by volume is peat moss, it will not be too much.

Greenhouse temperatures should be kept as close to 60 degrees day and night as possible. At temperatures much below 60 degrees the plants barely grow and will not blossom; at higher temperatures flowering is delayed and plants become weak.

Chrysanthemums are known as "short day" plants. This is why they blossom in the fall of the year when the hours of darkness become greater than the hours of daylight. Although it is entirely possible for any greenhouse grower to manipulate the amount of light his Chrysanthemums receive throughout the year and thus have flowers throughout the year, the effort and expense as well as the effect upon other plants he may be growing seem to suggest that the home-greenhouse owner would do better to stick to an autumn crop of Chrysanthemums and let them flower in their natural season. At other times of the year he might well augment the color display in his greenhouse by buying some Chrysanthemum pot plants from his florist. The actual mechanics of artificial lighting during the winter months and blackshading during the summertime are not relevant to the needs of most home-greenhouse owners, and those who desire specific information along this line should consult a commercial greenhouse manual.

Chrysanthemums are grown from cuttings, and the few that the average home-greenhouse operator would need can be purchased from a local florist with whom each home gardener should endeavor to develop the utmost rapport. Such cuttings should be benched during the months of April to July, depending upon the variety and the time it is expected to blossom. Most home greenhouses are relatively empty in early June, and this affords an ideal time to put in Chrysanthemums. The cuttings should not be planted any deeper than they stood in the rooting medium, for deep planting will delay plant growth. Most growers plant cuttings about seven inches apart in each direction whether they are planting pompons or the large mums, known commercially as standards since only one flower is allowed to develop at the top of each stem. Young plants should be misted lightly several times a day to encourage them into active growth and to keep them from wilting.

By mid-July the plants should be in vigorous growth. At this time they should be given what is called a soft pinch, which means that the very tip of each cutting should be removed. In that way the plants soon send out several stems instead of one. On pompons two to four stems are usually left to provide the flowers. On standards no pinch is made if a single flower is wanted from each plant. However, experience has shown that at least two large flowers, though not as large as a single one would be, can be grown from each plant by pinching and then selecting the two best stems. These require disbudding later when flower buds form so that only one flower is allowed to each stem.

CHRYSANTHEMUM PARTHENIUM
(*Matricaria capensis*), Feverfew

Feverfew is a small white-flowered member of the Chrysanthemum family native to Europe. In selected forms the flowers are double and up to three fourths of an inch across and are borne in thick clusters, making them very useful as cut flowers. They may be grown from seeds (or cuttings of particularly good varieties) sown in October to blossom in May. Transplant them twelve inches apart in each direction and pinch once to induce branching. Although the information may not be useful to the average home gardener, it is interesting to know that by giving them artificial light during the winter months, he can bring them into flower as much as two months ahead of their normal season.

CYNOGLOSSUM AMABILE, Chinese Forget-me-not

This particular flower with its Forget-me-not-like blossoms is best left for color in the greenhouse bench, since it does not stand up well when cut. Sow the seed in September, and the plants will come into blossom in March and April. Do not overwater. Space twelve inches each way. Cynoglossum must have a cool greenhouse, 45 degrees at night being about right.

DELPHINIUM, Delphinium, Larkspur

In home-greenhouse culture we are interested in two different types of Delphiniums, the annual *D. ajacis* and the perennial *D. cultorum*. They require completely different methods of culture with the exception that they both enjoy a cool greenhouse and soil with a *p*H of 6.0, somewhat more alkaline than is required for some other plants.

D. ajacis, Larkspur, is a native of Europe, but the beautiful varieties we have today with their salmon, blue, lilac, purple, white, pink, or rose double flowers bear but a superficial resemblance to the wild species. Larkspur foliage is finely divided, almost feathery in appearance.

Larkspur seeds should be sown any time from September to December for flowering in April and May. They should have two months at temperatures not over 50 degrees before they are given temperatures of 55 degrees or more. This is so that they will form a sturdy set of basal leaves before sending out flower spikes.

D. cultorum, the perennial Delphinium we think of as a garden flower, is best started in the spring and allowed to grow in pots in a cold frame during the first summer. They should be kept in the cold frame until February, then brought into the greenhouse, planted into benches, and forced into blossom during April and May. This type of Delphinium includes the huge Pacific Hybrids with their wealth of shades of blue, as well as pale pink and white. *D. belladonna*, a smaller-growing azure blue perennial, and *D. bellamosum*, its dark blue counterpart, are exceedingly worth while as greenhouse plants and should be treated in the same manner as *D. cultorum.*

DIANTHUS CARYOPHYLLUS, Carnation

There are men who spend their entire mature years growing Carnations and who readily agree that there is always something new to learn about their culture. Nevertheless, most of us with small greenhouses can do well enough with certain basic knowledge to coax Carnations to send out a continuing flow of fragrant blossoms. One thing that should be mentioned is this: Carnations do not make a spectacular crop, for only a few blossoms are in evidence at any one time. The fact that they flower almost without ceasing is in their favor, however. The spicy blossoms of Carnations come close to Roses in popularity. Varieties grown today are fully double in all shades of pink, red, yellow, and orchid as well as white. There are even varieties with petals of more than one color, a far cry from the five-petaled Carnations found growing as wildflowers in southern Europe.

Carnations grow best at a night temperature of 50 degrees, with day temperatures running to the low sixties. Bright sunshine is necessary for them to be at their best.

Named varieties of Carnations should be grown from cuttings made from side shoots of vigorous plants. Most growers make cuttings during the period from November to March. After rooting in sand (or other media), they should be planted about four inches apart in flats of fertile soil. When the weather is frost-free, they should be planted in an open garden to make as much growth as possible until the middle of July, when they should be dug and transplanted to benches in the greenhouse. It is important during all the period from the time that the cuttings are flatted until they are returned to the greenhouse from the field that they be pinched back regularly to encourage side branches to develop, since flower production is in direct relation to the number of branches on each plant.

Plants treated as noted above will come into flower in October and blossom continuously. Some growers keep the same bed blossoming for two seasons or longer, but nicer flowers are produced by growing new plants each year.

Carnations must be supplied with three sets of wires and cross strings to support them as they increase in height.

It is important to note that Carnations bear clusters of buds at the tops of the stems. If you want large flowers, it is necessary to remove all but one bud from each stem. Do this as early as possible so as to force all the strength into single buds. There are some miniature varieties now coming into vogue designed to be grown without disbudding. These give clusters of smaller but very graceful flowers.

DIDISCUS, see TRACHYMENE, this section.
ERYSIMUM ASPERUM, see Cheiranthus allioni,
this section.

EUPHORBIA FULGENS, Scarlet Plume

Scarlet Plumes are first cousins to Poinsettias and come from Mexico. Their brilliant orange-red flowers are quite small, but are borne in profusion along the tops of the arching stems, making them very effective cut flowers. Their season of bloom is from early in January through March.

They grow best in full sunshine with a minimum night temperature of 60 degrees. New plants are started from cuttings rooted in the spring and benched in fertile soil. They should be pinched back several times to induce branching.

Scarlet Plumes have a white latex inside the stems which exudes when they are cut. Sear the stems over a flame or dip the lower two inches of the stems in boiling water before arranging them, or the latex will plug the stems, and the flowers will wilt.

GERBERIA JAMSONII (known commonly, but not accurately as *Gerbera jamsonii*, Gerbera Daisy)
Gerberia, Barberton, or Transvaal Daisy

This unusual perennial Daisy comes from South Africa and can be grown in mild climates as a garden flower. Its leaves are all basal, and its salmon, pink, red, orange, yellow, or cream-colored flowers are borne on long leafless stems. Flowers are often three to five inches across, and there are double, as well as single, forms.

Gerberias may be grown from seed or from division. Seeds take about a year to develop into flowering-size plants. Sow in January to flower the following winter. Old plants must be divided each year, usually in June.

Gerberias like full sun and a minimum temperature of 55 degrees. They must have a light sandy soil and prefer one deeper than usually found in benches. You will find that a few plants grown in deep tubs or large pots will be very satisfactory as a source of long-lasting cut flowers.

GODETIA, Godetia, Satinflower, Farewell-to-spring

Godetias grow wild along the western coast of the United States, and from these native species have been developed some lovely hybrids with double or single flowers up to two inches across. The petals have a satiny texture and may be red, pink, white, or lilac in color.

Godetias will blossom in about four months from seed at any time of the year. They must have cool temperatures, however, 50 to 55 degrees being ideal. They tend to have rather soft growth in greenhouses so are better grown in shallow flats than in deep benches.

GYPSOPHILA ELEGANS, Annual Baby's-breath

The dainty airy-white flowers of the Annual Baby's-breath are very useful in bouquets and can be had in flower from May to August by making a succession of plantings every ten days from February to June. During the winter months artificial light is needed to induce them to blossom.

Grow them in shallow flats of sandy soil weak in nutrients at temperatures at 45 to 50 degrees.

IBERIS, Candytuft

There are two forms of annual Candytuft of real value as greenhouse flowers. Their similarities and differences are described below:

I. AMARA, Hyacinth-flowered Candytuft

This type of Candytuft has only white flowers, but they are fragrant and are borne in large terminal clusters like Hyacinths. They do not shatter when cut and will blossom at any time of the year in four to five months after planting. Sow in October or November to flower in February and March when they are especially appreciated. This Candytuft is sometimes called Rocket Candytuft and comes from Great Britain and Central Europe.

I. UMBELLATA

This is the Candytuft which gives us the clusters of lavender or rose flowers which are not fragrant and which shatter easily when used as cut flowers. It is native to the Mediterranean region and blossoms in a greenhouse only as the days get long in the spring. Plant them in January and February to flower in May and June.

Both varieties grow best in full sun with night temperatures of 50 degrees.

LATHYRUS ODORATUS, Sweet Pea

Perhaps the first thing you need to know if you want to grow Sweet Peas in the winter greenhouse is that you must specify seeds of winter-flowering varieties. Ordinary Sweet Peas will make nothing but leaves all winter long. If you prefer your flowers in the spring, be sure to get spring-flowering types.

All Sweet Peas like to grow in cool, deep, rich soil with night temperatures of 45 to 48 degrees. Often they are grown in ground beds, rather than benches, not only to give them deep soil, but also to allow for the fact that they often grow ten to fourteen feet tall. Sufficient overhead space is sometimes a limiting factor, but plants can be drawn down their string supports somewhat as they mature, allowing them to continue to grow upward. Excellent Sweet Peas can be grown in deep benches, however, if care is taken to see that the soil stays very moist except in prolonged periods of cloudy weather.

For blossoms from November to February sow winter-flowering types about the middle of July. For flowers from late December through March sow about the middle of August. If you want to have Sweet Peas in the spring, plant spring-flowering types early in November to blossom in April and May.

Sow Sweet Peas one inch apart in parallel rows six inches apart and thin the plants in the rows to two-inch spacing, selecting the strongest plants. One such planting across a bench is usually sufficient for most small greenhouses. If you desire to grow more of them, space your next twin rows about three feet away from the first ones.

Supports are easily made by running a tight wire close to the soil and another high above the plants and connecting them with strings spaced five to six inches apart. Wire netting can also be used.

Sweet Peas are native to Sicily. Their fragrant blossoms and delicate colors make them indispensable in any greenhouse large enough to allow them the room they need to grow.

LIMONIUM, Statice, Sea Lavender

The following forms of Statice are grown as greenhouse cut flowers:

L. SINUATA

This is the type of Statice that has clusters of tiny papery flower heads of blue, lavender, rose, or white. Sow seeds in January to have flowers in May.

L. BONDUELLII SUPERBA

Flowers of this Statice are similar to those above except that they are yellow in color.

L. SUWOROWII, Russian or Rat-tail Statice

The flowers of the Russian Statice are entirely different from the types mentioned above, being pale pink in color and borne in long slender graceful spikes, the spikes themselves being about the diameter of a pencil, but often over a foot long. They are very unusual and are lovely in arrangements. Sow seeds in October to flower from February until late in the spring.

MATHIOLA INCANA, Stock

The winter greenhouse can be graced with many fragrant flowers, but few are easier to grow or more satisfactory than Stocks. There are two types, the Column—that is, single-stem Stocks—and the Branching, of which Trysomic Pacific is a good representative. Both kinds have their place in the home greenhouse. The single-stem ones give long magnificent spikes of flowers; the others, short stems, but many of them. Stocks may be had in white, rose, lavender, or buff shades.

Stocks should be grown at 45 degrees at night and under 65 degrees in the daytime and should have full sun. Let the soil beneath them dry somewhat between waterings and try to keep the foliage dry if possible.

The length of time from seeds to blossoms varies with the time of the year that they are planted. Seeds sown in September and October will blossom in March and April, about six months after sowing. Seeds sown in mid-February will flower in late May or early June, about four months after sowing.

The best way to grow them is to sow the seeds directly in the benches, planting three or four seeds in "hills" four to six inches apart. When they sprout, thin to the best seedling in each hill. A point to watch here is this: Sow seeds of double varieties and thin the seedlings so that you leave the ones with the *pale green* leaves. Experience has shown that those with dark green leaves are apt to give less desirable single flowers.

Stocks grow wild in southern Europe.

MATRICARIA CAPENSIS,
see CHRYSANTHEMUM PARTHENIUM, this section.

MYOSOTIS, Forget-me-not

Blue flowers are always welcome in a greenhouse in the wintertime and none more so than dainty Forget-me-nots. They do best in a cool greenhouse with plenty of moisture. Sow seeds at any time from June to August and bench the plants about ten inches apart each way. Be sure to buy an early-flowering strain.

PANSY, see VIOLA TRICOLOR, this section.

RESEDA ODORATA, Mignonette

Here is a cut flower grown for its rich fragrance rather than its flowers. Mignonettes have been favorite garden flowers for generations. They are easily grown in a greenhouse, and a succession of plantings from July to November will give flowers from November until late spring.

Mignonettes do not transplant easily; so plant groups of seeds directly in the bench seven to eight inches apart and thin to the best plant of each group. Pinch back when six to eight inches tall to induce branching and disbud the branches to obtain one large flower spike from each branch.

Keep the soil moderately dry for best results and grow them at a night temperature of 45 to 50 degrees. Mignonettes are native to North Africa.

SALPIGLOSSIS SINUATA, Salpiglossis,
Painted Tongue

Most of us think of Salpiglossis as garden flowers. Commercial florists also feel that they should stay in that category because their straggly growth does not lend itself to automation. However, the home-greenhouse owner can indulge himself somewhat because his plants are grown for fun rather than profit. For that reason the velvety Petunialike flowers of the Salpiglossis belong in every home greenhouse. The plants came originally from Chile, close to the native habitat of Petunias, to which they show kinship in both foliage and flowers.

Modern Salpiglossis may be red, yellow, dark or light blue, or purple, veined with crimson or gold, or they may be white with a golden throat. Seed can be sown in September and the plants carried through the winter in a 50- to 55-degree house to flower in April, or they can be sown in January to blossom in May. The latter planting will give smaller plants.

STATICE, see LIMONIUM, this section.

TRACHYMENE CAERULEA (*Didiscus caerulea*),
Didiscus, Blue Lace Flower

Australia is the native home of the Blue Lace Flower, a member of the Carrot family. Its flowers are quite similar in shape to those of our Queen Anne's Lace, having flat-topped flower heads that are composed of many tiny, lacy flowers. The commonly grown form has sky-blue flowers, but there is also a white variety. This plant's foliage is finely cut and clearly shows its kinship to carrots.

Blue Lace Flower is not easy to transplant. It can be grown in light soil in benches, or in shallow flats, or even pots. Sow the seeds and thin out plants to stand about eight inches apart. If planted in August and grown at 50 degrees during the nights for two months, then at 60 degrees during the nights, it will blossom most of the winter.

VIOLA, Violets and Pansies

Few flowers bring back memories as do fragrant clusters of Violets or the friendly "faces" of Pansies. Although the plants are closely related, their cultures differ.

V. ODORATA, Violet

Greenhouse Violets are not the same as most garden Violets, but are hybrids of European species which grow and multiply by means of runners and seeds, rather than by seeds alone as do most native types. In mild climates, of course, these same Violets can be grown outdoors. Greenhouse Violets are fragrant as is implied by their botanical name *odorata;* there are many varieties both violet and white, single and double. Their greenhouse flowering season is from October until April.

After flowering, as the weather becomes warm in the spring, the plants send forth runners, and, strangely enough, though they cease blossoming in the normal way, they now send forth closed blossoms known as cleistogamous flowers, which are self-fertilized and produce viable seeds. Cuttings from these runners should be rooted in sand in May. In June set the young plants in beds of sandy soil containing about one-fourth well-rotted manure. Throughout the growing season this soil should be kept on the dry side to discourage disease from spreading under the thick canopy of leaves.

Violets must have a heavy shade in the summer and a light shade in the winter as well as very cool growing conditions. Temperatures of 40 to 45 degrees are considered to be ideal. These two factors somewhat limit the value of Violets as items for the average home greenhouse, but it is entirely possible to grow them either in a greenhouse or a protected cold frame provided they can be shaded and kept sufficiently cold.

V. TRICOLOR, Pansy

In selecting the type of Pansy to grow in a home greenhouse, one should consider several factors. One person may feel that huge-sized flowers are most important; another that a wide range of colors is more valuable. Some will surely choose the traditional greenhouse Pansy, which grows to three or four feet in height and must be supported by regular frames of wire and string. As a matter of fact, for most practical purposes a good strain of garden Pansy is superior for the home-greenhouse owner in the light of the care necessary to grow special greenhouse types.

Pansies will blossom all winter long if the flowers are kept picked and not allowed to go to seed. Keep them at a temperature of 40 to 55 degrees, and you will be very pleased with them. They flower more freely at high temperatures, but quality is not as good as that of those grown cool.

Sow seeds outdoors in July and transplant plants to benches about eight inches apart. Regular feedings will help produce large blossoms throughout the season.

SECTION 3. BULBS

All of the plants listed in this section do not grow from true bulbs. Many of them have underground tubers, rhizomes, or thickened rootstalks, but for the sake of convenience they are included in this grouping. Some of the plants become so large that they should be grown in tubs or large pots. Though their culture is given here, they are also listed under Tub Plants in Section 6.

ACHIMENES, see *Gesneriads*, Section 10.

AGAPANTHUS AFRICANUS, African-lily,
Lily-of-the-Nile

Although this plant is widely known as Lily-of-the-Nile, it may be that the name has a sort of chamber-of-commerce tinge, for the plant is really native to South Africa, thousands of miles south of the Nile River. At any rate, it is a fine large-growing, thick-rooted plant with long straplike leaves and tall flower stems topped by umbels of twenty-five to fifty or more porcelain-blue tube-shaped flowers. There is also a white form. African-lilies are very vigorous growers and must have a large pot or tub and rich soil in order to flower freely. They blossom during the summer and should be rested and repotted in a cool greenhouse in the winter. Failure to flower usually results from depletion of soil nutrients.

ALOCASIA

A shady tropical greenhouse is the proper home for Alocasias, with a warm moist atmosphere and humusy soil in keeping with that of their native East Indies. The plants are related to Caladiums and have similar arrowhead-shaped leaves, some of them reaching enormous proportions. There are two dozen or more types available, many with a metallic sheen to the leaves or with prominent white veining.

Alocasias make interesting subjects for a warm conservatory and give an atmosphere of the tropics. New plants may be grown from suckers that spring from the bases of old plants.

ALSTROEMERIA, Peruvian-lily

It would be interesting to know how these plants got their common name, for they are native to Chile and Brazil, rather than Peru. At any rate, there are many species and hybrids available, whose Lilylike flowers of red, yellow, or purple are borne in generous clusters at the tops of the stems. The insides of the flowers are often freckled with brown, adding to their quaintness.

While Alstroemerias may be grown from seed, the usual method is by root division. Such divisions planted in a bench in late summer and kept very moist all through the growing season will be in full flower during March, April, and May. Keep the temperature as close to 50 degrees as possible.

When the plants have finished blossoming, they die down to the ground. Save the roots in a dry place above freezing until the next planting season.

ANEMONE CORONARIA, Poppy-flowered
or St. Brigid Anemone

Biblical authorities believe that the lilies of the field, of which it was said that "Solomon in all his glory was not arrayed like one of these," were the flowers we know as Anemones. Basically their colors are the same as they always were, red, blue-purple, and white, but the shadings and combinations of the ones we have today are surely more colorful than those of the wild species. Anemones bear one flower at the top of each stem, and beneath the flower there is usually a little ruff of finely cut foliage. Flowers may be single or double in form and are very long-lasting as cut flowers.

Anemones grow from insignificant-looking, shriveled roots or from seeds. Seeds planted in April or May will begin to flower in October and continue all winter. If roots are planted, be sure to start them in light, well-drained soil in September. If kept at 45 to 50 degrees, they will blossom from January through March.

Although they can be grown in benches, some growers use flats or pots for their Anemones and feel that they flower more freely if the roots are somewhat crowded. In any event, be careful in watering so that the crowns of the plants do not stay wet any longer than necessary, for they are apt to develop crown rot.

After flowering dry off the tubers and save them for replanting in the fall.

ANTHERICUM LILIAGO, St. Bernard's-lily

St. Bernard's-lily is a European plant usually grown as a perennial in mild climates. Its white Lilylike flowers are rather small, but are borne on long loose clusters. Pot tuberous roots in early fall and grow plants in a cool sunny greenhouse.

ARUM PALAESTINUM, Black Calla-lily,
Solomon's-lily

The Black Calla-lily is an intriguing plant from its name only, if for no other reason. Actually the Calla-lilylike flowers are a very deep purplish black and the foliage arrowhead-shaped and a deep glossy green. The round bulbs should be potted when received during the fall. They will grow during midwinter and flower in the early spring. Let their foliage mature and the bulbs remain in the dry soil until the next planting season. As is implied in its botanical name, the Black Calla-lily is native to Palestine.

BEGONIA TUBERHYBRIDA,
Tuberous-rooted Begonia

There is little doubt but that gardeners sufficiently advanced to want a home greenhouse are already well acquainted with the charms of Tuberous-rooted Begonias. Every issue of national garden magazines seems to have several pictures of this most photogenic member of the Begonia family. Tuberous-rooted Begonias may be had in every color except blue and with single, double, ruffled, or frilled flowers, some so imitative of other flowers as to to be called Narcissus- or Camellia-flowered. In addition to the familiar upright forms there are magnificent varieties with a trailing habit of growth especially suited for hanging baskets.

While it is true that most of us think of Tuberous-rooted Begonias as growing from tubers exclusively, it is interesting to know that perfectly beautiful plants can be grown from seeds also. Plant the seeds in January to have flowering plants in May and June until frost; start tubers into growth in February and March for the same sort of results. You may divide tubers of select varieties if you wish and even make stem cuttings to increase your supply of plants.

Tuberous-rooted Begonias like cool, humid, partly shaded locations. Young plants in the greenhouse should have a 60-degree minimum at night, but during the flowering period they should be kept as cool during the night as possible. Cool moisture-laden breezes from the oceans on the east and west coasts have made these areas particularly suited to Begonia culture during the summer months.

Begonias are shallow-rooted plants and do best in a mixture of two parts loam, two parts peat moss, and one part well-rotted manure. They benefit from supplementary feedings during the growing season.

After flowering store the bulbs in a dry place at about 50 degrees until the next planting season.

BRODIAEA

Brodiaeas are unusual cormous plants which do well in sandy soil in a cool greenhouse in full sun. Pot the tiny corms in early fall for flowers in early spring. The flowers are about the size and shape of those of Flowering Tobacco, and the foliage is grasslike. After flowering leave the corms in the pots and let them stay dry over summer until the next autumn potting season.

B. IXIOIDES, Pretty-face

Many Brodiaeas come from the west coast of the United States; this one has salmon or yellow flowers streaked with purple.

B. UNIFLORA, Spring Starflower

This native of Argentina has white flowers tinged blue and has varieties such as *caerulea* with porcelain-blue flowers and *violacea* with violet-colored flowers. This plant is sometimes listed as *Milla uniflora, Triteleia uniflora,* or *Leucocoryne uniflora.*

CALADIUM, Fancy-leafed Caladium

During the summer months, when greenhouse flowers are scarce, it is particularly nice to have a display of colorful Caladiums either outdoors or in a shady section of your greenhouse. Two species from the jungles of South America, *C. bicolor* and *C. picturatum,* have been used to produce the modern varieties. Their leaves may be pink, red, white, or green, or any combination thereof, and are arrowhead-shaped.

Start the plants from dormant rhizomes during the spring by planting them in wet peat moss or sand until they sprout. Pot up immediately in a mixture of one-half peat moss and one-half sandy loam and grow them under a light shade. Night temperature should be 65 degrees.

In the fall the plants become dormant again, dying back to the ground. Save them by withholding water and laying the pots on their sides under a bench until next planting season.

CALOCHORTUS, Mariposa- or Globe-tulip

Over forty different kinds of Calochortuses are found on the west coast of the United States and Mexico, with colors ranging from cream and white through yellow and lavender to red. They grow from corms which should be planted in the greenhouse in early fall and grown at a 50-degree night temperature. They must have light well-drained soil. Dry off the corms after flowering and save for another year. They increase naturally by offsets of the old corms.

CLIVIA MINIATA, Clivia

Among the crowd stoppers at every spring flower show are the Clivias with their huge clusters of Lilylike orange or yellow flowers held high above their deep-green, glossy, strap-shaped leaves. As these South African plants increase in size, it is essential to shift them to very large pots or tubs. They should be handled carefully since they seem to resent root disturbance. Grow them in a shady warm greenhouse. They blossom in early spring.

COLOCASIA, Colocasia, Elephant-ear

Colocasias are very large-growing plants closely related to Caladiums and need similar culture. If given plenty of moisture and a rich soil in a warm location, plants easily become as tall as a man, with huge arrowhead-shaped leaves. If your greenhouse is too small for them, start the rhizomes early in the spring and transplant the young plants to your garden. They will make a tremendous growth. After the first frost dig the roots and store them over winter in a cool dry place. Taro, a staple food in the islands of the Pacific, is *Colocasia esculenta.*

CONVALLARIA MAJALIS, Lily-of-the-valley

The delightfully fragrant Lily-of-the-valley is grown only as a forcing item. The roots, technically called pips, should be discarded after they have produced a crop of flowers. The ordinary garden Lily-of-the-valley is not worth trying to force. One should buy large three-year-old pips from a florist supply house, preferably those that have been kept in cold storage (25 to 28 degrees) for a minimum of two months.

Plant the pips as close together as possible in sand or Sphagnum moss and grow them at a temperature of 75 to 80 degrees in a highly humid, heavily shaded location. The growth will elongate and be pale as it grows. When the flower stems are well developed, give the plants more light and cooler temperatures, but be sure to protect them from the sun.

CRINUM, Crinum, Crinum-lily

Crinums are usually grown as garden plants in mild climates and are infrequently seen in greenhouses because some types become quite large. Crinums have clusters of fragrant white, pink, or red Lilylike flowers from early spring to midsummer, depending upon the variety being grown. It is best to store the heavy roots without watering them in their pots under the bench from late fall until February or March; then water them and bring them into active growth. New bulbs should be planted high in pots and shifted to larger pots only when absolutely necessary. They need filtered light and abundant moisture. Bigeneric hybrids between Amaryllis and Crinums have resulted in *Amarcrinums*, grown in the same manner as Crinums. Crinums are native to tropical regions around the world.

CROCUS

Get a jump on spring by growing a few pots of Crocuses in your greenhouse. Plant the corms close together in shallow pots in the fall and store them in a cold place until midwinter. Bring them along in a cool greenhouse with plenty of moisture. If you keep them cool, you will be surprised at how long they stay in blossom.

DAHLIA

We do not propose that you grow Dahlias in your greenhouse, because they would take up too much room. However, a greenhouse is an ideal spot to use to increase your stock of new varieties. If you will start tubers in moist sand or light soil early in the spring and take cuttings from the sprouts, you will be able to increase the number of plants of choice varieties manyfold before the weather is warm enough to put them outdoors. Each rooted cutting will quickly grow into a full-sized plant and will have a crop of tubers beneath it in the fall. Dahlias can also be grown from seed and will blossom the first season from early planted seeds.

EUCHARIS GRANDIFLORA (*E. amazonica*),
Amazon- or Eucharis-lily

It surely is true that some plants give more pleasure than others; so it is with enthusiasm that I suggest that you grow a few Eucharis-lilies in your warm greenhouse. I have found that they do very well at 65 degrees at night in a shady house, where most of the other plants are Orchids. They grow from bulbs which flower more than once a year, sending out clusters of snowy-white, wonderfully fragrant blossoms widely grown by florists for use in corsages.

Plant the bulbs in large pots or small tubs so that you will not have to disturb them often. After each flowering period let the plants dry somewhat, but not to the point of wilting. After holding them in this condition for a month or so, increase watering, and a new set of flowers will come forth. The foliage is evergreen, and the plants will continue to flower indefinitely if you will repot them into fresh soil when it becomes necessary. Give them filtered light during the summer and full sun during the winter. Eucharis-lilies come from Colombia. Start new plants from division of the bulbs.

FREESIA

Freesias are winter-blooming bulbous plants from South Africa which have been grown for generations for their delightfully spice-scented flowers. Bulbs should be planted from August to November to have flowers from December through March. Plant the bulbs close together in regular greenhouse soil, and as the plants develop, give them a bit of support, for the stems are apt to be weak. A little brush stuck into the pot or flat in which they are growing will give ample support. Keep the plants moist and very cool. They do best at 40 to 50 degrees. After flowering let the foliage mature naturally and save the bulbs for planting again in the fall. Freesia blossoms are shaped like miniature Lilies and are borne in terminal clusters. Flowers may be white, yellow, pink, purple, brown, or orange in color. The white and yellow ones are usually the most fragrant. Freesias may be grown from seeds as well as bulbs. Sow seeds from March to June to flower from October to April.

GLADIOLUS

Before the days of modern transportation Gladiolus were regularly grown as greenhouse crops, but nowadays most of the winter blooms come to flower shops from growing fields in Florida, California, and the Rio Grande Valley in Texas. It is a real thrill, however, to grow Glads in a greenhouse, and surely you should start a few bulbs this way each year. Plant Gladiolus bulbs in a greenhouse bench in January or early February to have them in blossom in April and May. A night temperature of 50 to 55 degrees is ideal.

In addition to the ordinary Glads there are the Winter-flowering or Baby Gladiolus whose culture is somewhat different from that of the large varieties. Baby Glads, most of them hybrids of *G. tristis* and *G. blandus*, grow from very small corms about the size of Crocus corms. They should be planted in the fall and grown in a cool greenhouse. The blossoms of these Baby Glads are graceful open-faced flowers of white, pink, or red and are sweetly scented, especially in the evening. They grow to be about two feet in height.

All Gladiolus trace their ancestry to South Africa. After flowering the plants should be allowed to mature their foliage normally. Bulbs increase in number beneath the plants and may be saved from year to year.

GLORIOSA ROTHSCHILDIANA,
Glory-lily, Gloriosa-lily

Glory-lilies, which come to us from Africa, are wonderful items for the home-greenhouse gardener, their brilliant yellow-orange-red flowers causing a sensation among all who see them for the first time. Glory-lilies grow from elongated tubers, which may be planted from January to March for late summer and fall blooming. During the rest periods the stems die down to the ground. Store the bulbs in the pots without watering until the next planting season. Then replant them and force them into a new blossoming cycle. They do well in a moderately warm greenhouse, but will grow, though more slowly, in a cool greenhouse.

Glory-lilies sometimes need a bit of support for their slender stems. They have tendrils on the ends of their leaves which easily twine about slender stakes.

GLOXINIA, see *Gesneriads,* Section 10.

HAEMANTHUS, Blood-lily

If you can imagine fiery red balls of blossoms up to nine inches in diameter, then you can understand why Blood-lilies are grown despite their costliness. Blood-lilies come from South Africa as do so many of their cousins in the Amaryllis family. There are three species commonly grown, as well as many hybrids. They grow from large bulbs which should be potted in relatively small pots, considering the size of the bulbs. Plant them so that part of each bulb sticks above the soil. Plan to leave them in the same pot for three or four years, feeding them while they are in active growth with a complete fertilizer.

During rest periods keep the soil dry, giving just enough moisture to keep the bulbs from shriveling. When growth begins, gradually increase the amount of water available to the plants. Give the plants filtered light in the summer, full sun in the winter.

H. COCCINEUS sends out its flowers in early fall before its leaves. It grows its foliage during the winter and rests during the summer.

H. KATHERINAE also flowers in the spring, but its leaves are evergreen and are carried on the plants throughout the year.

H. MULTIFLORUS blossoms in the spring before developing leaves. It rests during the winter.

HIPPEASTRUM VITTATUM, Amaryllis

South Africa has yielded many lovely flowers for our gardens and greenhouses, but surely none more spectacular than Amaryllis. If you plant bulbs of some of the better hybrid Amaryllis, you can easily get magnificent clusters of flowers, with individual blossoms six to eight inches or more across. Amaryllis flowers are Lilylike in shape and may be pink, red, striped pink and white, or, rarely, pure white in color.

Bulbs are available from midautumn until early winter and should be planted in pots of no more than two inches' greater diameter than that of the bulbs. Use a soil composed of two parts heavy loam and one part well-rotted cow manure, plus one teaspoonful of bone meal to each pot. Set the bulbs, one to a pot, so that two thirds of each bulb is above the soil level. Firm the soil around them, but be careful not to injure the roots. Give a single good watering; then keep the soil barely moist until growth starts, at which time see that they have an abundance of moisture.

Amaryllis blossom in midwinter, usually before sending out foliage. After flowering they will send out long straplike leaves. Keep your plants in a sunny place and feed them twice a month with a complete fertilizer. From October until the beginning of the new year let them become quite dry. At that time they will be ready to blossom again. Keep them in the same pot for three years, scratching out some of the old soil each year and replacing it with fresh soil and a teaspoonful of bone meal. Amaryllis will grow at any greenhouse temperature, but do best at 60 to 65 degrees.

HYACINTHUS ORIENTALIS, Hyacinth

Most gardeners know that the familiar Hyacinth, so often called Dutch Hyacinth, is not a native of Holland, but comes from Asia Minor. The fact that the Dutch have done so much to bring forth new varieties of this lovely plant gives them good reason, however, to be associated in our minds with Hyacinths. In addition to the usual Dutch Hyacinths there is another form known as Roman Hyacinth, *H. orientalis albulus,* which sends up many slender

PLATE I

ST. BRIGID ANEMONES

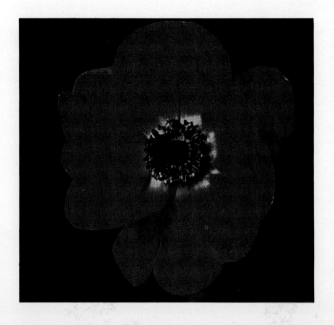

PLATE II

CYMBIDIUM ORCHIDS

CATTLEYA ORCHIDS

PLATE III

CATTLEYA ORCHID

AFRICAN VIOLETS

PLATE IV

AFRICAN VIOLET

CAMELLIA

PLATE V

AZALEAS

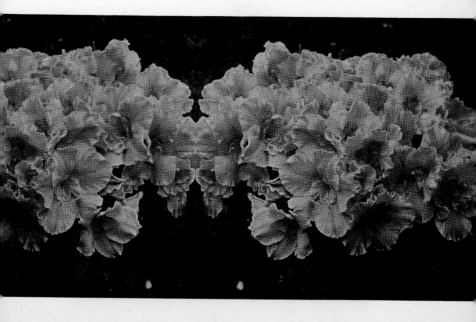

PLATE VI

EASTER LILIES

PLATE VII

CARNATIONS

PLATE VIII

GLOXINIAS

PLATE IX

TUBEROUS-ROOTED BEGONIAS

PLATE X

GERANIUM

GOLDBAND LILY

PLATE XI

ASTERS

CHRYSANTHEMUMS

PLATE XII

CHRYSANTHEMUMS

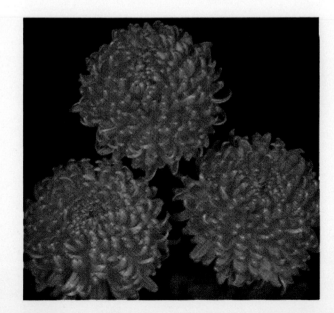

PLATE XIII

CHRYSANTHEMUMS

PLATE XIV

ACACIA

SWEETHEART ROSES

PLATE XV

TEA ROSES

PLATE XVI

POINSETTIAS

spikes of extremely fragrant flowers, usually white in color. The Dutch Hyacinths send forth one large spike followed by a secondary spike, which is somewhat smaller. Many colors are available in single and double flowers, including yellow, pink, red, lavender-blue, purple, and white.

Hyacinth bulbs must be potted up in the fall and stored in a cool dark place until roots make substantial growth. A cold frame or a garden trench is a suitable place to put bulbs while they are developing their root systems. Cover them with sufficient leaves or straw so that they will not freeze. Special "prepared" Hyacinths which have been given warm temperatures after being dug from the growing fields and before being placed on sale in the fall will start into growth earlier than others not so treated. It is possible to have Hyacinths in bloom as early as Christmas and to follow all through the winter with successive crops which have been allowed to remain in the cold frame until ready for forcing. Early Hyacinths must be allowed to stay in a dark place until new growth is about two inches tall, then gradually brought into the light, at which time the leaves will acquire their normal color. Hyacinths will stay beautiful for nearly two weeks if grown in a cool greenhouse. A special note about potting the bulbs in the fall is in order: Commercial growers never put Hyacinths in new clay flower pots. They always use old clay pots or plastic pots.

HYMENOCALLIS CALATHINA (*Ismene calathina*),
Peruvian Daffodil, Spider-lily

There are other members of the *Hymenocallis* or *Ismene* family to be had from certain sources, but the one mentioned above is readily available from most seed houses. Its fragrant blossoms are white and Lilylike and composed of twelve petals, six short incised ones and six long feathery ones. The plants grow from bulbs, which should be planted in the spring. Keep the plants moist from April to September, then dry for the balance of the year. The unusual flowers appear, two on the top of each stem, during the early summer.

IRIS

All of us have bought and enjoyed the lovely types of Iris sold by florists during the winter and spring months; thus it is interesting to know that they are easy to grow in a cool greenhouse. Technically known as Spanish, Dutch, or English Iris, they all spring from relatively small bulbs, which should be planted in pots, flats, or directly in benches in the fall of the year. Plant the bulbs one inch deep and three inches apart. Soil must be kept moist and temperatures cool. They do best if grown at a night temperature of no more than 55 degrees. Higher temperatures will cause bud blasting. Bulbs may be started in a cold frame and brought into the greenhouse at intervals to provide a continuous supply of flowers.

Particularly good varieties are Wedgwood, a medium blue; Imperator, dark blue; White Excelsior and Yellow Queen.

Although commercial growers sometimes produce flowers as early as December, they must use specially prepared bulbs and close temperature tolerances, which are not adapted to home-greenhouse culture.

As a special note on Iris culture it is well to know that once flats of Iris have been brought into the greenhouse, they should not be moved about until after the plants have flowered. Moving breaks roots and results in flowers' refusing to open properly.

ISMENE, see HYMENOCALLIS, this section.

IXIA

Ixias are small cormous plants from the Cape of Good Hope, grown for their lovely star-shaped flowers, which may be white, red, yellow, orange, lilac, purple, or green in color. They are borne on slender wiry stems and are good for cutting, but one must remember that they close at night. If left on the plants, the flowers last at least two weeks in a cool greenhouse.

Plant the small corms in the fall about an inch deep and two inches apart each way. Set the pots or flats in the cold frame and bring them into the greenhouse at intervals from December on for a succession of bloom. Grow them at 50 to 55 degrees with plenty of water. After flowering let the grasslike foliage mature and save the bulbs for another season.

LACHENALIA, Cape Cowslip

The name *Cape Cowslip* comes from the fact that this plant, like so many others familiar to gardeners, comes from the region of the Cape of Good Hope. European growers have hybridized Cape Cowslips for many years and have produced lovely plants with blossoms of red, yellow, or violet, often tinged with green. The flowers are somewhat bell-like and are borne along spikes that rise eight to ten inches above the basal leaves.

Cape Cowslips grow from small bulbs which should be planted one-half inch deep and one inch apart in pots during late summer. If placed in a shaded cold frame and allowed to make root growth, the pots can be brought into the greenhouse in November and December for flowering from December through February. It is important that they be grown in a cool greenhouse and that they be given plenty of moisture. After flowering let the foliage mature normally. Save the bulbs right in the pots of soil and do not water them. In August they should be replanted in fresh soil and started into another growth cycle. New plants can be grown from seeds, bulb offsets, and leaf cuttings. Some growers use Cape Cowslips as hanging basket plants, growing them in Sphagnum-moss-lined wire baskets.

LEUCOCORYNE, Glory-of-the-sun

These small cormous plants from Chile are very much worth growing in a cool greenhouse at 50 to 55 degrees. The starlike flowers are pale blue in color and are borne in clusters at the tops of the slender stems. They make long-lasting cut flowers for use in low bouquets. Plant the bulbs in the fall and give the same culture as Ixia.

LILIUM, Lily

When you think of greenhouse-grown Lilies, do you automatically think of Easter Lilies? No doubt most of us think of them first, but all too many would-be greenhouse amateurs let their thoughts begin and end with this one type of Lily. One has only to visit a flower show in early spring to see for himself the amazing exhibits of Lilies and to reflect that every plant in the show had to be forced in a greenhouse in order to realize that there is practically no end to the kinds of Lilies that can be encouraged to flower out of season in the protected climate of a greenhouse. It is surely true that you should grow a few Easter Lilies for the fun of it, but broaden your horizon and grow some of the colorful Lilies too. During the past few years Lily breeders have given us countless numbers of new strong-growing Lily hybrids, and it is these which you really should try in addition to the old standbys. Bulbs of hardy Lilies should be purchased as early in the fall as possible and potted up in greenhouse soil with provision for good drainage at the bottom of each pot. A layer of pebbles an inch deep at the bottom of the pots will take care of drainage. Use deep pots and plant the bulbs fairly deep so that stem roots will have a chance to grow. Put the pots in a cold frame and cover them with leaves or straw to keep them from freezing while they make a good root growth. Bring them into a cool greenhouse after the first of the year. Keep the soil moist; give the plants full sun and temperatures of 50 to 60 degrees; and let them come into flower slowly. After flowering let the plants mature their foliage. Repot before forcing again, or if you prefer, plant the bulbs in your garden.

Easter Lilies are easy to grow if one does not try to have them in flower right on Easter Sunday. The specialists who provide this miracle each season watch their temperatures closely, and even they have difficulties at times. A spell of dark cloudy or of unseasonably mild weather can upset the best-laid plans. Generally speaking, it takes 180 days from the time of planting to have an Easter Lily in blossom if it is grown at 60 degrees at night and the bulb was not "prepared" prior to planting. Prepared Lily bulbs are ones which have been given cold storage for five weeks before planting. Since these will blossom in 120 days, most commercial florists use them, but it is difficult to get the small quantity that an amateur would need unless he cultivates his local florist nearly as assiduously as he does his flowers. There are several strains of Easter Lilies, including Ace, Croft, Creole, Estate, Erabu, Giganteum, Harrisii, and Howardii, all derived originally from *L. longiflorum*, a species native to Japan.

Among Lilies that have been grown successfully for many years are the following:

L. AURATUM, Goldband Lily

Once you have seen the immense fragrant flowers of the Goldband Lily, you will no longer wonder why it is often used as one of the parents in breeding new Lily hybrids. The flowers of the species are white with crimson spots with a band of yellow down the center of each petal. It is not uncommon to have flowers ten to twelve inches across. Pot the bulbs in the fall and hold them in the cold frame until January or later; then bring them into the greenhouse at intervals to supply a succession of bloom.

L. BATEMANNIAE, Bateman's Lily

Bateman's Lily is another hardy Lily sometimes used for forcing. Its blossoms are of an apricot shade. Culture is the same as for *L. auratum*.

L. CANDIDUM, Madonna Lily, also Annunciation, Bourbon, Lent, or St. Joseph's Lily

Madonna Lilies have long been cherished for the waxy whiteness and the sweet fragrance of their blossoms, which out of doors usually open at the same time as Delphiniums. Pot the bulbs as soon as they are available in late summer and put them in a cold frame as noted with *L. auratum*. They make a rosette of leaves in the fall, which should not be smothered beneath too heavy a covering during the period before bringing them into the greenhouse. If they are brought into the greenhouse in January, they will flower in April.

L. REGALE, Regal Lily

There are many forms of Regal Lily hybrids differing somewhat from the original species, which has large open-faced white flowers with golden throats and rosy-purple tinges to the outsides of the petals. This Lily, like the Goldband, has figured in many of the better new hybrids. Treat in the same manner as *L. auratum*. Flowers will open in eight to twelve weeks after the bulbs are brought into the greenhouse, depending upon the temperatures at which they are grown.

L. SPECIOSUM, Speciosum Lily

The Speciosum Lily is one of those most commonly seen in flower shops, and the bulbs are available from commercial sources for forcing all through the year. If grown during the summer months, the plants should be given a bit of protection from the full sun. There are many forms of Speciosum Lilies. The one usually seen is *L. speciosum rubrum*, which has deeper pink flowers than *L. speciosum* and is called the Rubrum Lily. Another variant is *L. speciosum album*, whose pure white flowers are bridal favorites. The petals of all Speciosum Lilies are highly reflexed, giving them unusual charm.

L. TENUIFOLIUM, Coral Lily

This old-time favorite has small brilliantly scarlet, nodding, waxy flowers on relatively small plants. Culture is the same as for *L. auratum*.

Over the years many other types of Lilies have been grown, such as the Tiger Lily, *L. tigrinum,* but the newer hybrids are so much prettier that I would advise you to try them instead.

One last note about Lily culture. Once they have started growth, feed them twice a month with a complete water-soluble fertilizer. After flowering let the plants mature their foliage and either try forcing them again, though the results are not apt to be as spectacular, or relegate them to a place in your garden.

LIRIOPE, Lily-turf

Liriope and *Ophiopogon* are two similar Asiatic grasslike plants, which have been sold in mild climates as lawn substitutes under the name Mondo Grass. Although both forms have green foliage, each also has a green-and-white-foliaged variant, which is often used in the South as a ground cover. These plants are very useful in small greenhouses as filler plants since their foliage is carried throughout the year, and occasionally they have small lavender flowers. They will grow in any soil and do well in the sun or shade. Propagation is by division of the underground stoloniferous roots.

LYCORIS, Spider-lily

Spider-lilies are strange plants closely related to Amaryllis. They produce their foliage, die down, and then, out of the naked earth, they send forth tall leafless stems topped by clusters of Lilylike flowers of pink, red, or yellow. Bulbs should be planted so that the necks are above the surface of the soil. They resent being repotted, and care must be taken not to damage their roots. Propagation is by bulb offsets. *L. squamigera* (*Amaryllis hallii*) has pink flowers. It sends out its leaves in early spring, which mature, then die back and wither away. Flowers appear in late summer. *L. radiata,* the Red Spider-lily, produces clusters of red flowers, and *L. aurea,* the Golden Spider-lily, yellow flowers. These two species flower in late summer, then produce their leaves, which must be kept growing during the winter months. When the foliage matures, the soil must still be kept moist and warm, and when late summer arrives again, they will blossom. Spider-lilies come from Southeast Asia and look very much like Nerine-lilies, which are native to South Africa. They are often confused botanically and in trade offerings.

MUSCARI, Grape-hyacinth

Grape-hyacinths are among the easiest of the hardy bulbs to force in a cool greenhouse. Plant the bulbs in shallow pans as soon as they are available in the fall and set them in a cold frame. They make an abundant growth of foliage in the fall. Bring them into the greenhouse at intervals so as to have a continuing source of blooms. There are pale and dark blue, as well as white, varieties. Grape-hyacinths may be grown from seeds or from bulb offsets, but for normal purposes it is better to buy mature bulbs. After forcing they can be planted to permanent places in the outdoor garden. Grape-hyacinths are native to the Mediterranean region.

NARCISSUS, Narcissus, Daffodil, Jonquil

For the purposes of this discussion the Narcissus family will be divided into two classes only, not on the usual basis of the type of flower produced, but upon the hardiness characteristics of the species involved. The hardy Narcissus, which includes varieties of the King Alfred type with the large flowers as well as some of the cluster types, such as Laurens Koster, are best handled as follows: Pot the bulbs as soon as they are available in the fall, setting them close together in shallow pots or flats, and let them stay, protected from freezing, in the cold frame until you are ready to bring them into a cool greenhouse (50 to 55 degrees). They will come into flower very swiftly, and the bulbs may be ripened and saved for garden planting after the flowers have faded.

It should be pointed out that the longer that hardy bulbs can be left in the cold frame and the closer the forcing time is to their natural flowering season, the easier they can be encouraged to blossom. Also it should be noted that less time is necessary to force bulbs into blossom as one approaches their normal season. Generally, the earliest hardy Narcissus are brought into the greenhouse in mid-December to flower in January. An exception is that of precooled bulbs, which are available from commercial florist suppliers and which will flower in December from September plantings.

The second group to consider is the tender Narcissus of the Paper-white type. They should not have the cold outdoor treatment, but should be kept in a dark place for about two weeks so as to encourage root growth before bringing them into the greenhouse. They are often grown on window sills, but they are much more satisfactory when grown in the springlike atmosphere of a cool greenhouse. In addition to the Paper-whites, try the yellow Soleil d'Or. Unlike the hardy varieties, the bulbs cannot be saved for garden planting except in mild climates.

NERINE SARNIENSIS, Nerine-lily, Guernsey-lily

Nerine-lilies have luscious, spidery, pink-to-scarlet Lilylike flowers borne in clusters atop leafless stems. They are outdoor plants only in mild climates; so most northern gardeners find that the only way they can enjoy them is by having their own greenhouse. Their culture and appearance are similar to that of *Lycoris radiata,* with the exception that after foliage matures the bulbs must be left in the pots without moisture in full sun until it is desired to bring them into flower again. Their normal cycle is as follows: Plant bulbs in summer or early fall; blossoms will arise without foliage sometime between September and December. After the flowers die, the foliage grows and must be kept growing in a cool sunny greenhouse until it matures and turns yellow. Then comes the dry season as mentioned above. Flowering of plants in a group can be spaced somewhat by withholding water on some plants for a month or so after others have been started into growth. Since they do not like to have their roots disturbed, grow them several years in the same pots, feeding them monthly during the growing season with a complete water-soluble fertilizer. Propagation is by natural bulb increase. Nerines come from South Africa and are sometimes called Guernsey-lilies because they have become naturalized on the Isle of Guernsey in the English Channel.

OPHIOPOGON, See LIRIOPE, this section.

ORNITHOGALUM, Star of Bethlehem, Chincherinchee

Several of the tender Ornithogalums make fine bulbous plants for greenhouse use. All are of easy culture: Pot up the bulbs in the fall; give them a rooting period in a protected cold frame; then bring them into the greenhouse for flowering. The bulbs last indefinitely and increase by offsets. After flowering let the foliage mature and store the bulbs in the dry soil of the pots until the next autumn. Repot in fresh soil and start the plants off again on a new cycle.

O. arabicum has clusters of fragrant white flowers with black centers. *O. thyrsoides* is native to South Africa and has white flowers which last for weeks when cut. They are often sent to the United States and Europe as cut flowers. There is a yellow variety, *O. thyrsoides aureum*, which is also well worth growing.

OXALIS, Oxalis, Wood Sorrel

Oxalis are lovely small bulbous plants with Cloverlike foliage and small white, light and dark pink, or yellow flowers. The leaves fold together and flowers close at night and on cloudy days. They do well as small pot plants and as hanging basket plants. Give them full sun and abundant moisture in a well-drained soil while they are in active growth. After flowering let the plants mature and rest in dry soil until the next planting season. Bulbs should be potted up in early fall for winter flowering and allowed to rest during the summer months. Oxalis are often sold as mixed colors, but you may purchase them separately as follows: *O. Bowieana*, dark pink; *O. cernua*, yellow, sometimes called Bermuda Buttercup though it is native to South Africa, not Bermuda, and is not a Buttercup; *O. hirta*, deep rose; and *O. variabilis*, white, pink, or lavender.

POLIANTHES TUBEROSA, Tuberose

Tuberoses are grown for their delightfully fragrant, white Lilylike flowers. The name *Tuberose* is in allusion to the fact that it has tuberous roots and has nothing to do with the shape of the flowers. Strangely enough, Tuberoses have never been found growing wild, but botanists feel that they originally came from Central or South America. Both single- and double-flowering forms are cultivated, but the one most commonly grown is called Double Pearl.

Tuberoses are usually grown as summer flowers, but with a greenhouse one may have them in flower from May until late fall. Late summer flowers may be had by planting the tubers in May, and early flowers may be had by planting as early as January. Use only the largest bulbs you can buy and water lightly until growth starts. Grow them in full sun. Once bulbs have flowered, they are no longer useful, for the offsets must be grown to flowering size outdoors for at least one season before they can be forced. For that reason you may find it easier to buy new bulbs each spring. If you save your bulbs, store them over winter in a cool dry place.

RANUNCULUS ASIATICUS, Ranunculus, Persian or Turban Buttercup

Ranunculus are members of the Buttercup family and are native to Asia Minor. It is natural that yellow should be a predominant color among these gorgeous Buttercups, but plant breeders have also given us shades of orange, pink, and red, as well as white. Tecolote Hybrids are a commonly grown strain, noted for their large highly colored double flowers. Ranunculus may be grown from seed or tubers and should be given the same culture as *Anemone coronaria,* described earlier in this section.

SCILLA, Squill

If you are one of those who feel that a spring garden cannot be complete without the cheerful blossoms of the early Squills, then you should surely try some of them in your greenhouse and enjoy spring flowers for a longer period each year. Pot Squills in shallow pans in the fall and put them in your cold frame. Bring them into the cool greenhouse so as to have a succession of bloom. One of the easiest Squills to force is *S. sibirica,* Siberian Squill, whose startling deep-blue flowers rarely grow over four to six inches high. *S. nonscripta (nutans)* is known in England as the Wood Hyacinth and has blue or pink flowers, depending upon the variety. It grows ten to twelve inches tall and is good for cutting.

S. hispanica (campanulata), the Spanish Bluebell, grows as much as eighteen inches tall and has spikes of blue, pink, or white flowers. It is best to buy new bulbs for forcing and put the used ones into your garden where they will soon make a home for themselves.

SPARAXIS, Wandflower, Sparaxis

Sparaxis is closely related to Ixia and needs the same culture. Both grow from corms and produce swordlike leaves about one and one half feet tall. The flowers are lovely open cups of rose, red, yellow, or purple often with beautiful markings in the throats of the flowers. Sparaxis, like Ixias, are natives to South Africa.

SPREKELIA, Aztec-, St. James-, or Jacobean-lily

The Aztec-lily is an unusual summer-flowering member of the Amaryllis family, which bears bright red, somewhat Orchidlike, flowers atop slender stems before sending out its foliage. Plant the bulbs in the spring and, after the foliage has ripened, store the bulbs in a cool, dark, dry place until the next spring.

TRITONIA, Montbretia, Blazing Star

Montbretias look very much like miniature Gladiolus and are often grown in a similar manner in the summer garden. Home-greenhouse owners, however, may treat them like Freesias (which see for culture), planting them in the fall and having them blossom in a cool greenhouse in early spring. The flowers come in shades of yellow, orange, and maroon. They make fine cut flowers. Montbretias grow from corms about the size of those of Crocuses and are native to South Africa.

TULBAGHIA FRAGRANS, Tulbaghia, "Pink Agapanthus"

Tulbaghia is an uncommon bulbous plant from South Africa, which has the habit of growth of a dwarf Agapanthus, with long straplike leaves and flower spikes ten to twelve inches high. The leaves are evergreen, and the plant flowers nearly all through the year with clusters of very fragrant rosy-lavender blossoms. Try Tulbaghia for something out of the ordinary.

TULIPA, Tulip

It is unnecessary here to go into the charms of Tulips and their place as stand-bys in the winter and spring greenhouse. Although there are many colors and varieties available, not all of them force with equal ease. Choose Early Tulips for forcing in January and February. Darwins can be forced from late February on.

Pot the bulbs in October and November and place them in your cold frame so that they can become well rooted. Bring them into the greenhouse at intervals so as to have blossoms over a long period of time. Treatment as greenhouse plants is similar to that of Hyacinths, which should be consulted for culture.

Note that all spring bulbs do better if not brought into the greenhouse until late in January unless the bulbs have been given a period of precooling prior to planting. It is important to note that one must use large firm bulbs if large uniform flowers are desired. Do not scrimp on the quality of the bulbs you buy, for the flowers they produce will be in direct relationship to the bulb quality.

VALLOTA SPECIOSA, Scarborough-lily

The Scarborough-lily is another member of the Amaryllis family from South Africa grown for its large clusters of blood-red Lilylike flowers. Its culture is similar to that of the Amaryllis, except that it should not be allowed to dry out during its rest period. Although its foliage dies to the ground in its native habitat, it remains evergreen in cultivation. Care must be taken not to damage roots in transplanting the Scarborough-lily, and it should be grown in the smallest size pot possible that will accommodate the bulbs. Eventually the bulbs multiply, and the plant should then be grown in a tub. Give monthly feedings with a complete water-soluble fertilizer while in active growth and repot only when absolutely necessary.

VELTHEIMIA VIRIDIFOLIA, Veltheimia

Once you have seen a Veltheimia, you will not rest until you have a specimen for your greenhouse. The foliage alone, as is suggested by the name *viridifolia,* is particularly beautiful, being a glossy vibrant green, and the pendant yellow flowers hanging from the twelve-inch stem make the picture complete. Start the bulbs in the fall in a cool greenhouse, and they will blossom in the spring. Let the foliage continue to grow after flowering has completed. When the leaves finally shrivel, let the bulb stay in the pot without water until the following autumn.

ZANTEDESCHIA, Calla-lily

There are three main sections of the Calla-lily family which are considered to be greenhouse plants. The most common is the white Calla-lily, *Z. aethiopica,* and its more dwarf and freer-flowering strain *Godefreyana.* The Yellow Calla-lily is known botanically as *Z. Elliottiana,* and the Pink Calla-lily is *Z. Rehmannii.* (The Black Calla-lily is a different plant, *Arum palaestinum,* treated separately earlier in this section.)

Of the three Calla-lilies the easiest to grow is the white one. In any event, treat all of them in the same manner by potting up the tubers in rich soil in the fall, growing them at a temperature of 55 to 65 degrees with a great deal of moisture in full sunshine. Blossoms are effective either left on the plants or used as cut flowers. In the early summer withhold water and let the tubers become dormant. Repot in fresh soil in the fall and start them into growth again. You will find that they do very well when three or four tubers are planted together in a twelve-inch tub. They will make a fine showing throughout the winter season.

ZEPHYRANTHES, Zephyr-lily, Atamasco-lily,
Rain-lily, Fairy-lily, Flowers-of-the-west-wind

There are three colors available among the Zephyr-lilies, white, pink, and yellow. The plants are small, and the flowers are borne one at a time atop slender grassy stems. In nature they grow in moist places, and this must be considered when growing them in greenhouses. Start the bulbs in early spring and, after the foliage fades, keep the bulbs somewhat on the dry side, but not absolutely dry, until the next planting season. Various members of the *Zephyranthes* family grow wild from Virginia south to Argentina.

SECTION 4. VINES, CLIMBERS, AND TRAILERS
(See also Hanging Basket Plants)

In order to make this section about vines, climbers, and trailers of the greatest value to you, I have made abundant cross references with the next grouping, Hanging Basket Plants. As a matter of fact, how does one decide whether a plant belongs in one section or another? Often the line of demarcation is indefinite; thus I have made arbitrary decisions, based upon what I feel will be the manner in which you will most often use them. One thing is certain; among these plants will be found some of the most beautiful and intriguing ones known to horticulture. Most of them should be grown in containers of some sort. Not only will this provide portability, but it will restrain the rampant nature of some of the more robust species, causing them to devote less of their energies to foliage and more to flowers.

In this section and the one which follows, you will find many references to other plant groupings in which the cultural details of the plants will be found. Their inclusion here is simply an attempt to make it easy for a reader to locate plants suited for particular uses.

Be careful not to use too many vines or to let them grow in such a way as to shade your sun-loving plants. They can be given trellises to climb, or they can be allowed to find their way up the framework of the greenhouse. Many vines will benefit by being pruned quite often, not only to keep them within bounds, but to encourage flowering.

ALLAMANDA, Allamanda, Gold Cup

Any summer traveler to tropical or semitropical lands has seen the golden cups of Allamandas and wished that he could have such lovely plants in his own yard at home. If one has a greenhouse this is surely possible, for Allamandas have been grown in greenhouses for many years. There are several species, most of which have magnificent flowers. Perhaps the best of the yellow forms is the one known as *A. cathartica hendersoni,* a native of

Guiana. A reddish-violet species is *A. violacea.* It is not as strong a grower and does best when grafted onto the roots of the yellow Allamanda. Allamandas have beautiful large glossy leaves, which set off the flowers to great advantage. Grow them in large pots or tubs and keep them moist from early spring until they stop growing in the fall. Keep them on the dry side until January; then prune them back before new growth starts so that they will not become too large. During the growing season feed them regularly with a complete fertilizer. They like a rich humusy soil made up of two parts of good loam and one part each of leaf mold and well-rotted manure. Allamandas blossom profusely from late spring until autumn. New plants are easily started from cuttings.

BOUGAINVILLEA

Those who live in mild climates and have Bougainvilleas clambering over the tops of their porches might laugh at confining such rampantly growing plants to flowerpots. However, it may be done very happily, and the plants will cover themselves with huge clusters of brilliant paperlike bracts of purple, crimson, or tangerine from early until late spring. Plants should be cut back after flowering and encouraged to make new growth without becoming too tall. Feed them well when they are growing and pinch the tips of the stems to induce branching. If your greenhouse is of the lean-to type, you might want to plant a Bougainvillea in the soil and let it cover the unglassed side. Do not be afraid to cut it back if it grows too tall. Bougainvilleas are native to Brazil. Cuttings will root easily.

CEROPEGIA WOODII, Rosary Vine,
see *Hanging Basket Plants,* Section 5.

CISSUS, see *Hanging Basket Plants,* Section 5.

CLEMATIS

There are a great many species of Clematis, but for greenhouse purposes I suggest that you restrict your choice to the large-flowered hybrids, from which there are a great many to choose. Their colors range from white through many shades of pink to red, in addition to the lovely blues, lavenders, and purples. It is not at all unusual to have flowers five to six inches across or more, and the way that they are borne on delicate vines makes them all the more desirable. Give Clematis regular greenhouse soil, but add enough lime to it so that its reaction is neutral or a bit alkaline. Clematis should be given a support upon which to grow and should be fed and watered regularly during the growing season. New plants are easily rooted from cuttings made in the spring. Clematis grow best in a cool greenhouse in bright light. These choice vines are the result of hybridization among four Chinese and Japanese species.

CLERODENDRON, Glorybower, Bagflower, Clerodendron
Clerodendrons make fine subjects for a warm greenhouse and will flower almost continuously if kept growing with regular food and water. If one does not have sufficient room to allow them to develop into tall vines, they will accommodate themselves to living in small flowerpots and still flower freely. The blossoms of the most common species, *C. thomsoniae,* are crimson and white, borne in generous clusters on the ends of the stems. These West African vines never fail to arouse curiosity among greenhouse visitors.

COLUMBO AGENT, see SCINDAPSUS, this section.

CYMBALARIA MURALIS, Kenilworth Ivy,
see *Hanging Basket Plants,* Section 5.

FICUS PUMILA, Climbing Fig
Climbing Figs are small-leafed evergreen vines, which readily climb up any moist masonry or wire surface. The leaves lie flat and overlap like shingles. There is a variegated green and white type in addition to the more familiar green-leafed form. A humusy soil and an abundance of water will make Climbing Figs grow luxuriantly.

HEDERA HELIX, English Ivy
What comes to your mind when you see the words *English Ivy?*

It would be interesting to know, for there are dozens of forms of the English Ivy, all the way from the one that climbs castle walls to the delicate cut-leafed forms we use as decorative pot plants. Regardless of leaf shape, however, all of them thrive in a bit of shade and in rich humusy soil with plenty of water. Cuttings root very easily in moist sand. English Ivies can be grown beautifully as hanging basket plants, or they may be allowed to creep up masonry walls.

HOYA CARNOSA, Wax Plant, Porcelain Flower

Wax plants are climbing or trailing vines, which may reach eight feet or more in length. During the summer months they send out clusters of fragrant, waxy, long-lasting, star-shaped, pale-pink, dark-centered flowers. The flowers are borne on small spurs, which should not be removed since flowers come on them again and again. The plants like a warm moist atmosphere and a bit of shade. There is a form with variegated leaves as well as the more common green-leafed type. Wax Plants may be increased easily by rooting cuttings. They are native from China southward through the East Indies to Australia.

IPOMOEA, Morning Glory

It may seem strange to include Morning Glories among greenhouse plants, but you will be surprised to see how well they will blossom if the roots are confined to a relatively small pot. Try some of the Dwarf Bush Morning Glories for a lot of color on a sunny shelf in your greenhouse. Give them regular greenhouse soil and plenty of water. The seeds are hard and will germinate more quickly if you will nick their shells.

JASMINUM, Jasmine, Jessamine

There are many forms of Jasmines, but all are not suitable for the home greenhouse. Some grow to be forty feet tall, for example. The following species are suggested to give fragrance and flowers during different times of the year. All of them may be grown in pots, though rather large pots may be required as plants mature. They can be kept small by pruning, or smaller plants can be grown from cuttings easily rooted in sand in the spring. Jasmines can be grown in cool or warm greenhouses, provided that they have abundant light. Some types should be staked or trained against a wall for support as against the back wall of a lean-to greenhouse.

J. NUDIFLORUM, Winter Jasmine

Winter Jasmine blossoms from late winter to early spring, sending out its solitary yellow flowers from along its leafless stems. China is its native home.

J. OFFICINALE GRANDIFLORUM, Spanish, Poet's, or Catalonian Jasmine

This variety has fragrant white flowers, which are reddish on the outsides of the petals. It blossoms from June to October and is native to Kashmir.

J. PRIMULINUM (MESNYI), Primrose Jasmine

Yellow semidouble flowers with dark centers mark the Primrose Jasmine, which comes from China. It flowers in the springtime.

J. SAMBAC, Arabian Jasmine

The Arabian Jasmine is favored for its very fragrant white flowers, which turn purple as they age. The variety Grand Duke of Tuscany, developed in Italy, has double white flowers, which are particularly sweet-scented. Both of these types flower from early spring until late fall.

LANTANA MONTEVIDENSIS, Trailing Lantana, see *Hanging Basket Plants*, Section 5.

LATHYRUS ODORATUS, Sweet Pea, see *Cut Flowers*, Section 2.

MANETTIA, Brazilian Firecracker Plant

No plant could have a more aptly descriptive name than this one. Its tubular flowers are bright red and have a yellow tip and are borne throughout the year. Plants get as much as four to five feet tall and are very effective additions to a warm greenhouse. Ordinary soil and regular feeding will make them grow fast. New plants may be secured by making stem or root cuttings.

MONSTERA, Swiss Cheese Plant, Hurricane Plant

Monsteras are Philodendron relatives, which thrive in shady, warm, moist greenhouses. Give them a bit of food and a humid atmosphere, and your only trouble will be to keep them within bounds. The large leaves of mature plants are pierced with several irregularly shaped holes which give rise to the common name, Swiss Cheese Plant. Plants send out strong roots from along the climbing stems; so they are often grown on slabs of wood or Tree Fern.

PASSIFLORA, Passion-flower

There are several varieties of Passion-flowers which make handsome greenhouse vines. They grow so easily that one must be careful that they do not become too rampant. Since they are such strong growers, they are often grown in pots so that their vigorous roots can be restrained. Their flowers may be white with pink and purple on the insides of the petals, or they may be deep red. The flowers are curious and exotic, and a legend likening the flower parts to the crucifixion of Christ has given rise to the name *Passion-flower*. Various species of Passion-flowers are native from southern United States southward into South America.

Passion-flowers are easily started from seeds or cuttings in the early spring. As they increase in size they eventually need ten-inch pots containing a rich, well-drained soil. They blossom during the greater part of the year, but are usually cut back to the ground in January. At that time fresh soil should be added to replace as much as possible of the old soil. They should then be watered and started into a new growth cycle. A trellis of some kind must be provided upon which they can climb. Their tendrils easily cling to materials as thin as twine, and a few strands of twine may be just the support you want to give your plants.

PHILODENDRON

Philodendrons are too well known to need introduction here. There are hundreds of different kinds with various leaf sizes and patterns, but all are alike in their response to a moist, humusy soil, a bit of shade, and a warm humid atmosphere. Most Philodendrons are climbers so need some sort of support, such as a slab of wood with the bark attached, or a piece of Tree Fern stem. The self-heading Philodendrons do not climb, but spread out broadly as they mature, many of them becoming so large as to limit their usefulness in a small greenhouse. Over two hundred kinds of Philodendrons are native to the American tropics.

PIPER, Pepper

Three members of the Pepper family make interesting vines for the warm shady greenhouse. The most common is *P. nigrum*, from whose berries both black and white pepper are produced. Its leaves are tough and glossy and are pointed at each end. *P. ornatum* and *P. porphyrophyllum* have very attractive heart-shaped leaves mottled with pink and silver. Give them a moist humusy soil with filtered light. They are native to the jungles of the East Indies.

PLUMBAGO, see *Pot Plants,* Section 1.

POTHOS, see SCINDAPSUS, this section.

SAXIFRAGA SARMENTOSA,
see *Hanging Basket Plants,* Section 5.

SCINDAPSUS, Devil's Ivy, Marble Ivy, Columbo Agent

Scindapsus is a favorite foliage plant, often confused with Philodendrons since the habit of growth and the leaf shape are similar to that of the ordinary Heart-leaf Philodendron. The stems, however, are curiously square in profile, and the leaves of most horticultural forms are variously marked with cream or yellow streaks and blotches. Two species, *S. aureus* from the Solomon Islands and *S. pictus* from the East Indies, are commonly grown. Golden

Pothos is the name of one common florist variety, and Marble Queen is another. The leaves on young plants are two inches or so across, but as the plants mature the leaves become as much as two feet across. Give them filtered light, warm temperatures, a support to climb upon, and allow them to dry somewhat between waterings.

SENECIO MIKANIOIDES, German Ivy,
see *Hanging Basket Plants,* Section 5.

STEPHANOTIS, Stephanotis, Madagascar Jasmine

If most gardeners knew that they could grow only one vine in their greenhouse, there is little doubt but that they would choose Stephanotis. This is the waxy white, deliciously fragrant flower so much in demand for use in bridal bouquets and corsages. The vines are evergreen and easily grow to the height of a greenhouse, sending forth clusters of blossoms from spring until fall. During this time of the year they should be shaded very lightly, but they can stand full sun during the winter. Plants are easily increased by cuttings in the spring. In order to flower freely, Stephanotis must have a warm greenhouse with a night temperature of about 65 degrees.

THUNBERGIA, see *Hanging Basket Plants,* Section 5.

TOLMIEA, see *Hanging Basket Plants,* Section 5.

TRACHELOSPERMUM JASMINOIDES,
Star-jasmine, Confederate-jasmine

Star-jasmines are evergreen vines from China which have clusters of intensely fragrant white flowers in the spring and intermittently throughout the summer. The plants will do well in greenhouse soil, but are slow growing unless given a warm location. They can be trained to grow on a low trellis and clipped so as to stay within bounds. During the summer they need protection from the sun and do well if taken out of the greenhouse and plunged in a lightly shaded spot. Keep them in full light and on the dry side during their rest period of autumn and early winter. New plants can be started from cuttings in the spring.

TROPAEOLUM, Nasturtium

Ordinary Nasturtiums are common enough garden flowers, but they take on new beauty when grown in the protected environment of a greenhouse. Give them ordinary soil, but do not give them nitrogenous fertilizers as they will develop leaf growth at the expense of flowers. Nasturtiums may be grown as vines if one uses the giant *T. majus,* or as pot plants or hanging basket plants if one uses the dwarf types. The Canarybird Vine, *T. peregrinum* (*T. canariense*), has yellow feathery flowers and deeply lobed leaves and is a real climber, which will grow to ten feet or more. Give all Nasturtiums full sun. Nasturtiums are native to South America.

VANILLA, see Orchids, Chapter IX.

VINCA MAJOR VARIEGATA, Variegated Periwinkle, see *Hanging Basket Plants,* Section 5.

WAX PLANT, see HOYA CARNOSA, this section.

SECTION 5. HANGING BASKET PLANTS

The culture of many of the plants listed in this section is discussed elsewhere in this chapter; so in many cases only the names will be listed here. Do not take that as an indication that the plants are not suited for hanging-basket culture. As an example, one of the first plants in the list, *Achimenes,* is a marvelous plant for growing in this manner, but because it is a Gesneriad, its needs are discussed along with other related plants. Please note that hanging plants have a special charm in a greenhouse and add a touch seldom achieved in outdoor gardening. Somehow a visitor entering a greenhouse which has hanging plants feels that he has been transported into another realm close to paradise. In the following group of plants you will find some that like sunshine and others that demand shade, some that must be warm and a few which must be cool. Surely you will find a selection that you will consider indispensable to your greenhouse.

As an up-to-date suggestion for your hanging basket plants try potting them in plastic, rather than clay, pots. They hold moisture so much better than the clay ones that growth is more continuous and uniform. Chances are, too, that if you forget to water them for a day or two, they will still not suffer unduly.

ABUTILON, see *Pot Plants,* Section 1.

ACHIMENES, see *Gesneriads,* Section 10.

AESCHYNANTHUS, see *Gesneriads,* Section 10.

ASPARAGUS SPRENGERI, Sprengeri-fern

This South African member of the Asparagus family has fine-foliaged, drooping branches from one to two feet long, which by nature hang gracefully over the side of any container in which it grows. It is perfectly beautiful as an evergreen hanging-basket plant, and it becomes even more attractive when the tiny white flowers mature into bright red berries. This plant needs the same culture as *A. plumosus,* listed under Pot Plants, except that it grows best in a cool greenhouse at 50 degrees or lower. It can stand some shade and may be increased from seeds or from division of the roots. Besides the plants you hang, grow a few to use as greens for your cut flowers. They are superlative for this purpose.

BEGONIA, TUBEROUS-ROOTED, TRAILING, see *Bulbs,* Section 3.

BILLBERGIA, see *Bromeliads,* Section 8.

BROWALLIA SPECIOSA, Browallia

It is hard to imagine a more delightful hanging basket plant than a Browallia covered with hundreds of deep blue flowers. Browallias, natives of South America, do best in a warm greenhouse, 60 to 65 degrees or so. In cool temperatures growth is very slow. They can stand full sun or filtered light. I grow them close to the glass in a lightly shaded Orchid house, and they blossom throughout the year. Start new plants from seeds in July or August and pot about three plants to a shallow eight-inch pan.

CAMPANULA ISOPHYLLA, Falling Stars,
Italian Bellflower, "Star of Bethlehem"

The name *Star of Bethlehem* is usually applied to members of the Ornithogalum family, but this Star of Bethlehem is a late-summer- to late-autumn-blooming member of the Bellflower family, which needs to be grown in a cool greenhouse. There are both white and blue forms available, whose wide-open bell-like flowers are borne in such profusion as to hide the foliage. Start the plants from seeds or cuttings early in the spring and, as they grow, pinch them back so that the plants will become as bushy as possible. Do not pinch after the first week of June and from that time until late summer give them a lightly shaded location. Give them plenty of water during the summer months, but allow the soil to become fairly dry between waterings. After flowers fade in the fall, cut the plants back and grow them in a cool bright spot with relatively little water. It is necessary to feed these plants all through the growing season with a complete fertilizer. They are perennials and will live for many years. It is a good idea to repot old plants in fresh soil each spring. This species of Bellflower is native to Italy and is used as a rock garden plant in cool mild climates.

CEROPEGIA, String of Hearts, Rosary Vine

There are several species of Ceropegias known to botanists, but the one most often found in commerce is *C. woodii,* a delightful small vine which surely lives up to the name String of Hearts. The trailing stems which flow over the sides of the flowerpot are almost stringlike in size, and all along them are hung perfect little heart-shaped, mottled gray-green-pink leaves. Flowers are small, waxy, and pinkish purple. Allow the plants to dry somewhat between waterings and grow them in filtered light. They are native to Natal. New plants can be started from cuttings rooted in sand.

CISSUS, Cissus, Grape Ivy, Kangaroo Ivy

Three members of the Cissus family, grape relatives, are widely grown as house or greenhouse plants. All of them do best in filtered light. Soil should be allowed to become quite dry before you give them another drink of water.

C. antarctica from Australia has leaves somewhat the shape of those of Elms and is one of the toughest plants known. It will stand poor light and neglect and still stay apparently healthy. *C. discolor,* a jungle plant from Java, has interesting leaves shaped like spearheads. The veins are a soft green, and surrounding the center and side veins are sections that are a strange mixture of violet and maroon. Raised portions of the leaves close to the edges seem to have been brushed with molten silver. This plant may be allowed to climb a support, clinging by its tendrils, or it may be encouraged to trail over the sides of the pot. Pinching will foster compact growth. *C. rhombifolia,* Grape Ivy, a native of South America, has leaves that look much like those of Poison Ivy. It climbs by tendrils or may be allowed to trail.

COLUMNEA, see *Gesneriads,* Section 10.

CYMBALARIA MURALIS, Kenilworth Ivy

Kenilworth Ivy is a creeping vine from Europe, which has become naturalized in parts of eastern United States. Its leaves are roundish, less than one inch across, and have shallow scallops on their edges. Its lavender-blue flowers are tiny and have yellow centers. Kenilworth Ivy will grow in sun or shade and makes an interesting plant for use in hanging baskets or as edgings for window boxes in the summer. Since this creeping plant roots where it touches moist ground, new plants are easy to obtain.

DAVALLIA, Rabbit's-foot Fern, see *Ferns,* Section 9.

EPIPHYLLUM, see *Succulent Plants,* Section 7.

EPISCIA, see *Gesneriads,* Section 10.

FUCHSIA, see *Pot Plants,* Section 1.

HEDERA HELIX, English Ivy,
see *Vines, Climbers, and Trailers,* Section 4.

HELIOTROPIUM, Heliotrope, see *Pot Plants,* Section 1.

HOYA CARNOSA, Wax Plant,
see *Vines, Climbers, and Trailers,* Section 4.

LACHENALIA, see *Bulbs,* Section 3.

LANTANA MONTEVIDENSIS, Trailing Lantana

This Lantana is a much more refined plant than its relative *L. camara* (see *Pot Plants,* Section 1), but its cultural needs are the same. Trailing Lantana has a drooping habit of growth and blossoms throughout the year with a never-ending supply of lavender flower clusters. It will do best in full sun if given enough food and water, but can stand partial shade. As its botanical name would imply, Trailing Lantana comes from South America. Cuttings root quickly in moist sand. There are white- and yellow-flowered forms.

MANETTIA, see *Vines, Climbers, and Trailers,* Section 4.

NASTURTIUM, see TROPAEOLUM, *Vines, Climbers, and Trailers,* Section 4.

NEPENTHES, Pitcher Plant

Here is a true oddity for a home greenhouse, for Nepenthes are carnivorous plants which grow wild in the jungles of such far-off places as New Guinea, Celebes, Malaya, and the Philippines. The plants are climbers in their native habitat, but in greenhouses are best grown as hanging basket plants in warm shady greenhouses in company with Orchids. Certain leaves of the plants develop into huge "pitchers," as much as twelve inches deep, into which insects are attracted and where they are digested by a fluid. Grow the plants in pots containing one third each of Osmunda fiber, Sphagnum moss, and sand. After the plants have developed several leaves on their stems, pinch out the stem tips. This will force the last few leaves to produce huge pitchers.

ORCHID CACTUS, see EPIPHYLLUM, *Succulents,* Section 7.

OXALIS, see *Bulbs,* Section 3.

PELARGONIUM, Ivy Geranium, see *Pot Plants,* Section 1.

PLUMBAGO, see *Pot Plants,* Section 1.

SAINTPAULIA GROTEI, see *Gesneriads,* Section 10.

SANTOLINA CHAMAECYPARISSUS,
see *Pot Plants,* Section 1.

SAXIFRAGA SARMENTOSA, Strawberry Geranium,
Strawberry Begonia

The common names given this little plant are typical of the misleading nature of many popular plant names and are good examples why a person should know and use botanical names. This plant is a Saxifrage and has no connection with Strawberries, Begonias, or Geraniums! It is a beautiful plant and worthy of a name of its own. It is true that its habit of growth is somewhat like that of Strawberry plants, for it sends out runners with tiny replicas of the mother plants fully formed on them. This, of course, is the way to propagate them. The young plants should not be taken off the mature specimens unless needed for propagation, however, since the trailing beauty of the large plants lies in the host of young ones which surround them. The leaves are roundish in outline, dark olive green in color with occasional white markings above and reddish beneath, and both sides are abundantly covered with hairs. The variety *S. sarmentosa tricolor* has leaves with colorful markings of white, pink, and red and is not as strong a grower as the original species. Saxifrages must be grown cool in relatively poor soil and will stand considerable shade as well as bright sun. White flowers are borne in tiny clusters during the summer months. This member of the Saxifrage family comes to us from China and Japan and can be grown as a garden plant in mild cool climates.

SEDUM MORGANIANUM, Donkey's Tail

This most unusual Sedum has trailing stems up to three feet long, symmetrically clothed with tightly clasping, slender-pointed, three-quarter-inch-long gray-green leaves. Since it is a succulent plant, it should be grown in a sunny location and be given the same culture as other related plants (see *Succulents,* Section 7).

SENECIO MIKANIOIDES, German Ivy

German Ivy is an old-fashioned trailing or climbing plant, whose leaves look somewhat like those of English Ivy, except that they are pale green and thin in texture. The plant has small yellow Daisylike flowers. Grow it in a cool greenhouse in sun in the winter and in shade during the summer. It is an excellent plant for hanging baskets and for edging window boxes. Propagate from cuttings at any time. Although known as German Ivy, it is native to South Africa.

THUNBERGIA ALATA, Black-eyed Susan Vine, Clock Vine

Some folk say that certain plants have personalities of their own which are almost human, and it seems that the flowers of this Black-eyed Susan Vine might well come in this category. You can almost see "Susan" looking at you through her eyes. Actually the flowers are disclike in shape, an inch or more in diameter, and are colored white and shades of yellow to deep orange. Most, but not all, have dark centers. The plants are perennial, but are usually grown as annuals. Start seeds in midsummer for winter bloom and in spring for summer flowering. They will stand full sun or a bit of shade and are magnificent in hanging baskets and on the edges of window boxes. They are native to tropical Africa.

TOLMIEA MENZIESII, Pick-a-back Plant, Youth and Old Age

Pick-a-back Plant is a perennial herb native to the western coast of North America from Alaska to California and is grown as a pot plant or hanging basket plant because of its peculiar manner of sending forth young plants from the junctions of its leaf blades and petioles. The plants become luxuriant if grown in a cool, moist, shady location in humusy soil. The long leaf petioles hold the large, roundish, hairy leaves out far enough so that they drop gracefully over the edges of the pots. Flowers are tiny and greenish white in slender clusters.

TRADESCANTIA FLUMINENSIS, Wandering Jew
(See also ZEBRINA, this section.)

This type of Wandering Jew has green or green and white leaves and will grow in almost any moist soil in sun or part shade. It is a native of South America and, though quite common, is a very fine plant for hanging baskets. Cuttings root quickly in moist sand.

TROPAEOLUM, see *Vines, Climbers, and Trailers,* Section 4.

VALLOTA, see *Bulbs,* Section 3.

VINCA MAJOR VARIEGATA, Variegated Periwinkle

This green-and-white-leaved form of Periwinkle, which comes from Europe, is widely used in window boxes, hanging baskets, and similar places where trailing plants are desired. It has pale blue flowers about an inch across, but is usually grown for its decorative foliage instead of its blossoms. Plants are propagated from cuttings. They should be grown in moist soil with frequent fertilizings in order to get optimum growth. Periwinkles will grow well in either sun or light shade.

WANDERING JEW, see TRADESCANTIA and ZEBRINA, this section.

ZEBRINA PENDULA, Wandering Jew
(See also TRADESCANTIA, this section.)

Zebrina, whose name is an allusion to its zebralike, striped foliage, is a native of Mexico and is widely grown as a hanging basket plant, not only for its purplish-green leaves, but also for its small reddish-purple flowers. A more colorful form is *Z. pendula quadricolor,* with leaves striped green, white, and reddish purple. It will grow in sun or shade in almost any soil so long as it is moist. New plants may be had easily by rooting cuttings in moist sand.

SECTION 6. TUB PLANTS

Tub Plants may seem to be a strange title for a group of plants, and it is true that many of the plants listed here may be grown in small pots in their youthful stages, but in order to let them become large enough to be most effective, or, in some instances, large enough to blossom, it is necessary that they be given the root room that a large container affords. The word *tub* is used because it signifies a large rather shallow container, but here we mean to include also any large earthenware or plastic pots. Wooden tubs will quickly decay unless provision is made to fortify the wood by painting it with a preservative. Use copper naphthanate (trade name, Cuprinol), not creosote, mercuric compounds or pentachlorophenol, all of which preserve wood, but deter plant growth. You will be very pleased by the performance of large plastic pots, for they are impervious to decay organisms and do not require watering as often as other containers. No matter what container you use, make provision for drainage. Place a two-inch layer of coarse gravel in the bottom of the tub before adding soil. This is good insurance that plant roots will not become waterlogged.

ACACIA

Although Acacias grow in many parts of the world, the ones in which we are interested are native to Australia. They are grown outdoors in mild cool climates, such as along the California coast, as well as in cool greenhouses. Under greenhouse culture they blossom in early spring, usually March and April, at the time when spring flower shows are held. Their graceful sprays of fuzzy flowers have long been high lights of many springtime horticultural events. Plants are easily propagated from cuttings of firm new growth in early summer. Plants must be grown cool and moist and should be pinched back often to encourage a compact habit. During the summer months they benefit by being placed outdoors, but need a cool greenhouse during the balance of the year. A temperature at night of 40 to 45 degrees is ideal. If they are forced at higher temperatures, the buds shrivel and fall off. After flowering cut the plants back quite hard and during the growth season pinch back as noted above to foster bushy plants.

AGAPANTHUS AFRICANUS, African-lily,
Lily-of-the-Nile, see *Bulbs,* Section 3.

ALLAMANDA, see *Vines, Climbers, and Trailers,* Section 4.

ARAUCARIA EXCELSA, Norfolk Island Pine

Along about sundown one stormy day during World War II my ship passed close by that isolated speck of land in the South Pacific known as Norfolk Island, and I could not help but realize that this was the only spot on earth that the familiar Norfolk Island Pine grew until horticulturists of the nineteenth century found it and spread it into parlors around the world. In its native home it becomes a tree two hundred feet high and as much as ten feet in diameter, and it seems strange that it should be considered as a greenhouse or house plant. However, in its youthful stages the Norfolk Island Pine has a most beautiful, feathery, graceful nature and is well adapted to culture in a cool greenhouse or sunroom. It can stand partial shade and does best in moist humusy soil. Plants are grown from seeds or terminal cuttings.

BOUGAINVILLEA, see *Vines, Climbers,*
and Trailers, Section 4.

BUDDLEIA (BUDDLEJA), Butterfly Bush

All of us are familiar with the outdoor, summer-flowering varieties of the Butterfly Bush with their long spikes of pink, white, lavender, or purple flowers, but few know about the winter-flowering forms *B. asiatica,* with clusters of white flowers, and *B. farquhari,* a pink-flowered hybrid.

These shrubs are grown from cuttings taken in April. Young plants must be pinched back repeatedly to encourage branching until late in August, then allowed to grow normally. Buds form in September and October, and the plants blossom in January and February. After flowering cut the plants back to the ground and let them develop new tops for another season.

CAMELLIA

There is little doubt but that Camellias are the most useful evergreen shrubs for cool greenhouse culture. They blossom at any age—even rooted cuttings have been known to flower—and as they grow in size, they continue to send forth an ever-increasing number of flowers each year. There are Camellia varieties which blossom as early as October, and others whose flowers appear as late as April; thus with a few plants one may have Camellias in flower throughout the winter season. Blossom colors range from purest white through pink to dark red and wine red, as well as lovely combinations of pink and white, often with clusters of yellow stamens showing at the centers of the flowers.

Three species of Camellias and their hybrids account for most of the thousands of named varieties now grown. *C. japonica* is the large-flowered type so widely grown and loved in the South. Often the plants are called "Japonicas," rather than Camellias. The second group, now coming into prominence because of its huge flowers, consists of selections of *C. reticulata*. They make some of the finest varieties for greenhouse use. The third one is the slender, graceful *C. sasanqua,* whose flowers are light and delicate, not as full-petaled and heavy as those of other Camellias. It is not often grown in greenhouses simply because its flowers are not as showy.

All Camellias are related to Tea, *Thea sinensis,* and come from China and Japan. Camellias are best grown in tubs so that they can be placed outdoors during the summer months under light shade. A good Camellia soil is made up of two parts loam and one part each of peat moss and sharp sand. Well-rotted cow manure can be used in the mixture also, and when the plants are fed, they should be given a fertilizer which will tend to keep the soil acid. Cottonseed meal is an excellent fertilizer for Camellias. If the foliage turns yellow due to chlorosis caused by alkaline soil, water the plants with a solution made up of one ounce of iron sulphate to two gallons of water. Try to keep the night temperature at 40 to 45 degrees and the day temperature as cool as possible. They can stand sun during the winter months, but should have light shade in the summer. If the plants become too large, simply prune them back as far as you wish, and they will send out new branches. Do the pruning in the spring immediately after flowering, before the start of new vegetative growth.

CITRUS TAITENSIS, Otaheite Orange, Tahiti Orange

No one is sure about the origin of the small ornamental Orange, but botanists feel certain that it came from China, rather than Tahiti. At any rate, it is a fine evergreen shrub for the cool greenhouse, which sends forth a constant supply of deliciously scented flowers throughout the year, plus crops of small oranges. New plants can be started from seed or from cuttings. They should be grown in full sun with plenty of moisture and at a night temperature of about 50 degrees.

CIBOTIUM, Tree Fern, see *Ferns,* Section 9.

CLEMATIS, see *Vines, Climbers, and Trailers,* Section 4.

CLIVIA MINIATA, see *Bulbs,* Section 3.

CRINUM, see *Bulbs,* Section 3.

ERVATAMIA CORONARIA (*Tabernaemontana coronaria*), Butterfly Gardenia, Fleur D'Amour, East Indian Rose Bay, Crape-jasmine, Adam's-apple, Nero's Crown

With such a host of common names one would expect uncommonly beautiful flowers, and such is truly the case. The blossoms of the double-flowering *E. coronaria flore-pleno,* the form usually grown, are about two inches across and look like those of double white Oleanders. They have a wonderfully sweet fragrance, which has endeared them to flower lovers not only in their native tropics, but also around the world. The plants have much the appearance of Gardenias, with dark-green glossy foliage, and need much the same culture. They must be grown in a warm sunny greenhouse with a minimum night temperature of 65 degrees. If a regular feeding program is used and the plants are kept constantly moist, they will blossom throughout the year.

GARDENIA

It would be fine if I could blithely say that any person with a greenhouse can have Gardenias in flower throughout the year. In theory this is true provided one can maintain a night temperature of 62 to 65 degrees all of the time and a day temperature of 70 degrees or more. In practice this ideal situation, conducive to the formation of flower buds on Gardenias, may be met only at certain times of the year, except in parts of California near the coast where night temperatures do not become as high as they do in most inland areas. Thus in the South the flowering season is quite short because night temperatures throughout most of the year are above 62 to 65 degrees. In the Northeast the season is considerably longer because nights are cool during much of the year.

Gardenias prefer a soil mixture containing a great deal of organic matter. A good mixture contains one-half light loam and one-half peat moss, to which should be added a small amount of superphosphate. Soil *p*H must be maintained on the acid side, about 5.0 to 5.5 being considered ideal. If soil becomes alkaline, water the plants with a solution made of one ounce of iron sulphate to two gallons of water.

During the period of active growth Gardenias should be fed every other week with a solution of one ounce of ammonium sulphate to two gallons of water. They must have a humid atmosphere and full sunshine. In commercial establishments the walks are wet down several times a day during hot weather, and the plants are syringed often.

Bud drop is a frustrating experience when one tries to grow Gardenias and is brought on by allowing the plants to become too dry, or by failure to give them enough fertilizer as buds develop. The soil beneath Gardenias should stay moist at all times since even a brief dry period when buds are evident will cause them to fall.

GERBERIA DAISY, see *Cut Flowers,* Section 2.

GREVILLEA ROBUSTA, Silk-oak

Silk-oaks are graceful forest trees in Australia and have been planted as street trees in other mild climates, such as in California, but in greenhouses they are grown as pot or tub plants for their fine Fernlike foliage. They are easily started from seeds and do best when given plenty of moisture, a bit of shade during the hottest time of the year, and a minimum night temperature of 60 degrees.

HIBISCUS ROSA-SINENSIS, Chinese Hibiscus, China-rose

The Chinese Hibiscus is an Oriental shrub whose large single or double Hollyhocklike flowers may be white, a shade of pink, red, lavender, yellow, or orange, or a tawny tint between orange and red. Some of the flowers are deeply cut into feathery segments and look like giant spiders.

Hibiscus are often grown as summer-flowering shrubs. When treated in this manner, they are kept cool and on the dry side during the winter months. Early in the spring they are pruned back severely and started into active growth. Abundant flowers appear during the summer from current season's growth. However, if the plants are given continuous warmth, food, and plenty of water, they will flower without ceasing throughout the year. They need a warm greenhouse and can stand full sun, though they enjoy a bit of filtered light during the hottest part of the year. They grow best in a highly organic soil, even thriving in pure peat moss. Start new plants from cuttings in the spring.

MUSA, Banana

For a truly tropical effect in a warm greenhouse or conservatory nothing takes the place of a Banana plant. Bananas are the largest herbaceous plants in the world, some species reaching a height of forty feet. In the greenhouse we are mostly concerned with less robust species as noted below. They need a fertile humusy soil, constant moisture, and a night temperature of 65 degrees. They can stand full sun or a bit of shade. If there is not enough room in your greenhouse, you can grow the plants in tubs outdoors in the summer. Cut off the leaves, shake the soil from the roots, and store them in a cool cellar over winter, repotting them early enough in the spring to let them start growth in a corner of your greenhouse before setting them outdoors for the summer. Some of the ornamental, but not edible, Bananas are easily started from seeds sown in a warm location and given bottom heat. Otherwise Bananas are propagated from offshoots from the base of the main stem, which dies after fruiting. *M. arnoldiana* is a dwarf species from the Congo, that grows to a maximum height of ten to fifteen feet. *M. cavendishii* is the delicious Chinese Banana, which grows to only four to six feet and will set fruit in a greenhouse. *M. ensete,* the Abyssinian Banana, grows very tall, but is often used in conservatories that have plenty of headroom.

NERIUM, Oleander

In mild climates around the world Oleanders are mainstays in ornamental plantings. Likewise, they have been traditional house plants and tub plants for many years. Flowers are borne in huge terminal clusters and may be white, pink, cream, or red in color and in single or double form. The leaves are dark green and Willowlike in appearance. All parts of the plants are poisonous when eaten. They like a light soil enriched with peat moss and cow manure. New plants root easily from cuttings at any time of the year. Carry Oleanders through the winter as cool as possible and quite dry, giving them extra warmth and moisture as spring arrives. Set the plants outside for the summer, and they will blossom for months. After flowering trim them back somewhat to fairly heavy wood and let them make new vegetative growth. It is this growth which should be carried through the winter and which will flower the following year. Oleanders do best in full sun, but will tolerate a bit of shade.

PALM

There are many varieties of Palms which will grow in a home greenhouse. They should be given shade at all times and during the resting season from fall to spring only enough water to keep them alive. During the growing season, however, they should be watered abundantly and given regular feedings with a complete fertilizer. Palms should always be grown in pots which seem to be too small for them, for if given too much room, there is a possibility that the soil will stay too wet during their dormant season, causing their foliage to turn yellow. Palms are usually divided according to the type of foliage they produce, into two groups, those with fan-shaped leaves and those with feathery leaves. This method is used in the list below.

Palms with fan-shaped foliage:

Chamaerops humilis, European Fan Palm

Livistona chinensis, Chinese Fan Palm

Palms with feathery foliage:

Arecastrum romanzoffianum (Cocos plumosa), Queen Palm

Caryota (several species), Fishtail Palm

Chamaedorea elegans (Neanthe bella), Parlor Palm

Chrysalidocarpus (Areca) lutescens, Butterfly Palm

Howea (Kentia) belmoreana, Sentry Palm

Howea (Kentia) fosteriana, Paradise Palm

Phoenix roebeleni, Miniature Date Palm

Syagrus (Cocos) weddelliana

ROSA, Rose

The purpose of this book is to provide an authentic, practical guide for those who have home greenhouses, not to paint pictures of things that will not work out. This goal is restated here so that no one will think that the subject of Rose culture in the home greenhouse is being slighted. There are some wonderful Roses which can and should be grown in a small greenhouse, but they do not include too many of the large-flowered type that are usually sold by the dozen in flower shops. The chief reason I do not advise growing this type is that only a limited number of flowers can be expected from a given section of greenhouse at any one time. Any person visiting a large range of Rose greenhouses is immediately conscious of the fact that there are not many Roses to be seen. On the other hand, if one plants such Roses as Floribundas, there will be a constant supply of flowers throughout the year with long enough stems for home bouquets and delicate flowers for corsages. A half dozen large pots or tubs, each containing a good Floribunda Rose of a different color, will supply all the Roses most people will feel necessary and still leave room for growing a lot of other kinds of flowers. Then too, there is the idea of growing some of the tiny Fairy Roses, which can be accommodated in tiny pots and yet produce a wealth of miniature Roses.

For many years it was thought that a clay soil was the only type for growing Roses, but modern growers have shifted over to a soil very similar to that favored by other greenhouse plants, that is, one high in organic matter, such as peat moss or well-rotted cow manure, with a loose texture that will allow the ready passage of both water and air. Roses need a moist, but not sodden, soil at all times in order to continue to produce a steady supply of flowers.

Buy the best-quality Rose bushes you can find and pot them up early in the fall in containers large enough to accommodate the root systems without crowding. Set them in a cold frame or other protected spot and cover them with a blanket of hay or straw of sufficient thickness so that they will not freeze. About the first of the year bring them into the greenhouse, set them under a bench, cover them with moist burlap, and syringe the tops daily until new shoots are clearly evident. Then set them in a bright spot in the greenhouse and watch them develop. If they are given a night temperature of 55 to 60 degrees throughout the year, they will blossom continuously. Flowering will stop if active growth is interrupted by lack of food or moisture. In cutting flowers, try to leave as much foliage as possible on the plants, for the plants need it in order to manufacture food so that they can give more flowers.

STRELITZIA REGINAE, Bird-of-paradise Flower

The Bird-of-paradise Flower is a most unusual South African plant with strange, bird-shaped, orange-yellow flowers from which protrude blue "tongues." The plants do not blossom freely, and good-sized divisions often must be given excellent culture for two years or more before flowers appear. They are a novelty, which many will like to grow. If you try them, do not be disappointed if flower production is limited. Any good soil will serve them, but it should be firmed well about the plants. During the winter months give them full sun and keep the soil on the dry side. When growth starts in the spring, give them more water and feed them every two weeks with a solution made of one teaspoonful of ammonium sulphate in a gallon of water. Flower spikes are borne in spring and early summer, at which time and all through hot weather the plants should be shaded from the hot sun.

STREPTOSOLEN JAMESONII, Streptosolen

Streptosolens are evergreen shrubs from Colombia, which have long been favorite greenhouse plants cultivated for their clusters of bright orange-red flowers, which blossom in January and February. Cuttings rooted in the spring and grown in a good greenhouse soil take nearly a year to come into flower. Older plants should be cut back after flowering so as to encourage bushy compact plants for the next season.

SWAINSONA GALEGIFOLIA, Winter Sweet Pea

Swainsonas are not really Sweet Peas, but are shrubby relatives from Australia, which send out quantities of Pealike shortstemmed white, pink, or red flowers throughout most of the year. A good greenhouse soil with lime added will suit them well. Cuttings rooted in January will be large enough to blossom by midsummer and will continue to flower if grown in a cool bright greenhouse with plenty of moisture. If plants become straggly, they can be cut back hard and they will respond with compact new growth.

TABERNAEMONTANA, see ERVATAMIA, this section.

TIBOUCHINA, Glory Bush

Any person who has seen a Glory Bush in full flower surely will covet one for his greenhouse. The velvety deep-purple flowers may be as much as five inches across, and though they last only a day or two, there is always a supply of buds coming along. The leaves are very hairy, deep green, and turn red with age. Plants have a straggly nature and are often better if tied to a support than if allowed to grow normally. Plants blossom for about nine months out of the year if grown at 55 to 60 degrees. Always keep some young plants growing along from cuttings to take the place of the old ones, for once they are over two years old, they do not flower as freely as younger plants.

ZANTEDESCHIA, Calla-lily, see *Bulbs,* Section 3.

SECTION 7. SUCCULENT PLANTS, INCLUDING CACTI

It is interesting to note the small amount of space given over in most gardening books to the culture of succulent plants. It is not that flower lovers are not intrigued by them, but that they have found that many of the plants are not only armed with porcupinelike spines, but also with formidable tongue-twisting botanical names, both of which have served to keep them at bay. Some have been frustrated (or worse) when endeavoring to repot a Cactus, which has led them to picture themselves descending by parachute into the desert at midnight; thus they treat the entire family with more respect than admiration. Others have done their best to grow the plants and have never been able to get a flower. On the other hand, some folk who are much less enthusiastic about flowers have had outstanding success with succulents, and herein lies the crux of the story: More succulents are killed by kindness than by neglect.

Succulents, with but few exceptions, are plants from parts of the world where rainfall is sparse and the sun hot. Over the ages these plants have developed methods of survival during periods of drought. For example, many succulents have no leaves, but instead have transferred the functions of leaves to their stems. The stems are usually green with chlorophyll and do the job usually done by leaves in manufacturing food for the plants. The stems have stomata or breathing pores, but relatively few of them. This not only aids them in conserving moisture, but restricts the rapidity of their growth. Thus, from our point of view they are fine pot plants which are not quick to outgrow their usefulness.

Many succulent plants grow in bizarre shapes which aid their survival in hostile desert surroundings. Barrel-shaped Cacti, for example, have a remarkably small surface area exposed to the elements in relation to the weight of the plants. Many succulents are designed in an accordion fashion, being able to expand with favorable moisture conditions and contract when rainfall fails, living off the water stored within their cells. In addition to Cacti, with their multitude of spines, many other succulents have an abundance of hairs or bristles, which, in effect, help to shade the plants from the fiercest rays of the sun. Others have an outer layer of tough waxy cells which inhibit the loss of moisture.

Succulent plants may be divided into two groups, the most familiar being the desert types. In fact, it comes as a surprise to many to learn that some succulents come from the jungles, where they grow as epiphytes among the branches of the trees, sending their roots into the debris which collects among the crotches. A common representative of this second group is the familiar Christmas Cactus. The orthodox succulents are desert plants native to the dry parts of Asia, Africa, Australia, and the Americas. Although Cacti are now found in deserts all over the world, it is interesting to know that all except one insignificant form are native to the New World, being found all the way from British Columbia to Patagonia. Cacti brought to the Mediterranean region and parts of South Africa and Australia have grown so profusely that it is difficult to imagine that they are not truly native to the regions.

DESERT-TYPE SUCCULENTS

An understanding of the special needs of desert-type succulents is very important to anyone endeavoring to grow them in a greenhouse. The usual greenhouse is much too humid to suit most succulents of the desert type; so extreme care should be taken to see that they are given locations where they will get the maximum amount of sunshine, especially during the winter months. They must be watered as noted below, though out of the kindness of your heart you may want to give them more moisture. At this point remember that they are desert plants, accustomed to adversity and unable to cope with an abundance of water.

Desert-type succulents have very definite growth and rest periods, and this pattern must be considered when caring for them. Most kinds rest during the winter months and make their growth and send out their flowers during the spring and summer. They must be kept dry and cool (40 to 50 degrees) from October until late March or early April. It would be well to bear in mind that even if your plants are drier than they would like to be, they still are not apt to die; their growth will simply be slower, and they will stay at a usable size longer and not outgrow your greenhouse. Many who complain that their succulents never blossom have never allowed their plants a proper rest period.

HOW TO WATER DESERT-TYPE SUCCULENTS

As a yearlong watering program we suggest the following: In January and February give them no water unless it is needed to keep the plants from shriveling. In March give them light sprayings occasionally in the evening or early morning, corresponding to dews which the plants might expect if they were in their native deserts. In late March or early April they will begin new growth and should be given an increasing amount of water throughout the growing season, but the soil should be allowed to dry out between waterings. From May to August they should have less water, especially toward the end of the summer, so that they will mature the season's growth. In the period from September through December give perhaps one watering a month, but supplement it with sprayings to keep the plants from desiccating. When the term *watering* is used here, it means to set the pots in pails of water until they have ceased sending up air bubbles.

SOIL MIXTURES FOR DESERT-TYPE SUCCULENTS

Specialists in the culture of desert-type succulent plants have their own pet soil mixtures, but all of them strive, by the use of various materials, to arrive at a potting soil which is very well drained, nonacid and noncaking, one in which water cannot possibly be held for any length of time and in which there is no decaying organic matter. A variety of materials may be used, some of them uncommon in the cultivation of most other plants. It is not unusual to find succulent-plant growers using broken flowerpots, crushed bricks, ground oyster shells (available from poultry-feed dealers), old mortar from demolished buildings, and granular charcoal in addition to the ordinary materials such as sharp coarse sand, good loam, and well-rotted leaf mold. Many growers incorporate ground limestone, bone meal, basic slag, or hoof-and-horn meal into their soil mixtures. Such a diversity of opinion should not confuse, but give confidence that succulents are tough plants and can stand many diverse situations and still grow satisfactorily. As an easy-to-prepare soil try this: Mix together two parts of loam and one part each of coarse sharp sand and well-rotted leaf mold; to this add one-half part crushed charcoal, a liberal dusting of ground limestone, and a bit of bone meal. Remember that this soil mixture is for the desert-type succulents; the jungle ones, such as Christmas Cactus and others, will be treated separately and differently later in this section.

In the actual potting of succulents first fill the lower one fourth of the pots with coarse gravel; then set the plants rather loosely, not firming them as is commonly done for many other plants. Tapping the pots on a bench should settle the soil sufficiently. You will find that the spiny plants, such as Cacti, require the wearing of tough gloves, or, better still, the handling of the plants with tongs. Lightweight, rubber-tipped tongs such as photographers use in their darkrooms are ideal for handling the kinds of plants that try to "bite back." After potting do not water the plants for two or three days; then give them a drink and treat normally. Potting is best done in the spring just as new growth begins.

One last word about soil mixtures is in order. Root nematodes have an affinity for succulents; so it is well to pasteurize the soil before using it (see Chapter V).

THE CHOICE IS UNLIMITED!

Now we come to the kinds of desert-type succulents that you can grow in your greenhouse. Perhaps you already know that Cacti alone may have flowers of yellow, orange, crimson, rose, scarlet, copper, purple, or white, but not blue. Other succulents have flowers of nearly any shade you can imagine as well as some strange combinations of colors found nowhere else in the plant kingdom.

There are entire books written on the culture and varieties of succulents, as well as organizations whose members are particularly interested in these plants. Since we have noted the basic cultural needs of the various desert-type succulents, we shall now simply list the botanical names of many of the kinds available from growers.

Succulents other than Cacti which need bright light: *Aeonium, Agave, Aloe, Bryophyllum, Caralluma, Cotyledon, Crassula, Echeveria, Euphorbia, Faucaria, Fenestraria, Kalanchoe, Kleinia, Lithops, Mesembryanthemum, Pachyphytum, Pleiospilos, Sedum, Sempervivum,* and *Stapelia.*

Succulents other than Cacti which need filtered light: *Ceropegia, Gasteria, Haworthia, Huernia,* and *Pedilanthus.*

Cacti, all of which need bright light: *Aporocactus, Astrophytum, Cephalocereus, Cereus, Chamaecereus, Cleistocactus, Echinocactus, Echinocereus, Echinopsis, Gymnocalycium, Hylocereus, Lemaireocereus, Lobivia, Mammillaria, Melocactus, Notocactus, Nyctocereus* (*N. serpentinus* is one of several plants known as Night-blooming Cereus), *Opuntia, Pachycereus, Parodia, Rebutia,* and *Trichocereus.*

One genus of Cacti, *Pereskia,* needs filtered light.

It should be borne in mind that the lists above are not meant to be all inclusive, but simply representative of the kinds of plants available. Succulent fanciers will find many others listed by those growers who specialize in this type of plant.

EPIPHYTIC CACTI

Among the branches of the jungle trees in Central and South America live some of the most beautiful members of the Cacti family. Unlike their brethren of the desert, these plants are accustomed to moisture and a humid atmosphere. Situated as they are, growing in the accumulation of rotting leaves lodged among the branches of the trees, they nevertheless enjoy excellent drainage even though moisture may be abundant. Unlike their dry-land cousins, these Cacti are not exposed to the sun, but instead live under the canopy of the branches above them. They belong to a group of plants which botanists know as epiphytes. Epiphytes are plants which grow upon other plants, but are not parasitic upon them. Sometimes they are called air plants because they receive their moisture and food without actually putting their roots into soil, though in the case of the plants we are about to describe the leaf mold in which they grow serves as their soil. An example of a common true epiphyte is Spanish Moss, which is often seen growing on telegraph wires in the South, deriving all of its nourishment from the air. This plant, by the way, never fails to draw interest from visitors to a home greenhouse. Tie a few strands of the moss to a wire and hang it from a rafter; it will grow without further attention.

Epiphytic Cacti are at home with Orchids. They need the same filtered shade and mild temperatures. If grown at 60 degrees at night, they will do beautifully for you.

SOIL MIXTURES FOR EPIPHYTIC CACTI

It goes without saying that plants whose ancestors grew in patches of decaying vegetation among tree branches need a soil which has a large proportion of leaf mold. It must also be very well drained and must supply a steady, though mild, source of nourishment for the plants. For your epiphytic Cacti use a mixture composed of three parts coarse (not sifted) old leaf mold, one part good loam, one part sharp sand, and one part well-rotted cow manure. Add a sprinkling of bone meal, but not too much since this type of Cacti needs acid rather than alkaline soil.

Pot your plants lightly, as with other Cacti. Give them one drink and then no more until the soil has become quite dry. From that time forward keep the soil barely moist, not wet, and during the time of the year when they are resting, maintain a somewhat lower moisture level.

The following epiphytic Cacti are available from commercial sources; some, in fact, you may already have as house plants or can get as cuttings from a friend's plant.

EPIPHYLLUM, Epiphyllum, Leaf-cactus,
sometimes called "Orchid Cactus"

This particular plant is not an Orchid, of course, but a true member of the Cactus family. Sometimes it is listed as *Phyllocactus* or *Phyllocereus,* the former name being one used in Europe. The latter is in reference to the fact that most present-day Epiphyllums are in reality hybrids between true Epiphyllums and other types of Cacti. Whatever their background or name, however, they represent some of the most spectacular flowers grown today. The blossoms are Cactuslike, being composed of many overlapping petals, and have open centers with prominent stamens, which add to the attractiveness of the flowers. What astonishes the novice is that the "small" flowers of Epiphyllums are from two to six inches in diameter, while the large ones are the size of a dinner plate. Colors range from white through cream, yellow, pink, rose, brilliant red, orange, bronze, purple, and orchid, as well as combinations of these colors.

Epiphyllums are unusual among Cacti in that most do not have spines, though some plants have occasional clusters of hairs along the soft green angular or flat stems. Since these plants are by nature accustomed to living in trees, it is easy to see why some varieties make unusually beautiful hanging-basket plants when they are in blossom.

There are literally hundreds of named varieties of Epiphyllums available, including night-blooming, as well as day-blooming, varieties.

SCHLUMBERGERA and ZYGOCACTUS,
Christmas, Crab, and Easter Cactus

The two families of Cacti *Schlumbergera* and *Zygocactus* are so alike superficially and in their culture that they are grouped together for our purpose here. There is even a question among authorities as to which one ought to be called the true Christmas Cactus. Since certain varieties of these plants may blossom any time from early fall until Easter time, it may well be that those who say their Christmas Cactus will not flower for Christmas have, in fact, a plant whose normal flowering time is not December.

At any rate, the plants themselves grow by linklike segments, roughly oval, wavy-edged, and flat, which are actually the stems serving also as leaves. The type usually thought of as the Christmas Cactus has smoothly oval links, and the Crab Cactus has typical clawlike appendages on the forward edges of each link.

Of course, it is the flowers for which these plants are primarily grown, and they are truly lovely no matter what season they appear. Each blossom seems to be composed of two flowers, one set within the other. Colors have an electric quality and may be red, orange, nearly white, or some shade of pink, with the pink varieties being the most common.

Frequently the question is asked, "Why doesn't my Christmas Cactus blossom?" The answer in most cases is that the plant has not been allowed to have enough cool temperature. In order for flower buds to form the plants must have cool nights in the fall of the year with temperatures between 55 and 65 degrees. When plants are kept warm all the time (70 to 75 degrees or more), they never blossom.

Although I shall not go into the culture of other epiphytic Cacti in this book, those interested might try growing such plants as *Rhipsalis, Disocactus, Chiapasia,* and *Pseudorhipsalis,* all of which need growing conditions very similar to other epiphytic Cacti.

PROPAGATION OF SUCCULENTS

Succulents, including Cacti, may be grown from seeds, cuttings, offshoots, and leaves and in many cases may be grafted as well. Many kinds, especially many Cacti, germinate very readily if grown in a warm place. Cacti grown especially for flowers, such as Epiphyllums, take a minimum of three years to mature from seed.

PLATE 15   Every home-greenhouse owner ought to try a few Dendrobium Orchids. This *Dendrobium nobile* is from the author's greenhouse.

PLATE 16 The Miltonia is known as the Pansy Orchid, and is an interesting and desirable type to enhance the beauty and scope of an amateur's collection. Pansy Orchids bloom in bright combinations of red, pink, and white.

Courtesy Neil McDade, Rivermont Orchids, Signal Mountain, Tenn.

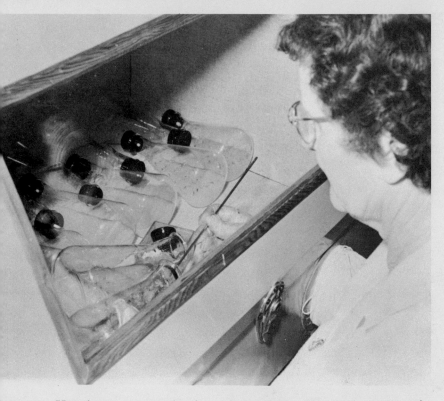

PLATE 17 Here is one reason why the author suggests that certain aspects of orchid culture be left to the experts! In this photograph, tiny seedlings are being transplanted from a seed flask after initial germination, to a "transplanted flask." About 35 plants will be placed in the transplanted flask, where they will grow large enough to be planted into a seedling flat or small pots. This flasking case is sterilized with alcohol before each use, and the technician uses plastic gloves to prevent contamination.

Courtesy Neil McDade, Rivermont Orchids, Signal Mountain, Tenn.

PLATE 18 The most critical decision any Orchid grower makes is in dividing his plants. This shows a proper division, leaving each part of the plant with healthy pseudobulbs and roots to insure good growth.

Courtesy Neil McDade, Rivermont Orchids, Signal Mountain, Tenn.

PLATE 19 When a Cattleya is repotted, it must be properly staked and tied. This young plant is in fir bark with a small layer of gravel at the bottom for drainage. It is tied with fine thread to each lead so the plant will grow upright. Notice the front lead is about centered in the pot, while the back, or oldest part of the plant, is against the edge of the pot. This allows for proper growth of new leads, which always form in front. Notched pots are especially recommended for Orchids.

Courtesy Neil McDade, Rivermont Orchids, Signal Mountain, Tenn.

PLATE 20 Make full use of greenhouse space by hanging some of your Orchids on rigid overhead supports. Mature Cattleyas respond particularly well to this treatment. During the summer months, hang them outdoors under trees.

Courtesy Neil McDade, Rivermont Orchids, Signal Mountain, Tenn.

PLATE 21 *Cypripedium insigne,* a Ladyslipper Orchid, flowers freely each year in the author's greenhouse.

PLATE 22 Vanda Orchids are easy to grow in a warm greenhouse.

Author's photo.

Desert-type Cacti and many succulents are grown for their unusual plant structure, thus are interesting from the time they begin to pop out of the ground.

Succulents are particularly easy to grow from cuttings, and this method is recommended for those who want flowering-sized plants in the minimum length of time, or who want hybrid plants with especially nice flowers. Since the plants are juicy, it is necessary that the cut surfaces be allowed to dry before placing the cuttings in sand to root. It may seem cruel to you to let cuttings lie on a bench for days, but succulents are so susceptible to rot that this policy is the only sound one.

Certain of the Kalanchoes and Bryophyllums mature miniature plants around the edges of their leaves, sometimes while the old plants are growing or if the leaves are severed from the old plants. They are so tenacious of life that in certain species leaves can be pinned to a curtain, for example, and tiny plants will grow from the leaf margins.

It is common practice to graft various types of Cacti together, and some unusual, as well as grotesque, specimens often result. Consult special literature about Cacti to learn what species are compatible.

SECTION 8. BROMELIADS

It may come as a surprise to you to learn that you enjoy eating the fruit of a Bromeliad, for it is among this group of plants that Pineapples belong. All Bromeliads are native to the Western Hemisphere from southern Florida down through Central and South America. More than forty genera and one thousand species have been catalogued by botanists, many with such slight differences in growth or inflorescence that the experts often disagree as to their actual relationship.

Although most Bromeliads are tree dwellers by nature, they are not parasitic on trees, but are true epiphytes or "air plants," using the rough bark of jungle trees as lodging places for their roots. Others grow on bare rocks, and a few even grow in the soil beneath forest trees. Since they come from the tropics, it is easy to see why they do best in a warm greenhouse, though they are tough enough to grow in temperatures as low as 40 degrees at night.

Tough is a good word for Bromeliads, for their foliage, typified except in rare instances by a rosette of leaves like that atop a Pineapple, is harsh and stiff, though usually borne in a graceful arching manner that belies its rigidity. Many kinds of Bromeliads have sharp teeth or rough serrations on the edges of their leaves. The leaves themselves are usually the chief reason for growing Bromeliads, for, while many have exotic flowers, their foliage is in itself bizarre and intriguing, often weirdly marked with zones of bronze or cream. Because of the rosette habit of growth of most Bromeliads, there is formed in the center of each plant a watertight funnel, which has given rise to the common name Vase Plant. In nature this "vase" collects and holds rain water for the plant's use, and this should serve as a guide to their culture; they enjoy moisture on their foliage, especially during their active growing season. Even when they are resting, the best method of watering them is to syringe the leaves with a fine rainlike spray of warm water.

Few plants are as undemanding as Bromeliads. As a soil they prefer peat moss, Sphagnum moss, chunks of charcoal, Osmunda fiber (which is the roots of Ferns often used as a potting medium for Orchids), ground fir bark (another Orchid potting medium), or any other highly organic soil. Often they are not grown in pots at all, but simply fastened to chunks of bark and hung in the greenhouse.

Bromeliads can stand adversity, thus have long been used as dish garden plants subject to shallow soil and neglect. Most species thrive in filtered light, although some can stand full sun. They are at home in company with Orchids, which demand protection from the sun, as well as in bright greenhouses.

Anyone can have a Bromeliad in his greenhouse by the simple expedient of lopping off the top of a Pineapple. Let it dry for a day or two; then root it in sand and pot it in a humusy soil. You will be pleased at the rich greenness of its foliage and the ease with which it can be grown.

An outstanding exception to the rule that Bromeliads grow from rosettes is the Spanish Moss (*Tillandsia usneoides*), which grows from any available perch in the tropics. A few strands hung in a warm greenhouse will soon grow long and luxuriant.

Bromeliads are usually grown from basal offshoots, but they may easily be grown from fresh seed as well. Seeds should be sown on a moist medium (commercial growers often use a piece of blotting paper), which is kept under highly humid conditions. A closed glass jar or a shallow plastic covered dish make good containers in which to start Bromeliads from seed. Seeds sprinkled lightly on a bed of moist screened Sphagnum moss will sprout readily. Set the newly seeded container in a spot where it will get filtered light. Bromeliad rosettes die after flowering, but not before sending out a group of offsets, from which several new plants may be grown.

Certain Bromeliads have outstandingly beautiful flowers, a fact which will be brought out in the following paragraphs devoted to specific members of the family.

AECHMEA

Aechmeas are among the most commonly grown epiphytic Bromeliads and have a rosette type of growth and leaves of various shades of green and greenish red as well as green and white combinations. The exotic flowers are usually red and yellow, often with touches of blue.

ANANAS, Pineapple

In addition to the edible Pineapple with its green foliage, there are varieties with leaves striped green and cream. Pineapples will grow well in any soil rich in organic matter. Give them full sun or filtered light.

BILLBERGIA

Billbergias are epiphytes with rosettes of mostly gray-green foliage and pendant clusters of red, green, and blue flowers. They do well as basket plants suspended from the rafters of a warm greenhouse.

BROMELIA

This namesake of the Bromeliad family grows too large for most greenhouses, but it is often grown as a hedge plant in the tropics. Its long tough leaves are edged with sharp spines.

CANISTRUM

Canistrums have a typical Bromeliad rosette form of growth with showy orange or greenish-white flowers.

CRYPTANTHUS

Cryptanthuses are my favorite Bromeliads. They have long, narrow, wavy leaves spreading in all directions from a low basal rosette. Someone has likened their appearance to that of a starfish. Leaf surfaces of Cryptanthuses are often rough to the touch and of various shades of green, beige, and tan, usually with zebralike markings across the leaves. Their small white flowers are borne close down toward the centers of the plants.

DYCKIA

Most cultivated Dyckias have narrow spiny-edged leaves growing in a typical rosette form. Blossoms are usually yellow or orange.

GUZMANIA

Guzmanias have small flowers, yellow or white in color, but, springing from between scarlet bracts on large central spikes as they do, they are extremely attractive. Guzmania foliage may be green, purple, or wine-red, often with a deeper color on the lower surfaces.

HECHTIA

A typical Hechtia has a dense rosette of spiny-edged narrow leaves which recurve toward the base of the plant. Flowers are usually orange or white.

NEOREGELIA

The inner leaves of Neoregelia rosettes have a strange way of turning brilliant red or purple in advance of the flowering period.

There are many kinds of Neoregelias; one, *N. spectabilis,* is called the Fingernail Plant because the tips of its leaves are of a brilliant red hue.

NIDULARIUM

The name *Nidularium* comes from the Latin word for nest, referring to the fact that its flowers are borne close down in its nestlike rosette of foliage, the inner section of which turns a brilliant red prior to the flowering period.

TILLANDSIA

Tillandsia usneoides, Spanish Moss, has been mentioned previously in this section. In contrast to the stringy growth of the Spanish Moss, most other Tillandsias have a more or less rosette type of foliage; some have large paddle-shaped inflorescences of pink or red bracts, from which spring lavender flowers.

VRIESIA

Vriesias have smooth-edged basal rosettes of various shades of green, often spotted or marbled with other colors. Flower spikes are paddle-shaped, made up of many bracts, mostly purple, red, yellow, or maroon in color, from between which the individual flowers arise. A common name for one Vriesia, *V. splendens major,* is Flaming Sword.

SECTION 9. FERNS

I have forgotten now the name of that South Pacific island where I first stepped ashore after months at sea and found the ground beneath the Coconut Palms carpeted with the waving fronds of the Sword Fern. It was a veritable paradise with its soft warm air and dappled shade, redolent with the fragrance of the tropics after a gentle rain. This type of atmosphere is what many of us experience every day if we have a warm shady greenhouse in which to grow the tender Ferns of the equatorial regions. There are many lovely Ferns that can be grown in home greenhouses, and the list which follows is only a sampling. It will fill the needs of most home gardeners and may even encourage them to grow more exotic types.

As you already know, Ferns revel in a soil which is high in organic matter. Many growers use a soil which is one-half peat moss, one-quarter loam, and one-quarter sharp sand. Others use such materials as leaf mold, Sphagnum moss, charcoal, Osmunda fiber, and broken flower pots in their mixtures. The object is to attain a soil which is largely organic, thus highly retentive of moisture, yet one in which water will not stand, for, despite their affinity for moisture, tropic Ferns need good drainage.

Ferns are unlike flowering plants in that they do not have seeds, but produce on the reverse sides of certain of their fronds tiny spores which serve as seeds, though they differ in many ways from true seeds. Spores may be sown on a moist sifted-soil mixture similar to that mentioned above and will eventually become large plants. However, it is possible to get literally thousands of Ferns from the amount of spores you can hold on the tip of a spoon. What the average home-greenhouse owner would do with a thousand Ferns poses quite a dilemma; so we suggest that you limit your Fern growing to individual plants that you buy to enjoy for their own beauty. One Boston Fern, if allowed to mature fully, would fill in the end of a small home greenhouse.

Actually the Boston Fern mentioned above is not usually propagated by spores. The wild type may be, but it is rarely grown; the horticultural forms, which are mutations, are grown from runners which are produced on the plants in the summertime. Not all Ferns produce runners; some have tiny plants develop among their fronds, thus are said to be viviparous. Others "walk" by sending out plants at the tips of their fronds where they touch the soil. Certain kinds are best propagated by division; so the choice is wide, but for the average small greenhouse the question is usually not how to get more Ferns, but how to keep the present ones within bounds.

The following ten Fern families offer a wide selection and include most of the types commercially available. It should be pointed out that certain of them have many varieties which afford a wide diversity of frond shape and texture. The Boston Fern, as an example, has had over one hundred mutations brought into commerce in the last half century, though most of them are no longer grown.

ADIANTUM CUNEATUM, Maidenhair Fern

The Maidenhair Fern is native to Brazil and has been grown for many years as a greenhouse plant. It has slender black stems and delicate wedge-shaped leaflets. There are several forms of Maidenhair Ferns with various shaped and colored foliage, all of which are nice for growing in the warm greenhouse. They grow one to two feet high.

ALSOPHILA AUSTRALIS, Australian Tree Fern

If you grow a Tree Fern in your greenhouse, you must be prepared to eventually throw it away . . . or get a bigger greenhouse. As young plants, however, Tree Ferns are very graceful and desirable. Their fronds eventually grow five to ten feet long and in Australia they become eighty feet tall.

ASPLENIUM NIDUS, Bird's Nest Fern

Unlike many Ferns, the Bird's Nest Fern does not have typical divided foliage, but has long apple-green tongue-shaped fronds which unfold from a "nest" of brown hairs at the center of the plant. This type of Fern is greatly admired and is one of the choicest for a warm greenhouse. Try not to allow water to stand in the nest, or it may cause rotting of the crown. Bird's Nest Ferns grow one to two feet high and are found in tropical regions around the world.

CIBOTIUM SCHIEDEI, Mexican Tree Fern

Mexican Tree Ferns are the ones most commonly used by florists in church decorations. They are usually set in tiltable stands so that their lovely pale green fronds can be displayed to best advantage. They are slow-growing and can be long-time residents of a small greenhouse. Average plants have a spread of four to six feet and can be grown on a pedestal with other shade-loving plants beneath.

CYRTOMIUM FALCATUM, Holly Fern

The Holly Fern is surely one of the nicest of the small Ferns for the home greenhouse. Its fronds are divided into segments somewhat similar in shape to that of Holly and are very shiny. The plants grow from one to two feet in height and hold their fronds upright. They are native to the tropical jungles of Asia and Africa.

DAVALLIA FEJEENSIS, Rabbit's Foot Fern

The Rabbit's Foot Fern is an old-time favorite not only for its graceful fronds, but also for its creeping brown hairy rhizomes, which give rise to its common name. It comes from the Fiji Islands and is very decorative.

NEPHROLEPIS EXALTATA BOSTONIENSIS,
Boston Fern, Sword Fern

The story has been told many times about the origin of the Boston Fern. It appeared as a chance seedling among a shipment of Sword Ferns being sent from Philadelphia to a Boston greenhouse about 1894. It so happened that this Boston Fern, beautiful in its own right, soon developed a series of mutations unlike the parent plant. Within a few years there were dozens of variations of the Boston Fern, many with fronds so finely divided as to appear almost like moss. Any type of Boston Fern is easy to grow and very beautiful.

PLATYCERIUM BIFURCATUM, Staghorn Fern

The Staghorn Fern is an exception among Ferns in that it is an epiphyte, thus grows on the rough bark of trees in the jungle instead of in the soil. In the greenhouse it is usually grown on a man-made pocket of Osmunda fiber or fir bark anchored to a board and tied to the damp shady wall of a warm greenhouse. Its common name comes from the way in which its flat, deeply cut foliage resembles a stag's horns. It is native to Australia and some of the Pacific islands.

POLYSTICHUM ADIANTIFORME, Leather Leaf Fern

The Leather Leaf Fern grows with much the same creeping habit as the Davallias, but has coarser, tougher leaves. The foliage is often used to supply a touch of green to flower arrangements and will last for weeks in water. The Leather Leaf Fern is found in tropical Asia and Africa.

PTERIS, Table or Brake Fern

There are literally dozens and dozens of leaf types among the Table Ferns, all of which are different from one another. Some have foliage boldly marked with white and silver, others have crested fronds, and others have finely divided foliage. The Ferns usually grown in the center of Poinsettia pots to camouflage bare stems are Pteris. They are low in stature, durable, and inexpensive. They are native to tropical and semitropical areas around the world.

SECTION 10. GESNERIADS

Many gardeners can remember when African Violets were rarities and Streptocarpus sounded like some sort of an infection, but times have changed rapidly, for now the Gesneriads are riding high and are without doubt the most popular family of flowering house plants today. The ease with which such plants as African Violets can be grown and flowered has led plant collectors to search the world over for related plants, hoping to find others that would become as widely salable. It is a fact, however, that not all plant cousins are equally attractive, and though the list of Gesneriads is now impressive, some of the plants are what many of us would call weedy. Others are particularly lovely and easy to grow, and as the supply becomes more plentiful, they will doubtless be grown by many flower lovers. In the pages that follow you will find specific cultural information on the five most commonly grown Gesneriads: *Achimenes,* sometimes known as Monkey-face Flower; *Episcia,* called Flame Violet though the name is misleading; *Gloxinia* (botanically *Sinningia*); *Saintpaulia,* the familiar African Violet; and *Streptocarpus,* the Cape Primrose. In addition, I have described seven other interesting Gesneriads in detail and have listed most of the others currently available, though some are difficult to locate. You will notice in the list that some plant names have synonyms which reflect the confusion in nomenclature and identification of some of the plants not only among those lately brought from the wild, but even among species long known to botanists.

It should be noted that besides the Gesneriads mentioned here, there are others which must be grown outdoors, some preferring alpine conditions, a far cry from the comfortable surroundings most of the family enjoy.

All of the plants in this section are Gesneriads which grow under conditions of filtered light, warm temperatures, and moist humusy soil as noted in detail immediately below.

GROWING CONDITIONS FOR GESNERIADS
Temperature and Humidity

Gesneriads are native to various tropical regions around the world, and this one fact is the most important to keep in mind in determining the conditions under which they can be grown in cultivation. In order to help them do their best, we must try to duplicate the warm moist air of the tropics in our greenhouses. No doubt, the chief reason that African Violets have become so popular as house plants is that they like our warm centrally heated homes, even though the atmospheric humidity is not as great as they might wish. You will be amazed at how luxuriantly Gesneriads of all kinds will grow in the salubrious atmosphere of a warm greenhouse. Ideally the temperature should range from 65 to 70 degrees at night to 70 to 80 degrees in the daytime with a relative humidity of 50 to 60 per cent.

Light

At the same time one considers the temperature and humidity needs of Gesneriads, one must not overlook the amount and quality of the light they require. As a group, they are plants which grow beneath the shelter of trees in their native lands, and this same filtered light is needed when they are grown in greenhouses. Experiments have shown that African Violets, for example, flower most profusely when given about 1100 to 1200 foot-candles of light for eighteen hours each day. As a rule of thumb for greenhouse or window-sill culture one can consider that if there is enough light coming into a shaded greenhouse or house window on a sunny day so that one can barely see the shadow of his hand, then the light is about right. Plant growth, of course, is the real indicator of light conditions. Leaves which show bleaching, excessive coloration, or sunburn mean that plants are receiving too much light. On the other hand, long slender growth with wide spaces between the leaves and few flowers are signs that plants need more light.

Soil

Most Gesneriads are accustomed in nature to a moist well-drained soil composed to a large extent of decaying leaf mold. Under pot culture we attempt to supply them with a soil which is similar, but, we hope, even more conducive to good growth than that supplied by their natural habitat. Grow Gesneriads in a soil mixture made of two parts good loam and one part each of well-rotted leaf mold, peat moss, and clean sharp sand (not beach sand). You will find that commercial growers use such materials as well-rotted cow manure, composted organic matter, perlite, and even volcanic sand in their mixtures. The purpose is to supply a fertile organic-filled soil which is at the same time both retentive of moisture and well drained. If you do not want to prepare your own soil, you will find that the prepared African Violet Soil sold at florists will be suitable for all your Gesneriads. As an aid in disease and insect control it is a wise precaution to pasteurize all soil for Gesneriads as described in Chapter V.

Fertilizers

Gesneriads are not heavy feeders, but they should have a steady mild source of nutrients at all times. Part of their nourishment, of course, comes from the breaking down of the abundant organic matter in the soil mixture, but it is advisable to feed established plants once a month, *during their active growing season only,* with a mild solution of a complete, water-soluble fertilizer.

Moisture and Resting Periods

Most Gesneriads go through alternate periods of active growth and rest. Certain ones such as the plant we call Gloxinia (botanically *Sinningia*) die to the ground and spend part of each year as dormant tubers. At the other extreme are some of the modern African Violet hybrids, which will blossom without ceasing if given good growing conditions. Thus it is that moisture requirements of Gesneriads must be viewed in the light of the various stages of growth of the individual plants. When in active growth Gesneriads need a moist, but not sodden, soil; when resting they should have less water, but not be allowed to desiccate.

As to the water itself, it is important that its temperature be close to the temperature of the air about the plants. I suggest that, as pointed out in Chapter III, you have both hot and cold water connections in your greenhouse with a mixing faucet so that you can easily give them water at the correct temperature. The question is often asked as to whether the leaves should be wet or not. Of course in nature the leaves are wet with every rain, but the tropic rains are warm ones. Here, then, is the answer: Warm water, close to air temperature, will not hurt Gesneriad foliage especially if the plants are in diffused light. Too cold or too hot water on the leaves will cause ugly blotches that detract from the beauty of the plants.

Progagating Gesneriads

Anyone who has ever rooted a leaf from an African Violet in sand, water, or vermiculite can vouch for the ease with which it can be done. Similarly, most other Gesneriads can be propagated by leaf cuttings. Of these, certain ones can also be grown from stem cuttings and others by division of crowns or tubers. Growing Gesneriads from seeds is an intriguing part of horticulture. The seeds are as fine as dust, and one needs to be careful not to breathe on them, or they will blow away. Sow them on top of a sifted mixture of pasteurized Gesneriad soil. Moisten the soil lightly and cover with a piece of glass or plastic and set the container in a warm place out of the sun. I have found that covered plastic dishes or small shallow bottles are ideal containers in which to start small quantities of Gesneriad seeds.

Insect Problems

About the only insect which really bothers Gesneriads is the Cyclamen mite, but this pest is a tough one to control. It lodges deep within the crowns of the plants and is difficult to reach and to kill, once it has been reached. A systemic poison, such as sodium selenate, which is placed in the soil to be absorbed by the plant, is one effective way to control Cyclamen mite. Another way is by the use of Kelthane, a relatively new insecticide, which is a specific for Cyclamen mites. Consult labels for directions and especially for precautions before using any insecticide.

FIVE EASY-TO-GROW GESNERIADS

ACHIMENES, Achimenes, Monkey-face Flower

Achimenes are lovely summer-flowering Gesneriads from Central America, which grow from conelike rhizomes. They are slow to start and during that time the soil should be kept somewhat on the dry side. Once they begin to grow, the soil should never be allowed to become dry until it is time for the plants to go into their rest period. Achimenes blossom freely all summer with unusual open-faced flowers of white, pink, red, lavender, or purple, often with golden-yellow throats. After flowering has ceased, dry the plants off and save the conelike roots for another season. Achimenes are good for hanging baskets or shady window boxes and are of very easy culture.

EPISCIA, "Flame Violet," Episcia

Episcias are among the most beautiful and easily grown of all Gesneriads, and while many have interesting scarlet, pink, yellow, white, or lavender flowers, they are more commonly grown for their extraordinary foliage. Their leaves may be any shade of green or bronze, often with metallic markings and a quilted texture. The plants may be grown in hanging baskets, as regular pot plants, or as ground covers in warm shady conservatories. Episcias are native to Central and South America.

GLOXINIA (botanically *Sinningia*)

There is a bit of confusion regarding the name of the plant we all know as Gloxinia. There is, you see, a plant whose botanical name is *Gloxinia,* also a Gesneriad, but not too closely related to the florist type of Gloxinia. Usage has given the name Gloxinia to the plant whose botanical name is really *Sinningia*. It is all very much mixed up, but Gloxinias as we know them are worth the trouble. Their blossoms are large, velvety, and bell-shaped, mostly held upright so that their beauty can be appreciated.

Gloxinias are often grown from seed; sow seed in January to flower in midsummer. It is easier, however, to buy tubers and start them into growth at any time of the year. After flowering the plants die down and rest as dormant tubers. Keep the tubers only moist enough so that they will not shrivel during dormancy. When they start new growth, repot them in fresh soil and in a short time they will flower again. Gloxinias last indefinitely. Many tubers twenty or more years old still produce magnificent crops of flowers each year.

Gloxinias are native to Brazil, and all the native species have slipper-type flowers. The original plant with the bell-type flowers appeared as a mutation in an English greenhouse many years ago. It was used in breeding work to give us the modern beauties we know today.

SAINTPAULIA, African Violet

African Violets need no introduction to flower lovers, for many amateurs grow not only dozens but even hundreds of them on the window sills of their homes. Few plants are of easier culture or blossom as freely as the better of the modern African Violet hybrids. It is interesting to grow some of the wild species of African Violets from which the present plants are descended. About ten species of African Violets are represented among the wild plants, one of the most interesting being *S. grotei*, a trailing plant with pale-violet flowers. It is ideally suited for planting in hanging baskets in a warm shady greenhouse. African Violets are native to that section of East Africa known as Tanganyika. If one follows the instructions previously given for Gesneriad culture, he will be able to grow magnificent African Violets.

STREPTOCARPUS, Cape-primrose

There are many species of Streptocarpus native to the same general area of East Africa to which African Violets are indigenous. However, the ones most worthy of culture in home greenhouses are the improved hybrids, notably the Wiesmoor hybrids. These lovely plants have rather long narrow quilted basal leaves and astonishingly large open-faced blossoms of many shades of pink, rose, crimson, blue, and purple, as well as white. Sow the tiny seeds in January, and the plants will begin to flower in August and continue until October. Cut the plants back after flowering and you will get another crop of flowers in the spring.

SEVEN UNUSUAL GESNERIADS FOR THE FANCIER

AESCHYNANTHUS (*Trichosporum*),
"Lipstick Plant," Aeschynanthus

Aeschynanthuses are trailing members of the Gesneriad family from the East Indies. They have waxy dark green leaves, and most species have small scarlet two-lipped flowers which give rise to the common name "Lipstick Plant."

ALLOPLECTUS

Alloplectuses are upright-growing plants from South America, which become quite large. Most types have hairy leaves and stems. Flowers are small and yellow and not very conspicuous.

COLUMNEA

Most Columneas are trailing plants with brilliant red flowers and waxy green leaves. At least one species has yellow flowers and another pink ones. Many species have prominent red hairs on the stems, which add to their attractiveness. These rather new-to-horticulture Gesneriads are native to Central and South America and make beautiful hanging basket plants.

KOHLERIA (*Isoloma, Tydaea, Sciadocalyx*)

Many plants now called *Kohleria* were formerly known as *Isoloma* and have been grown in conservatories for many years. There are upright, as well as trailing, Kohlerias with velvety leaves and small red, and occasionally pink or white, flowers. They are native to Central and South America.

NAUTILOCALYX

Nautilocalyx are large coarse-growing Gesneriads with mostly bronze crinkled foliage and small yellowish flowers hidden in the axils of the leaves. They are native to the basin of the Amazon River in South America.

RECHSTEINERIA (*Corytholoma*)

Rechsteinerias are similar in many ways to Gloxinias in that they have soft fuzzy leaves and grow from tubers. Like Gloxinias, they die back to the tubers after flowering and rest in that dormant fashion. Most Rechsteinerias send up an erect central stem from which spring the nodding scarlet, or less commonly pink, flowers.

SMITHIANTHA (*Naegelia*), "Temple Bells"

Once Smithianthas become better known, they will surely be widely grown for their velvety heart-shaped leaves and clusters of nodding bell-shaped flowers of red, pink, or yellow. Like Achimenes, they grow from a scaly rhizome and must rest completely part of each year.

ALPHABETICAL LISTING OF GESNERIADS NEW TO OR RARELY FOUND IN COMMERCE

Campanea, Chirita, Chrysothemis, Codonanthe, Cyrtandra, Dia-

stema, Didymocarpus, Drymonia, Gesneria, Gloxinera (bigeneric cross between *Sinningia* and *Rechsteineria*), *Gloxinia* (botanical, not florist type), *Hypocyrta, Koellikeria, Nematanthus, Petrocosmea,* and *Titanotrichum.*

SECTION 11. BEDDING PLANTS

The term *bedding plants* has been given to those plants, mostly annuals, which are grown under glass during early spring months so that they will be of blossoming or near-blossoming size when the weather becomes mild enough for them to be grown outdoors. Most of the bedding plants of the season are planted during the months of January, February, March, and April, and these notes about their culture are meant to be used in conjunction with seasonal notes in Chapter XII, "What to Do and When to Do it."

Good bedding plants should be short and stocky, and this kind of growth can only be achieved under cool-greenhouse conditions (night temperatures of about 50 degrees) and bright sunshine. Seed should be planted at 60 to 65 degrees, however, and kept at this temperature until young plants are above ground. Plants should be transplanted from the seedbed as early as they can be moved so that they will not crowd one another. They should get most of their growth in a greenhouse, especially the early-planted ones, but as soon as outside weather moderates, they should be moved to a cold frame. Here their growth will harden and the transition from the cold frame to the open garden can be made without shock. Cold frames need to be covered at night, of course, in cold weather, but the sashes can come off on bright days when the temperature is 45 degrees or more so that the plants can get the benefit of full sunshine and fresh air.

For countless years bedding plants were grown in flats or clay pots, but within the last few years there has been a tremendous change-over to the use of pots molded from peat moss. These peat pots have several advantages, not the least being that the pots are planted right into the garden soil, and the roots eat their way through them so that the plants suffer no setback whatsoever. Of course, clay pots are still used, and if you have them on hand, so much the better. They do need to be cleaned each year, however, and they are much heavier to handle and dry out faster between waterings. Plants grown in flats must be dug out to be planted in the garden, thereby having some of their roots broken, which tends to check their growth.

In determining when to sow seeds of tender plants, one must consider his own growing area and plant seeds sufficiently in advance of the last expected frost so that plants will be of the correct size to set outdoors when that date has passed. Since all plants do not grow at the same rate, the lists below have been compiled so that you can anticipate your needs. It cannot be emphasized too much that it is a mistake to plant too early, for then plants become crowded, leggy, pot-bound, and woody. Such plants suffer such a setback to their growth that they never catch up with plants grown without any check.

During the spring plants get a great deal of sunshine and grow at a tremendous rate. Use the schedule below to calculate when to plant various species.

GROUP A   These plants take from seven to nine weeks from seeding until they are large enough to plant outdoors:
Fibrous-rooted Begonias, Dwarf Impatiens, Browallia, Lobelia, *Mesembryanthemum, Mimosa pudica* (Sensitive Plant), Petunia (fringed, ruffled, and double-flowering types), Scarlet Sage, Verbena, and *Vinca rosea* (Periwinkle).

GROUP B   Plants which take from six to eight weeks from sowing to planting-out size:
Ageratum, Sweet Alyssum, Globe Amaranth, Arctotis, China Aster, Bells of Ireland, Blue Lace Flower, Castor-bean, Cardinal Climber, Cathedral Bells, Cosmos (yellow), Dusty Miller, Lupine, Cape-marigold, Nemesia, Nicotiana, Petunia (bedding types), China Pinks, Portulaca, Annual Phlox, Salpiglossis, Snapdragon, Stock, and Strawflower.

GROUP C   Plants which take from four to five weeks from sowing to planting-out size:

Many of these plants can be sown in a cold frame rather than a greenhouse, or, by waiting a few weeks, may be planted directly in the open garden. Those planted in the garden often catch up with those started earlier indoors, particularly if growth of indoor plants is allowed to harden too much. Some of the plants in this group appear also in Group B. This is accounted for by the fact that later sowings grow very fast because of more sunshine and higher temperatures.

Sweet Alyssum, Globe Amaranth, Arctotis, Balloon-vine, Calendula, Celosia (Cockscomb), Annual Chrysanthemum, Clarkia, Cleome, Cornflower, Cosmos, Cynoglossum, Swan River Daisy, Winged Everlasting, Forget-me-not, Gaillardia, Godetia, Gomphrena, Marigold, Nemophila, Petunia (bedding type), Scabiosa, Schizanthus, and Zinnia.

SECTION 12. PERENNIALS TO FORCE IN THE GREENHOUSE

It is possible to encourage many perennials into growth in home greenhouses, and an idea of the number of them may easily be gained when one visits a spring flower show. There a great many of the plantings have perennials in full bloom though the backgrounds may be of shrubs and evergreens.

The important thing to bear in mind when forcing perennials is that they will not force until they have had a taste of cold weather. This normal part of their life cycle is easily met by letting the plants spend until the first of the new year in cold frames. After that time they may be brought inside and grown either in benches or pots. By far the best method is to grow the perennials in pots during the late summer and fall so that their roots will be well established. Then when they are brought into a cool greenhouse (45 to 50 degrees at night), they flourish in the spring-like atmosphere. Here are some that you will enjoy forcing: Alyssum (perennial types), Astilbe, Balloon-flower, Bleeding

Heart, Campanulas, Columbine, Coral-bells, Daisies (Esther Read, English, and Painted), Delphinium, Foxglove, Leopard-bane, Lilies, Lungwort (Pulmonaria), Phlox (especially the white Miss Lingard), Primroses (particularly the Polyantha type), Tritoma (Red Hot Poker), Trollius, Virginia Blue-bells, and Wallflowers.

CHAPTER IX

ANYONE CAN GROW ORCHIDS

Over the years since men first began to cultivate Orchids, there have been hundreds of books written on their culture. Most of the literature has been of a technical nature, and it has only been during the past few years that books directed toward the amateur have appeared in print.

It is well known that some men and women have devoted all of their adult years to the cultivation of Orchids; thus it is with trepidation that I enter into company with this august body of experts. These very professionals, of course, would be the first to admit that there are questions about Orchid culture to which they have not yet found the answers. How, then, can I justify the title of this chapter, "Anyone Can Grow Orchids"? Surely part of the answer lies in the fact that Orchids are tough plants and will not die because you mistreat them now and then. I am convinced that after applying the basic cultural information given in this chapter, you will soon be able to do as I did this morning. Before sitting down to my typewriter, I stepped into my own home greenhouse for a few minutes to relax and get into the mood for writing. For the fun of it I noted the Orchids then in blossom. There must have been a hundred of them altogether on plants representing eight different Orchid families. When I reflected on how little care they had demanded during the past year, I could not help but realize that they had given me more in return for my efforts than had any other group of plants in my greenhouse.

There was a time when Orchid culture was actually conducted behind locked doors, and only a few men were allowed to work with the plants. Until a few years ago this mantle of secrecy was still draped about Orchids, but this is no longer true. The American Orchid Society, for example, publishes a wonderful monthly magazine devoted to the culture of all sorts of Orchids, and there are regional Orchid societies throughout the country. Nowadays the dissemination of information is stressed by those who grow plants for sale to home-greenhouse operators. Any person who is really serious about his Orchid growing will soon read all of the literature available, for the "Orchid bug," once it bites, inflicts one with "orchiditis" forever after.

Botanists say that there is little doubt but that the Orchid family is the largest in the world, with representatives growing from Arctic regions to the equator. Nearly all of the ones we usually think of as Orchids and surely all those grown commercially in greenhouses are native to tropical or subtropical regions. Most of the ones that we grow come from the jungles of Central and South America or from Southeast Asia and the islands of the East Indies as far south as northern Australia.

After seeing the magnificence of Orchid flowers, some people are distinctly shocked to see the plants from which the flowers came. Orchids have a real claim to some of the most beautiful flowers in the world, but most of them have rather ordinary foliage. It is also a fact that most Orchids do not flower throughout the year, but often spend ten months of the year without blossoms. When someone starts to grow Orchids either in the home or in a small greenhouse, he should have these bits of information. He should be careful to choose plants that will blossom at the time of year when he will be able to enjoy them. I have mostly types which blossom in the fall, winter, and spring, for the summer months bring outside flowers of equal beauty. When you see a picture of a

whole group of Orchids in blossom in someone's home, remember
that the picture was either posed for the occasion, or at least that
the plants will be without flowers for most of the rest of the forth-
coming year. This should not be construed to mean that you
should not grow Orchids, for as an Orchid hobbyist I have a personal interest in them and am particularly anxious that you try
some for yourself.

Why is it that there is always someone who asks for a black
Orchid? Perhaps the mystery writers are to blame, for there is no
such thing in nature. There are dark brown and dark purple flowers which someone with an elastic imagination might call black,
but the only black Orchids you find will have been dyed. All too
many people feel that all Orchids are orchid, but nothing could
be farther from reality. It is possible to find all colors imaginable
and many that defy description with mere words.

There are many plants which serve men with no utilitarian purpose, and Orchids come close to this category, except that they
quench our souls' thirst for loveliness and give meaning to Emer-
son's "Beauty is its own excuse for being." Except for vanilla,
derived from the ripe seed pods of *Vanilla planifolia,* and salep, a
starchy tapiocalike food made from the tubers of certain Orchids,
their usefulness lies in their ability to lift our thoughts above mun-
dane things.

Very often when an Orchid blossoms in my greenhouse, I trans-
fer the plant into my study where its beauty as well as fragrance
can be appreciated at close range. So many times visitors have
come into the room and asked the source of the delightful scent
even though they could see the Orchid plant in front of them. They
were not aware that Orchids may be fragrant as well as beautiful.
They had been brought up on florist blooms which lose their
fragrance when kept under refrigeration.

Orchids are unique in many ways, not the least being the ease
with which various genera will hybridize. Thus plant breeders
have been able to produce some of the most unusual flowers known
to horticulture. For example, a *Cattleya* may be crossed with a

Brassavola, giving rise to a *Brassocattleya;* that plant may in turn be crossed with a *Laelia,* bringing forth a trigeneric hybrid named *Brassolaeliocattleya.* This strange state of affairs is analogous to crossing an Apple with a Rose and that combination with a Plum! Strange, wonderful, and intriguing are Orchids, and the more one learns about them, the more fascinating they become.

A recent author, recognized throughout the world as a horticultural authority, has pointed out a fact long known to Orchid growers: that Orchids are tough plants and will tolerate conditions less than ideal and still give a great deal of satisfaction to their owners. Although Orchids may do best under certain conditions of temperature, moisture, and humidity, even their tropical homelands occasionally suffer from storms, excessive moisture, dry spells, and even chilly nights. Thus one who contemplates growing Orchids for the fun of it should be encouraged to know that with a greenhouse he is bound to have considerable success if he will follow a few general principles as set forth below.

How Orchids Grow

In order to simplify the discussion of Orchid culture it is first necessary to understand a few general principles pertaining to their growth habits. The entire Orchid family, with but few exceptions, can be divided into those plants which make a continuous growth from one stem, called *monopodial* Orchids, and those whose new growth arises from side buds, called *sympodial* Orchids. A Vanda Orchid, which grows upward year after year, sending out its flower spikes from leaf axils, is an example of a monopodial Orchid. A Cattleya Orchid, whose rhizomes proceed horizontally in a zigzag manner with flower clusters terminating at the top of each new leaf, typifies the sympodial group.

The monopodial and sympodial Orchids are further divided into two groups each, depending upon whether they are terrestrial or epiphytic. To confound those who would assign plants their niches in conformity to man-made laws, Vanda Orchids begin life as terrestrials and as they mature become at least partially epiphytic in nature.

Another term you soon encounter when discussing Orchids is pseudobulbs. It refers to the bulbous, above-ground storage stems common to many species of Orchids. Since they are not true bulbs, they are called pseudo (or false) bulbs.

Potting Media for Orchids

It should be a "required course" that each would-be Orchid grower visit a dozen commercial establishments before starting in with his own plants. The only problem seems to be that he might end his tour in a state of utter confusion, for he would surely find a difference of opinion among those who grow Orchids for a living. It would not be uncommon to find Cypripedium (Lady-slipper-type) Orchids growing in Osmunda fiber in some green-houses, fir bark in others, and plain gravel in others. As far as the amateur could see, all the plants would be flourishing, which brings up the real crux of the matter. Orchid growing is to this day still more of an art than a science. Many materials may be used, but in the final analysis skill and attention to detail will determine the extent of one's success.

It is essential, before discussing actual potting media, to understand the structure of Orchid roots, because they are so different from those of most garden plants. In nature many Orchids grow among the branches of trees, and their roots either cling to the rough bark or dangle in the air beneath the plants. As anyone knows, ordinary plants must have their roots in soil, or the plants will quickly die. The difference here lies in the way in which the Orchid roots are made. Upon examination of an Orchid root one of the first things that will be noticed is that the roots are practically the same diameter for their entire length. They have no root hairs, and they rarely branch as freely as do roots of other plants. Also it will be seen that the roots are grayish-white in color and of a peculiar firm-yet-soft texture. The "working part" of an Orchid root is the tiny tough core, and the soft spongy outer layer is composed of multitudes of cells which readily take up water and hold it for use by the plant. Such spongy roots simply cannot be confined in ordinary soil or in a sodden mixture, or they will rot. They must have free access to air just as do those of the wild plants growing in the jungle. The most important characteristic of any Orchid potting mixture is an open texture which will allow the free passage of air and water.

The type of potting medium you choose for your plants depends to some extent upon where you live. In England, for example, growers use a mixture of dead Polypoly Fern roots and live Sphagnum moss. Some growers of Orchid seedlings have had phenomenal success in starting their seeds in a mixture of agar and tomato juice! We suggest, however, a more prosaic approach to home Orchid culture. The following potting materials are commonly used by both amateurs and commercial growers: Osmunda fiber, fir bark, gravel, and Tree Fern stems. Each of these materials is discussed in detail below.

Osmunda fiber, or "Orchid peat," was for a great many years the only material used as an Orchid-potting medium. It is a tough, wiry brown-to-black material, actually the roots of our native Ferns *Osmunda regalis* and *O. cinnamomea*. It has much the consistency of matted horsehair and allows for a relatively free movement of air and water. It does not decay very rapidly. Orchid roots do not derive a great deal of nourishment from it, but they do thrive when potted in Osmunda and are watered and fed properly. Nowadays many growers are getting away from the use of Osmunda chiefly because it requires skill and considerable time to repot Orchids in it in contrast to fir bark, now the most widely used Orchid-potting medium.

Fir bark as an Orchid-potting medium has a rather unique history. A few years ago a west coast lumber company hired a group to find a use for the tremendous piles of bark they accumulated each year in the course of their operations. Someone reasoned that since Orchids naturally grow on the bark of trees in the jungle, this material might have a use as a substitute for the long-used Osmunda. Trials soon showed that Orchids responded wonderfully to bark culture, and, best of all, the bark could be handled easily and quickly by inexperienced persons. It is simply scooped up in one's hand and put around the plants in the way that ordinary soil is used. Osmunda, on the other hand, requires the use of a potting stick, considerable strength, and real finesse. Within a very few years a great many growers shifted over to bark culture. It is my opinion that it is the most satisfactory medium for use by the average amateur for most Orchids. It is necessary to augment the relatively low-nutrient content of fir bark, pine bark, or any other bark by the use of fertilizer. Fertilizer for bark culture must be high in nitrogen because, during the process of the decay of the bark, the decay bacteria use up extra nitrogen, thus making it unavailable to the plants. Special bark fertilizers are sold; be sure to use one of them according to directions on the label.

Some growers with a scientific mind reasoned that the only use any medium served Orchid plants was to hold them upright and that the maximum amount of drainage and air circulation about roots would be served by the use of an inert material such as coarse gravel. Others used coarse grinds of poultry grit, for example, and found that plants did beautifully, provided that they were watered regularly with a nutrient solution. Such an exotic approach should instill within the mind of a reader that Orchids are tough and adaptable plants, and about the only thing they cannot stand is to have their roots constantly submerged in a water-soaked, air-excluding mass.

Those who live in Hawaii have at their disposal a natural source of Tree Fern stems, which are composed of tough wiry fibers of much the same consistency as Osmunda Fern roots. Orchid plants in the Islands are often simply fastened to a piece of stem and allowed to shift for themselves. They are fed, of course, and grow luxuriantly in that gentle climate. Tree Fern stems are shipped all over the world from Hawaii, and you may try some of your plants on this material if you wish.

Orchid Benches
It has already been seen to what extent it is necessary that Orchid roots be exposed to the air; thus it should be no surprise to you to find that they are grown on benches made of widely spaced

slats or on wide-mesh hardware cloth so that the air can circulate freely about the plants. Many Orchid benches are built in steps so that back-row plants will have as much light as possible. The area beneath benches is often taken up by huge tanks of water in commercial greenhouses so that there is a constant supply of moisture being evaporated into the atmosphere. Others spread coke or gravel under benches and wet it down often. Since Orchid houses have a constantly high humidity, it is wise to build the benches of the most rot-resistant material possible. Heart redwood or cypress will last for many years.

Control of Atmospheric Moisture

We have written previously of the unusual roots of Orchids and their affinity for air. Of course, these roots are the means by which the plants take up moisture and nutrients, and though they need an abundance of fresh air, the air must have a high moisture content or the roots will dry out and die. A relative humidity of 40 per cent to 70 per cent is a workable range in which most Orchids will thrive.

Orchid leaves are unlike those of most other plants too, in that the stomata or breathing pores are fixed and do not open and close to meet changes in the outside atmosphere. Unless there is moisture in the air, the open stomata will allow an excess of cellular moisture to be lost to the surrounding air.

During warm weather, on sunny days especially, it is necessary to water down the walks, to sprinkle the plants with a foglike blanket, and to wet the walls and benches. Such sprinkling should be done on a rising temperature so that plants will have time to evaporate any moisture on their leaves before going into the cooler night temperatures. As an alternative, an automatic humidifier can be installed to maintain the proper moisture content of the atmosphere.

Treetop Living

How long has it been since you climbed a tree? Don't you remember the exhilaration of the height and the freshness of the breezes up there? Now, this is the very atmosphere to which most of our greenhouse Orchids are suited. They do not want stagnant air, but fresh air, and certain of your success with Orchids will depend upon their receiving it. Open the greenhouse ventilators a crack for a while even on cold days and let there be a circulation of air in your greenhouse.

The very thought of treetop living brings out forcibly the fact that your Orchids will benefit by being put outdoors in the summer. Hang them from branches of a tree or erect a support of some kind so that the air can sweep around them freely. The growth they make beneath the filtered shade of a tree during the summer months will be tough and seasoned, the very kind of growth to give the most flowers.

The Relationship of Light to Thrifty Growth

There is no mystery to the cultivation of Orchids. They require moisture, food, warmth, air, and light, as do all other plants. They differ from other plants only in the proportion of each that they need. All Orchids are not alike in their needs. Some require considerable shading all through the year. Others can stand full sun, and the majority can stand sun during the winter months but need some protection from intense heat during the summertime. Orchids will flower most freely when they receive the maximum amount of light they can take without burning. That means with Cattleyas, for example, that the foliage should not be a deep "healthy" green, but a yellow green. Too much shade means few flowers. Give your plants enough light even at the risk of a bit too much sun. I use a shading compound on my greenhouse glass during the summer months and let it wear off during the winter. Late in the winter I apply a light coating again and add to it as the sun becomes hotter.

Temperature Requirements of Orchids

When one tries to grow Orchids from many parts of the world where climatic conditions vary to a marked degree, it would be reasonable to suppose that difficulties would arise regarding a way of adjusting a single greenhouse to the needs of dissimilar plants. In commercial practice Orchids are usually segregated so that each type receives its optimum growing conditions. In a small greenhouse a person soon finds that there is a definite difference in temperatures in various parts of the greenhouse, and by putting cool-loving Orchids in cool sections and warmth-seeking ones nearer the source of heat it is possible to accommodate a great variety of Orchids. The element of compromise must be part of the game when one grows flowers for the fun of it and tries to cram everything under the sun into one small greenhouse.

It is well to know what temperatures the various Orchids would like to have so that one may have a sensible approach to their best culture; therefore, the following lists will serve as a guide. The commonly grown Orchids listed below are classified according to their ideal minimum temperatures. Temperatures should fall each night to within the range given if the plants are to do their best. Remember that minimum temperatures always refer to the lowest night reading and that daytime temperatures may climb much higher without injury to the plants, except for some special species such as *Odontoglossum*, whose special needs are noted below.

Cool Temperature Orchids (50- to 55-degree nights)

Coelogyne	*Lycaste*
Cymbidium	*Miltonia*
Cypripedium (green-leaf type)	*Odontoglossum**
Dendrobium (deciduous type)	*Oncidium*
Epidendrum	*Vanilla*
Laelia	

Intermediate Temperature Orchids (55- to 65-degree nights)
Brassavola
Brassocattleya (bigeneric hybrids)
Brassolaeliocattleya (trigeneric hybrids)
Calanthe

*Odontoglossums require cool night temperatures throughout the year and must be grown either in northern areas or in air-conditioned greenhouses.

Cattleya, species and hybrids
Cyrtopodium
Dendrobium
Epidendrum
Laelia
Laeliocattleya (bigeneric hybrids)
Miltonia
Oncidium
Sophrolaeliocattleya (trigeneric hybrids)
Sophronitis

Warm Temperature Orchids (65- to 75-degree nights)
Cycnoches
Cypripedium (mottled leaf)
Dendrobium (evergreen type)
Oncidium
Phalaenopsis
Vanda (strap-leaf)

Immediately it will be seen that the names of certain Orchids appear in more than one list. This is due to the fact that many Orchid genera have innumerable species. For example, over five hundred different kinds of Epidendrums have been discovered. Some grow in steaming jungles and others high on the cool slopes of the Andes. In addition, it must be mentioned again that Orchids are adaptable, and it will be found upon experimentation that a wide variety of plants can be grown together despite the fact that their needs are not met exactly.

Specific Cultural Notes for Orchid Genera
The balance of this chapter will be devoted to specific usable information about the kinds of Orchids you will probably want to grow in your greenhouse. They are listed alphabetically, and in most cases the culture is given under the first-named representative of a group. In other cases, such as *Cattleya* hybrids and generic crosses in particular, the culture is given under the most representative member of the group, here under *Cattleya.*

BRASSAVOLA

One particular species of Brassavola, *B. Digbyana*, has been of great value in the production of hybrid Orchids. This species has rather large flowers, greenish white in color, with tremendous fringed lips. It is the ability to transmit the distinctive lip to its progeny that has made this species of so much value. When Orchid growers speak of a flower as having a "Brasso lip," it is sufficiently descriptive to anyone who has once seen a *B. Digbyana* or one of its hybrids. *B. Digbyana* flowers in the spring and is native to Honduras.

Two other species of Brassavolas are sometimes grown: *B. cordata*, a smaller-flowered Jamaican form without a fringed lip that blossoms in the early fall, and *B. nodosa*, sometimes called Lady of the Night, whose white flowers, also without fringed lips, appear in the autumn. This species is exceedingly fragrant in the evening and comes from Central America.

Brassavolas need much the same culture as Cattleyas, which see, except that they can stand more light and need less water.

BRASSOCATTLEYA

Brassocattleya Orchids are bigeneric hybrids between *Brassavola* and *Cattleya* species. They usually combine the large size of the *Cattleya* parent with the huge fringed lip of the *Brassavola*. Culture is the same as for *Cattleya*. In Orchid literature the name is abbreviated to *Bc*. *Brassocattleya* Orchids, because of their hybrid origin, may flower at any time of the year.

BRASSOLAELIOCATTLEYA

This tongue twister is a trigeneric hybrid combining the species of *Brassavola*, *Laelia*, and *Cattleya*. In catalogues you will find the name shortened to *Blc*. Plants with this ancestry may flower at any time of the year and should be given *Cattleya* culture.

CALANTHE

Calanthes are terrestrial Orchids grown for their long arching sprays of yellow, rose, or white flowers. There are both evergreen and deciduous species, but the deciduous ones are those most often grown. They flower in midwinter from leafless bulbs, then go into a rest period. They should be divided each year so that only one pseudobulb is planted in each pot. Give them a mixture of one part leaf mold, one part sand, and two parts good loam. Set the bulbs so that only the bases are in the soil. Water sparingly until growth starts, then freely all summer. Fertilize them every two weeks during the vegetative period with a mild fertilizer. When foliage dies down in the fall, withhold water until flower spikes begin to develop. Calanthes come from Malaya and need considerable shade. In the summer they can be grown under the shade of trees outdoors and moved into the greenhouse in the fall.

CATTLEYA

To some people, trying to describe a Cattleya Orchid is easy, for it is the Orchid that looks like an Orchid. Cattleyas are usually seen nowadays as hybrids, and the huge flowers of orchid, lavender, pink, white, yellow, cream, or red are indicative in many cases of the parentage of the plants from which the flowers came. There are about forty species of Cattleyas outside of the thousands of hybrids, and a beginner will find that they are easy to grow and inexpensive to buy. After a while, though, one's interest soon turns to the gorgeous hybrids. To any who say, "Oh, I like the small Orchids better," I suggest a close examination of a cluster of one of today's Cattleya hybrids. Just this afternoon I found that one of my new seedlings had opened its first blossoms, four of the most beautiful flowers I have ever seen, pure snowy white in all their petals except for the splash of lavender on the lips and the touch of gold at each throat. Don't be a scorner of large Orchids; try them and you too will be captivated by their elegance.

Throughout this section you will find references to Cattleya culture. This is a way to grow them that I know works well. I pot my plants in fir bark, coarse, medium, or fine, depending upon the size of the plants. Tiny seedlings get the fine grind, and the more advanced plants the coarser ones. I put broken flowerpots into the bottom third of a pot, add some fir bark with a sweeping motion, set the plant in the pot, and fill in with more bark, being careful to set the rhizomes at top-of-the-bark level, and leaving about one-half inch of space at the top of the pot for watering.

Newly planted Orchids are apt to be wobbly when first set in fir bark, and since plants usually need to be tied up anyway, I suggest that you buy stake clips which fit over the edge of the pot. The clips hold a wire stake upright, and the leaves of the plant can be tied with soft string to the stake. As an inexpensive alternative, bend one end of a piece of stout wire so that it will fit flush inside the bottom of the pot, with the upright portion of the wire extending ten to twelve inches above the top of the pot. Plant as noted above, and the wire stake will be securely "rooted" beneath the plant and conveniently located to make tying easy.

As a general rule, Cattleyas should be repotted when they begin to grow over the edge of the pot. Do the job after flowering, just prior to the development of new roots. Such a job usually needs to be done every two to three years, depending upon the vigor of the plant. Never divide a plant into less than four pseudobulbs and, when planting, determine the direction the plant wants to grow and plant it so that it will have the greatest possible room for development before repotting will be required again. This means that the older pseudobulbs should be crowded against the side of the pot with the growing point, or "lead," as it is called, headed for the other side of the pot across a bed of fir bark.

As I have mentioned previously, it is necessary to feed Orchids planted in fir bark. Use a regular fertilizer prepared for this purpose. Many growers use a simple nitrogenous fertilizer, ammonium nitrate, at the rate of one teaspoonful to a gallon of water. Plants may be watered with this solution every other watering, the alternate watering being of plain water.

Plants growing in fir bark should be watered once or twice a week, according to prevailing conditions. The bark should never be allowed to get completely dry, because it is very difficult to get it wet again. When plants have finished flowering and are resting, water should be applied sparingly, only often enough to keep the bark from drying out. This applies particularly to newly repotted plants, and it is at this time that regular misting of the foliage will do much to help plants become re-established.

COELOGYNE

There are many kinds of Coelogynes, but the one most often grown for its wonderful white flower clusters is *C. cristata*, which is native to low elevations in the Himalayas. It is a cool-growing Orchid which does well when grown in the same manner as Cattleyas, or somewhat cooler. Flowers are borne in the period from January to April each year.

CYCNOCHES, Swan Orchid

The most familiar member of the Cycnoches family is *C. chlorochilon*, a lovely chartreuse-colored beauty, whose gracefully curved flower center easily reminds one of a swan. Swan Orchids flower in late fall or winter after their leaves have fallen. Give them much the same conditions as *Phalaenopsis*, except reduce watering during the dormant period. Cycnoches are native to Colombia and Venezuela.

CYMBIDIUM

It is not at all uncommon for a lady to wear her Easter Cymbidium corsage again on Mother's Day, for these Orchids are among the longest-lasting of all and are not at all difficult to grow. Cymbidiums are terrestrial plants and may be grown in a mixture of one third each of peat moss, sand, and fir bark. They need a light shade except during the winter months, when they can take full sun. I grow my Cymbidiums in large tubs and move them outdoors in the summer so that they get plenty of fresh air and the light shade of open trees. The potting mixture for Cymbidiums should stay moist, but not wet. If you give your plants an outdoor vacation during the summer, return them to the greenhouse when the nights get down to the forties. In mild climates Cymbidiums make fine garden plants. Commercial growers often plant out Cymbidiums in ground beds, but home-greenhouse operators will, no doubt, be happier with their plants if they can move them about occasionally. The flower spikes carry from a dozen to forty flowers that last from six to eight weeks on the plants. Cymbidiums are cool-growing Orchids and will not do well in a warm greenhouse. Give them regular feedings during their active growing period. Cymbidiums blossom from late fall until late spring, depending upon the plant. Flower colors range from pure white through chartreuse to many shades of tan, often with maroon spots or blotches on the lips. For those with very small greenhouses we recommend the miniature Cymbidiums, delicate in size of plants as well as flowers.

CYPRIPEDIUM, Cypripedium, Lady Slipper Orchid

If you want to be correct about the botanical name for this flower, you should call it *Paphiopedilum*, for the name Cypripedium really belongs to the native wild Lady Slipper Orchids of Europe and North America. However, if you wish to be understood, call it Cypripedium, or even "Cyp." Few other flowers of any kind are as long-lasting, either on the plants or when cut, as are Cypripediums. There are varieties which flower as early as September and others as late as June, with the majority of them coming during the winter months when they are most apt to be wanted and appreciated. Colors range from snow-white to butter-yellow, green, brown, and maroon-red, and each flower has the appearance of having been freshly varnished. They are wonderful!

Perhaps you have already noticed that Cypripediums appear on the list of cool Orchids and again on the list of warm ones. This is because there is a definite separation of species between the cool-loving plants, which have clean green leaves, and the warmth-seeking ones, which have mottled foliage. To confuse us, though, there are now hybrids between the two groups, but Orchid catalogues carefully point out the needs of these plants of mixed ancestry.

Cypripediums have long been grown in Osmunda or in rich composts high in organic matter, but nowadays a great many of the Orchid catalogues state clearly, "All our Cyps are grown in fir bark." It has been my own experience, too, that they are ideally suited to fir-bark culture. The bark should be kept quite moist, and the plants should be fed regularly with an Orchid fertilizer. The warm Cyps do well with Phalaenopsis and enjoy the shade and high humidity. I have found that they prosper in the warm section of a Cattleya house, but the cool ones do not blossom well unless given 50- to 55-degree nights. The ancestors of the green-leafed types came from the foothills of the Himalayas, where temperatures often fall to freezing, but the mottled-leafed ones are native to the tropical atmosphere of the islands of the East Indies.

CYRTOPODIUM, Cyrtopodium, Cow Horn Orchid

The Cow Horn Orchid gets its name from its huge pointed pseudobulbs, shaped like horns, which are large enough to do justice to nearly any bovine. The tawny yellow, chocolate-barred flowers, in contrast, are small, from one to one and one-half inches across, but are borne in great numbers on long sprays during the spring of the year. The bulbs send out long cornlike foliage during the summer, which matures and drops off in the fall. The plants grow well in any composty soil or in plain fir bark and never fail to arouse interest among greenhouse visitors. This Orchid is native from Florida to southern South America.

DENDROBIUM

If you wish, you can have a greenhouse full of nothing but Dendrobiums, all different, for there are over six hundred wild species, to say nothing of the countless hybrids now available. Right away it should be said that there are two classes of Dendrobiums, the cool-growing ones and the warm ones. The warm ones may be grown at intermediate temperatures with Cattleyas, but the cool ones must have night temperatures of 50 degrees or so in the fall in order to initiate flower buds. Both types of Dendrobiums are of the easiest possible culture. Give them very small pots and set them in fir bark. The warm group, typified by *D. phalaenopsis*, comes from the jungles of New Guinea and that area of the Pacific and grows nearly all the time, sending out long spikes of white, purple, or lavender flowers at any time of the year.

These plants should be fed regularly and kept moist, warm, and shaded. They do well with Phalaenopsis. The cool type, of which *D. nobile* is the most common example, has a different growth pattern. After flowering, the plants go into a vegetative period, sending up long slender pseudobulbs, which maintain their leaves about a year and one half, losing them during their second autumn. At that time the plants must be kept cool and on the dry side until flower buds form, then watering can be increased.

No plants are easier to grow than the Nobile type of Dendrobiums. My plants hang on wall brackets in the cool side of my greenhouse year after year with no attention other than food and water, and they flower profusely every February and March. This Nobile type forms clusters of flower buds along the length of its pseudobulbs; so when they open, the plants are nearly hidden beneath the flowers. Colors are mostly white to pale lavender, often with dark centers.

In addition to the Nobile group there are others which need similar culture; they are known as the Yellow Pendant Dendrobiums. Their flowers are borne in long sprays and are magnificent. They should be given practically no water from October until March, at which time they send out their flower spikes; then watering should be resumed. *D. aggregatum,* variety *majus,* is a lovely dwarf-growing species with orange flowers, and *D. chrysotoxum*, a fine golden yellow one, you will surely enjoy.

EPIDENDRUM

Epidendrums form another huge group of Orchids with over five hundred wild species recorded, though all of them are not generally grown. There are two types of growth among Epidendrums, sympodial and monopodial. The plants described immediately below are sympodial, have pseudobulbs and sprays of lovely, though small, flowers, and need the same culture as Cattleyas. *E. atropurpureum* bears small, long-lasting, fragrant flowers in the spring, whose sepals and petals are brown and whose lips are pink, rosy lavender, or purple. *E. cochleatum* seems to blossom all through the year, sending out delicate flowers with green sepals and petals and dark, almost black, lips. *E. fragrans* is surely one of my favorite Orchids. The flowers are small and greenish white with lavender bars on the lips. If a single flower of this lovely Orchid is open, there is sufficient fragrance to fill an entire home greenhouse with an exotic perfume. *E. Mariae* is sometimes called Mariae Ames, but at our house we call it our "Anniversary Orchid," for it always blossoms in July. Its delicate flowers with their chartreuse petals and huge snow-white lips make beautiful and unusual corsages. Plants rarely grow over six inches tall. *E. tampense* is a Florida native whose tiny greenish-white flowers cover the plants each spring and summer. *E. vitellinum,* variety *majus*, is another miniature Epidendrum with bright orange-red flowers.

The second group of Epidendrums, those with monopodial growth characteristics, is best typified by the Reed Stem Hybrids. They carry their blossom clusters atop slender reedlike stems and continue making more flowers in the clusters as the old ones mature and drop off. There are many colors ranging through shades of red, yellow, orange, rose, and lavender. My plants are potted in fir bark and hang in full sun in the coolest part of the greenhouse and blossom without ceasing throughout the year. They grow so luxuriantly that they soon overrun the pots and send down aerial roots three feet or more long, but the plants continue to grow and blossom without visible means of support. This ought to be a good recommendation for any beginner. Try *E. O'Brienianum* if you want an easy-to-grow type. My plants are never without clusters of orange-red flowers.

Epidendrums have been crossed with other genera, chiefly with Cattleyas, giving rise to *Epicattleya* Orchids. Usually these display much of the Epidendrum growth habits, but the flowers have Cattleya coloration.

LAELIA

There are many species of Laelias and innumerable hybrids between Laelias and other members of the Orchid family, particularly with Cattleyas and Brassavolas. They require conditions similar to Cattleyas, except that they need more light. The Mexican Laelias, such as *anceps*, *autumnalis*, and *majalis*, like to be cool. Laelia flowers are shaped much like those of Cattleyas, and among the species may be found those with white, lavender, purple, or yellow flowers.

LAELIOCATTLEYA

These Orchids are hybrids between Laelias and Cattleyas and among this group are found many of the fine firm-textured modern hybrids. The abbreviation *Lc*. appears before the name of any plant of this ancestry. Culture is similar to that given Cattleyas, and flowering season is irregular because of the hybrid nature of the plants.

LYCASTE

Lycastes are Central American Orchids which do best in cool temperatures, light shade, and constant moisture with perfect drainage. In the summer they benefit by being put outdoors. Keep them somewhat on the dry side when dormant. Flowers appear during the winter and spring and do not look like conventional Orchids. The lips are abbreviated, and the flowers look somewhat like Tulips. The most commonly grown species *L. Skinneri* has rosy-white flowers. *L. aromatica* has fragrant orange flowers.

MILTONIA, Miltonia, Pansy Orchid

As the name implies, the Pansy Orchid does not have flowers usually considered typical of the Orchid family. They resemble Pansy flowers not only because they are flat and shaped like Pansies, but because they have a blotch of color at the throat of each flower in a Pansylike manner. Most Miltonias are cool-loving plants, which need considerable light and constant moisture during their growing period and need to be comparatively dry while resting. The plants are small in stature, but produce many flowers in shades of pink, rose, red, or yellow with "masks" or blotches of contrasting colors.

There is another group of warm-growing Miltonias which does well under Cattleya, or intermediate temperature, conditions.

Flower petals of this group are usually narrower than those of cool-growing Miltonias and look more like Odontoglossum flowers.

Miltonias flower easily in small-sized pots and will do well potted in fir bark or Osmunda.

ODONTOGLOSSUM

Unless the reader is willing to install a mechanical cooling system for his greenhouse or lives in a section of the country with very cool summers, he had better forget trying to grow most Odontoglossums, as beautiful as they are. Until the advent of air-conditioned greenhouses, all sorts of schemes were worked out to try to keep temperatures down during hot summer weather. Growers knew that their Odontoglossums would suffer so much from one heat spell that they could not grow out of it in a whole year of ideal temperatures. Night temperatures should be about 40 to 45 degrees, and day temperatures never over 70 degrees. Odontoglossums flower from midwinter until early summer and have tremendous sprays of stunning flowers of nearly every color imaginable.

Several Orchid catalogues now list a few warm-growing Odontoglossums which are well worth a bit of effort. The ones listed are *O. cervantesii, O. pulchellum, O. rossii,* and *O. schleiperianum.* They need the same culture as Oncidiums.

ONCIDIUM, Oncidium, Butterfly Orchid, Dancing Ladies

Oncidiums surely deserve a place in any greenhouse, not for the size of their individual flowers, but for the gracefulness of the slender sprays of blossoms that flutter in the slightest breath of air. There are dozens of species and hybrids available with flowers of yellow, brown and yellow, or rose. Oncidiums do well when grown with Cattleyas, except that they like more light. Give them plenty of water when they are growing and keep them dry during their rest period. You may have Oncidiums in blossom throughout the year by choosing species or hybrids with various blossoming seasons.

PHALAENOPSIS, Phalaenopsis, Moth Orchid

I find it hard to dispute the person who contends that the members of the Phalaenopsis family are the most beautiful flowers in the world. They achieve their beauty by a simple uncluttered grace and purity of color that makes other flowers seem garish in comparison.

Phalaenopsis do not have pseudobulbs in which to store food and water; so they must be kept moist at all times. They need warm temperatures, 65 degrees or so at night, and quite a bit of shade. Provide them with a high humidity and a regular feeding program, and even the young seedlings will blossom at a tender age. Phalaenopsis will often blossom two or three times a year. If you pick the flowers, leave the flower stalk on the plant, and it will usually send out more flowers.

Most people think of Phalaenopsis Orchids as being white, but there are lovely pink, as well as yellow, ones too. The flowers last for weeks on the plants and are easy to grow.

Fir bark makes a good potting medium for Phalaenopsis. It must be kept quite moist at all times. If you will treat your plants as I have suggested, they will have a wealth of flowers, firm healthy leaves, and a general aspect of well-being that is a joy to behold.

SOPHROLAELIOCATTLEYA

This trigeneric cross has resulted in many fine hybrids whose flowers tend to pick up red shades from the Sophronitis ancestry. Grow the plants as you would Cattleyas.

SOPHRONITIS

These little Orchids, closely related to Cattleyas, are rarely offered for sale in catalogues and do not blossom freely, though they grow congenially with Cattleyas. They are mentioned here because they have been used extensively to introduce a bright red color into hybrids which produce flowers of Cattleya size.

VANDA

For many years Hawaii had nearly a monopoly on the production of Vanda Orchids, and the flowers were, and still are, shipped by air to the mainland to be given away at all sorts of public and private gatherings. The plants from which these particular Vanda flowers come are not the same type as the Vandas usually grown in greenhouses. They are terrestrial plants with cylindrical leaves and are called Terete Vandas. They require a great deal of sunshine and rarely blossom freely in greenhouses.

The other form of Vanda, the strap-leaved Vanda, is the one which is so popular today. This is a monopodial Orchid, which grows onward and upward, sending out sprays of flowers from between its leaf axils as it grows. Some of the newer hybrids are among the most beautiful Orchids in the world. My son, looking at a single Vanda flower, said it looked like a ship's propeller, and the description is an apt one, for the five petals and sepals so evenly overshadow the tiny lip as to make it inconspicuous. Flower colors range from white through shades of cream, yellow, red, blue, purple, buff, and tan, with combinations difficult to describe. Many modern hybrids have flowers three inches across in full sprays. They are long-lasting and truly hard to surpass, yet easy to grow.

Give Vandas a warm place with a good deal of light. I hang my Vandas from the greenhouse roof so that they will get as much light as possible through the shading and grow them in fir bark which is kept moist all through the year. The plants continue to send out flowers without regard to the season. Feed them as you would Cattleyas, and they will grow luxuriantly.

VANILLA

Vanilla, the last Orchid on our list, is a climbing vine with cream-colored Cattleya-shaped flowers which last only a day or two. The flowers are fragrant, however, and it is from ripe seed pods of this plant that true vanilla is extracted. Give the plants a humusy soil or fir bark, plenty of water, half shade, and a support upon which to climb.

As a final word on Orchid culture I want to stress the fact that they are not hard to grow and that everyone with a greenhouse should surely have some Orchids. Somewhere in the dim past it was rumored abroad that Orchids require seven years of tedious culture to produce their first flowers. This thought has served as a deterrent for those who felt that their patience would not hold out that long. It may indeed take seven years to get an Orchid to blossom if one starts with seeds, but why start with seeds? Do you grow your Apple trees from seeds, or your Rose bushes? It is equally as silly to think that one must grow his Orchids that way. The idea I want to get across is this: Start your Orchid collection with mature plants that are of blossoming age. You will find that they need not be expensive and that caring for your first plants will give you a bit of experience before you add to your Orchid holdings.

When you have grown Orchids for a short while, you will be tempted to buy some seedlings. Humor yourself at this point, for they are inexpensive, and if they have good parentage, you will get some marvelous flowers. Do not go through the process of starting your own plants from seed, for this is a business of its own, and unless you have room for the thousands of seedlings, all more or less alike, that you would get from a single sowing, what in the world would you do with them? Buy a plant of this cross and a plant of that to lend variety to your collection. It is a great hobby and an absorbing one.

CHAPTER X

BATTLE OF THE BUGS

When I first started to write Chapter VIII, "Plants You Can Grow in Your Greenhouse," I listed after each plant all the types of insects and diseases which could possibly attack it. The result was frightening, and I soon bordered upon hypochondria. It seemed as though there were hordes of bugs lying in wait to pounce upon each tender plant. As a matter of practical gardening I knew that this was not true, but the effect was so real that I decided to group all the troubles here together where we could examine them and see what need be done to keep them under control. It should be stated here and now that it is much easier to control insects and diseases in a greenhouse than it is outdoors, for in a greenhouse one can corner them and exterminate them. The amount of spraying, dusting, and fumigating that is necessary is very slight. The main idea is to have a program of preventive control, and your troubles will be at a minimum. If you institute a system of spraying, for example, so that every week or ten days your plants get a light application, you will always have disease- and insect-free plants.

It is particularly important that your plants be sprayed thoroughly during the early fall, for that is the time that many plants are being brought in from outdoors, and they are sure to harbor a few uninvited guests. Then, too, ventilators are open often during the fall, and insects find their way inside to spend a cozy winter. Careful sprayings in the fall will do much to keep the insect population to a minimum.

No doubt you will buy plants or be given plants during the winter season. Often these plants will have a few bugs on them. Aphids particularly seem to come in this way. If you wait until you notice them before you apply control measures, they may have spread to other plants, making your task more difficult and extermination more uncertain. It is one more reason why you should have a regular program.

Disease prevention is another phase of good greenhouse management and to a large extent has to do with keeping the atmosphere of the greenhouse of low enough humidity so that moisture will not condense upon the foliage, for if it does, conditions are ideal for the spread of many kinds of leaf diseases. Likewise, during cold weather and on cloudy days one should be careful about splashing water on foliage. During bright dry weather it will soon evaporate, but under cloudy conditions it may remain for hours, providing perfect conditions for the spread of infections. Watering should always be done on rising temperatures and early enough in the day so that the foliage will be dry before nightfall. It is imperative that plants get fresh air not only to provide them with the carbon dioxide they need, but also to provide a circulating, rather than stagnant, atmosphere. Do not hesitate to open ventilators a bit for a while each day even in cold weather, for this is one secret of good culture.

It cannot be stressed too strongly that the insecticides and fungicides used nowadays to control pests of all sorts are extremely dangerous to handle. They are poisonous and should be kept out of reach of children, and directions for their usage should be followed meticulously. This is particularly true when they are used in a small greenhouse where one cannot stand on the windward side as one can outdoors. It is a good practice to wear gloves when mixing the poisons, to pour the powders into water carefully so that there will not be a dust to inhale, and, last but most important, to arrange for a speedy exit when you do the spraying. Start at one end of the house and work swiftly toward a door which you can close securely and lock or at least put a sign on so that someone else will not walk in until the poisons have settled. If you have a freestanding greenhouse, you will find the use of a smoke fumigator very satisfactory. There are types to control various kinds of insects. Select the kind you need, open the top and put in a lighted sparkler, and retire swiftly. Fumes will penetrate every crevice in the house. For that very reason I do not recommend that this type of control be used for greenhouses attached to dwellings. The fumes will easily pass the most tightly sealed door.

In applying poisons it is well to wear a mask or respirator, to wear old clothes that can be laundered, and to do the job in company with another person so that in case of accident you can get immediate assistance. Respirators for greenhouse use are manufactured by Ray-O-Vac Company, Wilson Products Division, Reading, Pennsylvania.

Modern Insecticides and Fungicides

Later on in this chapter you will find a section devoted to a description of specific insects, but here it should be noted that many of the modern insecticides and fungicides control a wide range of insects and diseases, and though there may be certain instances where you will need to use one preparation alone for a particular problem, the chances are that a mixture of a good insecticide, a good fungicide, and a spreader such as a household detergent will give ample control. (See general-purpose spray below.)

In the discussion of the poisons it will be seen that some of the ones commonly used in commercial work have been left out. It is simply because they are such violent poisons and must be used under such controlled conditions that it would be folly to suggest them to home-greenhouse owners.

It is well known that certain insects, particularly red-spider mites, build up strains which are resistant to given insecticides;

so if there is a severe infestation of them, use a poison specifically made to kill red spiders, but different from the one you have used in previous sprayings.

The following insecticides and fungicides are recommended for home-greenhouse use:

Poisons	Insects Controlled
Aramite	Red-spider mites
Chlordane	Ants, sow bugs, pill bugs, springtails
DDT	Chewing insects, thrips, soil pests, white flies, scales
Kelthane	Cyclamen mites, red-spider mites
Malathion	Aphids, chewing insects, scales, thrips, mealy bugs, white flies, red-spider mites
Metaldehyde	Slugs, snails
Nicotine sulphate	Aphids, sucking insects
Pyrethrum	Aphids, sucking insects
Rotenone	Aphids, sucking insects
Sodium selenate	Foliar nematodes, Cyclamen mites, aphids
Tedion	Red-spider mites
Ferbam	Fungus leaf spots, rusts, botrytis blights
Wettable sulphur	Fungus leaf spots, mildew
Zineb	Fungus leaf spots, rusts, botrytis blights

A general-purpose spray which will do a good job of controlling insects and diseases in the home greenhouse can be made of two level teaspoonfuls each of 50-per-cent Malathion, 50-per-cent DDT, and Ferbam, plus one-fourth teaspoonful of a household detergent in one gallon of water. It should be applied each week or ten days for constant protection. Do a thorough job when spraying to be sure that you get good coverage of the undersides of leaves. The sprayer should send out the material in a fine mist so as to do as complete a job as possible.

A final word of caution about poisons is in order. Some of those mentioned above cannot be used on food plants; so *read labels carefully and follow manufacturers' suggestions.*

PLATE 23 A home greenhouse is unalloyed joy during the dead of winter. How many plants can you identify in this cool greenhouse?

Courtesy Aluminum Greenhouses, Inc., Cleveland, O.

PLATE 24 With a bit of planning, your home greenhouse can be as lovely as this one during the winter months.

Courtesy Aluminum Greenhouses, Inc., Cleveland, O.

PLATE 25 An autumn scene in a home greenhouse. After the Chrysanthemum season has passed, they will be replaced by a succession of colorful spring-flowering plants such as Azaleas, Daffodils, Tulips, and others of the owner's choosing.

Courtesy Lord & Burnham, Irvington-on-Hudson, N.Y.

PLATE 26 There is no limit to the variety of plants that can be grown in a home greenhouse.

Courtesy Lord & Burnham, Irvington-on-Hudson, N.Y.

Common Greenhouse Insects

Aphids. Aphids, or plant lice, as they are sometimes called, are tiny insects, usually green or black in color, that congregate near the growing tips of plants and suck the juices from the plant cells. Several controls are listed above.

Cyclamen mites. Cyclamen mites cause a great deal of damage to many ornamental plants, particularly to Cyclamens and African Violets, often causing a twisting and malformation of new leaves. Infected plants do not blossom, or if they do, they have poor flowers. These mites are very hard to kill, but Kelthane will do the job. It must be directed into the crowns of the plants, where the mites live.

Mealy bugs. These insects appear to be little balls of cotton fluff and are covered with a waxy coating which resists the penetration of some insecticides. Before the discovery of some of the modern insecticides they were difficult to irradicate. Malathion will control them easily.

Nematodes or eelworms. These are microscopic threadlike creatures that infect either roots or leaves of plants. Soil nematodes are controlled by soil pasteurization as discussed in Chapter V. Foliar nematodes may be controlled by the use of sodium selenate on certain plants, and they may be kept from spreading by destroying plant refuse and by keeping foliage dry.

Red-spider mites. These are among the most common of insects and thrive in the warm sheltered environment of a greenhouse. They are extremely tiny, about the size of the point of a pin, and in severe infestations cover the leaves, particularly on the undersides, with a fine web. They injure plants by sucking out cell juices. Several controls are noted above.

Scales. Several kinds of scale insects infect greenhouse plants. All are sucking insects which have a shell of some kind that protects them from most of their enemies; however, Malathion or DDT will penetrate the shells and kill the scale insects beneath.

Slugs and snails. These slimy creatures thrive in warm moist greenhouses and can raise havoc with plants by eating seedlings and by eating holes out of mature plants. Methaldehyde used in a bait form is very effective in their control. They feed at night and usually hide under flowerpots or in other dark places during the day.

Springtails. Many an Orchid amateur has lifted a pot or poured water into a pot and been shocked to see the surface come alive with tiny, white, bouncing, wormlike creatures. It is not known how much damage they do, but Chlordane will get rid of them.

Thrips. Thrips are extremely tiny insects which rasp out sections of leaves and flowers and are particularly fond of Gladiolus. Control them with DDT or Malathion.

White flies. These little fellows have a very descriptive name and have a host of relatives. When an infected plant is touched, the air suddenly becomes filled with the tiny flies. Control can be effected with DDT or Malathion.

Common Greenhouse Diseases

Rather than go through a long list of diseases of fungal or bacterial origin, it seems better to suggest that each greenhouse owner use a general-purpose spray as noted above, which will do much to control this type of infection. Diseases such as damping-off are covered in Chapter V, and such leaf and stem infections as anthracnose, leaf spot, botrytis, and rust are controlled by the use of a good fungicide. Sulphur is a specific material to use in case of mildew infection.

Answers to Your Specific Problems

All too many amateurs are not aware of the number of plant scientists upon whom they may call for free information about disease and insect problems. State colleges, county field stations, and experiment stations have trained men and women who will gladly inspect your plants if you will send or take a sample to them. They also do soil analysis work, for which there is little or no charge.

CHAPTER XI

GREENHOUSE STRETCHERS

There never was an amateur greenhouse owner who did not feel at times that his greenhouse should have been made bigger. This feeling is most prevalent in the spring when his greenhouse is already full, and he knows it is time to start seedlings for his outdoor garden. It is not always possible or practical to build a bigger greenhouse; so it is comforting to know that there are other ways of meeting the emergency. Commercial growers and estate gardeners learned long ago that they could grow a number of plants earlier in the spring and later in the fall by the use of hotbeds and cold frames. Certain tender plants could be carried over winter if given the protection of a cold frame; a cold frame provided an ideal frost-free place in which to store spring-flowering bulbs before bringing them into the greenhouse for forcing; and hotbeds and cold frames afforded a place to put unsightly plants that had finished their blossoming season, yet needed protection for the balance of the cold season.

Hotbeds and Cold Frames

Hotbeds and cold frames are identical except that one has heat and the other does not. Essentially they are low glass- or plastic-covered structures which are inexpensive to build and heat, and though they are not too easy to work in, they do provide a very satisfactory answer to the need for an expanded growing area at certain times of the year. Figure 3 illustrates the construction details of a modern hotbed.

The standard size for cold frames and hotbeds has always been six feet in width by three, six, or more feet in length in multiples of three feet. That is simply because standard hotbed sash comes in three- by six-foot sizes. There is no reason, of course, why home hotbeds must be of a standard size. If one has a few discarded storm windows, he can make a frame to fit the material on hand.

The first thing to consider when building a hotbed or cold frame is the location, which ought to be on a well-drained site facing south if possible. Most units are excavated more or less in order to benefit from the protection of the earth around them. Often they are excavated somewhat and also built up somewhat so that they are easier to work. Sides may be made of wood which has been treated with copper naphthanate so that it will resist rot, or of masonry, which is more expensive but also more permanent. The back of the bed is usually eighteen to thirty inches high, and the

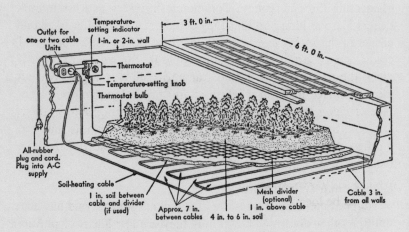

Cutaway view of hotbed illustrating the use of electric soil-heating cable. Courtesy National Greenhouse Co., Pana, Ill.

front twelve to twenty-four inches high so that the sash has a slope which will catch the sun's rays and which will also carry off rain. Inside, the earth level is six to twelve inches from the glass at the front of the bed and six inches farther from the glass at the back of the bed because of the slope of the glass. A bed made particularly for holding bulbs for late forcing or for special purposes may well be considerably deeper, but this is the depth to use for normal growing plants.

Modern Heating for Hotbeds

It used to be that all hotbeds were heated by the fermentation of strawy horse manure, an item few gardeners, amateurs or professionals, can buy these days. This is the day of the electrically heated, thermostatically controlled hotbed, and its ease of maintenance and dependable heat have made plant culture relatively simple. One may even buy devices which will open and close hotbed sash in answer to temperature needs.

Soil-heating cable may be lead- or plastic-covered and is laid about six inches beneath the top of the soil. It is protected from damage by tools by being covered first with two inches of soil, then with a layer of one-half-inch-mesh galvanized hardware cloth before the top four inches of soil in which the plants are to grow are added. A special type of thermostat may be buried in the soil (not over a heating cable), or may be partly in and partly out of the soil. This may be set so that the soil will be heated to the desired temperature. For most crops a soil temperature of 70 to 75 degrees will give rapid growth.

In addition to heating a hotbed, there must be some arrangement made for cooling it, for the sun alone will quickly raise the inside temperature too high on sunny spring days unless ventilation is given. Usually this is a manual operation. The sash can be blocked open to allow some of the heat to escape. A thermometer should be located so that it is easy to read, yet is not in the direct sun. Temperatures inside the hotbed should not be allowed to rise above 85 degrees.

Since the beds will lose heat at night, many growers cover them with straw mats or tarpaulins during the hours of darkness.

It is impossible to state exactly how much it will cost to operate a hotbed using electricity, but experience has shown that the average three- by six-foot hotbed uses one to two kilowatt-hours of electricity per day.

Pit Greenhouses

What would you do if you lived in Boston or Montreal and had a group of large-growing plants whose nature was too tender to allow them to survive the winter outdoors? There are three possible choices: You could bring them into a greenhouse; you could leave them outdoors to die; or you could put them in a pit greenhouse. A pit greenhouse is just what the name implies, an excavated section of the earth covered with glass. When the earth is excavated to a depth of six to eight feet and the glass cover is flush with the surface of the soil, there is remarkably little loss of heat during the winter months. During darkness the glass should be covered with straw mats or even heavier protection, and the rays of the sun should be admitted during the daylight hours. Such a shelter rarely needs auxiliary heat to keep it above freezing and makes a marvelous place to store large tender shrubs and, of course, acts as a bulb cellar for starting spring-flowering bulbs. Side walls should be of masonry, and the structure should be built in a well-drained location so that it will not collect water during spring rains.

CHAPTER XII

WHAT TO DO
AND WHEN TO DO IT

In a sense this chapter may be the most valuable part of this book, for timeliness is of the very essence in horticulture. One cannot wait until blossoming season before planting seeds. Every job has its season, and it is imperative for those who are unfamiliar with growing plants under glass that they have a usable, practical, down-to-earth guide. Although these instructions begin with the calendar year, there is every reason to believe that most home-greenhouse gardeners will actually begin their year at another season. The preparation for winter flowering must begin during the summer months. Then too, most greenhouses are constructed at that time of the year and will be stocked for their first season of winter beauty several months ahead of time. In using these directions, then, begin where you are and refer again and again to previous sections of the book for specific instructions pertaining to the care of the plants mentioned in this chapter under the tasks of each season.

JANUARY

Your greenhouse in January should be an unalloyed joy, for it truly offers a sanctuary from the wintry blast. Flowers coming in the dead of winter have more than their usual charm. It is a time to capitalize upon the work that you have done in the months past, but it is also a month of preparation for the future. One of the pleasures of January is that it is the time of the year when seed catalogues arrive. Look through them carefully not only for the newer varieties that have won All America Awards, but also for the time-tested and, in many cases, unusual plants that everyone does not grow. Above all else in your selection of seeds and plants, be careful to buy from reputable dealers and look askance at bargains. Be prepared to pay a fair price and, without a doubt, you will be happy with the ultimate result. It costs no more to provide heat and food for a good strain of plants than for an inferior one. The most costly purchase is the one which does not produce satisfaction.

Miscellaneous Greenhouse Duties for January

Since this is one of the months of the year when you will get the most enjoyment from your greenhouse, you will do well to augment your collection of flowering plants with selections from your local florist. He will doubtless have plants in full flower that you did not have time to start for yourself earlier. You will be pleased to see how long flowering plants will stay beautiful in a greenhouse.

This is the time of year to prune back such plants as Allamandas and Passion-flowers. Cut them back and repot them if necessary and start them into a new growth cycle.

From mid-January on start to bring in a succession of spring-flowering bulbs which you set in your cold frame last fall. Early Tulips, Hyacinths, Daffodils, Crocuses, Snowdrops, Squills, Chionodoxas, and Grape Hyacinths all force easily in a cool greenhouse. Let shoots of Hyacinths and Tulips become three to four inches tall in a dark place before bringing them into the light, or invert opaque paper cones over them to keep them in darkness until they make sufficient top growth. Hyacinths will blossom in three to four weeks and Tulips in four to six weeks if kept at 50 to 55 degrees at night.

Bring in Azaleas from cold frames at intervals so as to have a succession of bloom. It takes six to seven weeks at 60 to 65 degrees for Azaleas to blossom. Lower temperatures will serve them better, but it takes longer to get blossoms. When new growth starts, feed them every other week with a solution of one ounce of ammonium sulphate to two gallons of water.

Rose bushes, potted last fall, can be brought into the greenhouse from the cold frame now. They will blossom in the early spring.

Shift Calceolarias and Cinerarias to their final pots early this month. They will flower from February until April. Cinerarias must not be allowed to become pot-bound. Grow them in a cool greenhouse.

Poinsettias that have finished flowering should be cut back slightly and laid on their sides under a dry bench until late April or May, at which time they may be cut back severely, watered well, and grown on for the production of cuttings.

Gloxinia tubers started now and grown at 60-degree nights will be in full blossom in June and July.

All sorts of hardy Lilies can be brought in from the cold frame now. Regal Lilies will flower in March and April and Madonna Lilies in April and May.

Easter Lilies should be making good growth at this time of year. Beginning in the third week in January commercial growers feed their Easter Lilies every other week with a solution of one ounce of nitrate of soda to four gallons of water.

Iris should be kept moist, and the flats in which they are growing should not be moved from one place to another. Root breakage often results in blind buds.

Gladiolus in storage, if not previously treated, should be dusted with DDT to control thrips. Gladiolus planted in the greenhouse now will blossom in May.

Dahlia and Canna tubers in storage should be inspected for rot. Cut away decayed areas and dust the cuts with sulphur.

Now is the time to start Caladiums into growth. They need high temperatures to initiate growth, about 85 degrees, then should be grown at 75 degrees with a bit of protection from the hottest sun.

Fragrant Tuberoses for summer flowering should be planted now. It is also time to plant tubers of Gloriosa-lilies. They will flower late in the summer.

Root cuttings of Geraniums now. When roots are one-half inch long, pot into soil. Pinch out tops so that they will become bushy. They will begin to flower in May. This is also a good time to take cuttings of Fuchsias, Lantanas, and Carnations.

Sow seeds of perennials. Many will be large enough to blossom this summer. Delphiniums, especially, do well when planted at this time of year. They flower in midsummer on vigorous disease-free plants.

Do not neglect insect and disease control. Spray with an all-purpose spray every week or ten days, skipping plants that are in bloom.

Orchids, especially Cattleya hybrids, should be beautiful this month. Consult Chapter IX for specific instructions. Most Orchids should be repotted after flowering if they have overgrown the containers in which they have been growing.

Seeds to Sow in January (mostly for greenhouse flowering)

Plants	Time of Flowering
Baby's-breath, Annual	April
Begonia, fibrous-rooted	Continuous, starting May
Begonia, Tuberous-rooted	July until frost, outdoors
Candytuft, Hyacinth-flowered	May
Candytuft, Umbellata-type	May
Cherry, Jerusalem	Fruit in December
Chrysanthemum, Annual	May
Clarkia	April, May
Cornflower	May
Gloxinia	August, September
Impatiens	Continuous, starting May
Larkspur	June
Lily, White Queen	15 months after sowing
Marigold, African	May
Pansy	April, May, outdoors

Plants	Times of Flowering
Petunias (ruffled, fringed, double)	May until frost, outdoors
Salpiglossis	May
Snapdragon (single-stem)	Late May, June
Statice	May
Stock	May, June
Streptocarpus	August, September
Sweet Peas (spring-flowering)	April to June

Seeds to Sow in January (for planting out in gardens)

Since readers of this book will be living under varying climatic conditions, I refer you now to Chapter VII, Section 11, Bedding Plants, wherein is listed groups of plants according to the length of time it takes them to attain planting-out size. Use this guide in conjunction with your last frost date in determining when to plant various kinds of annuals.

FEBRUARY

In February your greenhouse should be overflowing with color, for all sorts of plants will have responded by this time of year to the additional sunshine of the coming spring. It is the time in most greenhouses to sow seeds of some of the slow-growing annuals for planting in the garden later. If you and your greenhouse are new to each other, it would be a good idea at this time to read once more the notes given last month. If you find that you have neglected to do certain jobs, this is the time to get them out of the way.

Miscellaneous Greenhouse Duties for February

Easter Lilies should show buds six weeks before Easter. If you find that your plants are ahead or behind schedule, adjust temperatures accordingly. Feed them every two weeks with a solution of nitrate of soda, one ounce to four gallons of water.

With the increase in sunshine plants will require more water each day. Easter Lilies, Cinerarias, Hydrangeas, and Cyclamens particularly need attention in this regard.

Along with the more robust plant growth of the season comes

an increase in insect activity also. Spray regularly and watch especially for aphids on plants recently brought into the greenhouse. Spread bait around the benches and under them to control slugs and snails, for they will raise havoc with young seedlings.

This is the time to start tubers of Gloxinias, Tuberous-rooted Begonias, Achimenes, and Caladiums into growth. Tuberoses started now will flower in June. Gloriosa-lilies will blossom in late summer.

You should bring in pots of spring-flowering bulbs from the cold frame so as to have a steady source of color in the greenhouse. Last month was too early to bring in Darwin Tulips, but from now on they will force easily.

Bring in hardy Lilies from the cold frame for late spring flowering. Although they are rarely grown commercially, they make unforgettable additions to the homelike surroundings in an amateur's greenhouse.

Perennials will force easily now. Delphiniums brought in now will be in full flower in early May. Polyantha Primroses are especially nice when brought in for early bloom. After the weather moderates, they can be planted in the garden again.

Roses of many kinds can be brought in from the cold frame now. Do not fail to grow some of the tiny Fairy Roses. They are exquisite miniatures and very lovely in a small greenhouse.

Watch the level of sunlight on your Orchids this month. It is time to give them a light shading. You will need to add additional shading as the hot weather approaches.

One of the nicest small plants for forcing in a home greenhouse is the sweet-scented *Daphne cneorum,* Rose Daphne. Have a few potted plants in your cold frame each fall and bring them into the greenhouse for a real breath of spring. The foliage is tiny and gray-green, and the blossom clusters are pink with much the same fragrance as that of wild Mayflowers.

Your cutting bed should be a busy place at this time of year. Plants of all descriptions root readily in the spring. Now is the time to take Carnation cuttings for benching in June. It is also not too late to make Geranium cuttings. The plants will not be large by May, but they will grow rapidly in your garden and be colorful all summer.

Do not sow seeds of bedding plants too soon. It is a mistake to start them so early that you have to check their growth waiting for the outdoor weather to become warm enough to plant them in the garden. Consult the guide under Bedding Plants, Section 11, Chapter VIII, to know when to plant the various species.

One of the most difficult of the slow-starting annuals to get to germinate in warm weather is Bells of Ireland, *Molucella laevis*. Many commercial growers sow their seeds in flats and set the flats in the cold frame for four to six weeks, or even over winter, then bring them into the greenhouse. Treated in this manner, they germinate fast and evenly.

Gladiolus bulbs may be planted among bench crops such as Snapdragons and will blossom in May and June.

Old Bouvardia plants which finished blossoming in the fall may be cut back now and repotted in very sandy soil. If kept moist, they will soon produce a fine crop of cuttings. Make the cuttings with a bit of the old stem attached, root them in sand, then pot them up and grow them in the greenhouse until warm weather. At that time put them outdoors for the summer and bring them into the greenhouse for flowering in the fall. All during their growing season pinch out the stem tips often to induce compact growth. Make no pinches after the end of August.

Seeds to Sow in February (mostly for greenhouse flowering)

Plants	*Time of Flowering*
Begonia, fibrous-rooted	Continuous, starting May
Begonia, Tuberous-rooted	July on, outdoors
Candytuft, Hyacinth-flowered	May, June
Candytuft, Umbellata-type	June
Cherry, Jerusalem	Fruit in December
Cyclamen	Small plants, 12 to 14 months
Kalanchoe	Large plants, January, February
Marigold, French	April
Primrose, Obconica type	December, January

Plants	*Times of Flowering*
Snapdragon (single-stem)	June
Stock	May, June
Sweet Peas (spring-flowering)	April to June
Thunbergia	All summer

MARCH

March is not the time for procrastination if you have a home greenhouse! This is one of the busiest times of the year, for seeds must be planted now so that plants will be ready for the outdoor gardening season soon to come. This is the season when greenhouses are bursting at the seams and plants all seem to come into flower at once. In order to make more room available for seedlings, it is a good idea to place high shelves close to the glass. They especially like the bright light this type of situation affords. During spring and fall when outdoor temperatures are cool even though the sun is bright, a home-greenhouse owner is particularly thankful if he has installed automatic ventilation. As the sun slides from behind a cloud, temperatures rise very fast, and ventilators must be opened and closed often to keep the inside temperatures favorable to plant growth.

Miscellaneous Greenhouse Duties for March

Sooner or later this month, depending upon where you live, it will be warm enough to place some of the hardier plants in protected, but unheated, cold frames. Such plants as garden varieties of Carnations, Snapdragons, and Stocks will stand considerable cold. Move them out of the greenhouse so that you will have more room for the tender species. As the season advances, you will be able to move more and more plants to the cold frame so that they can become somewhat acclimated to outside weather before going into the garden.

This is the month in which most gardeners plant the bulk of their flower and vegetable seeds. It must be remembered that the tiny plants are extremely delicate, and care should be taken that they never suffer from lack of water. At the same time they cannot stand being in soil which is constantly wet. Use discretion, bearing in mind that shallow pots and seed flats dry out rapidly. Try to arrange your watering schedule so that the plants go into the night with the surface of the soil and their leaves dry.

When young seedlings are transplanted from the seedbed to flats or pots, they need protection from the sun during the hottest part of the first few days until their roots have become re-established. A piece of newspaper laid over the plants affords a cheap and effective temporary shade.

It is important that plants which need protection from the sun be given a bit of shade from now on. Cyclamens, for example, as well as African Violets and Ferns need shading from now until autumn. Orchids should have extra shade provided to compensate for the increased light.

All plants in the greenhouse will use more water now, especially on sunny days. In order to keep up the humidity it is a good idea to wet the walks occasionally. Be sure that all foliage is dry before nightfall.

Many of the large tub plants can be repotted at this time of year. It is not always necessary to repot, however, for many times quite a bit of old soil can be scratched out of the pots and replaced with fresh soil to tide the plants over until another season.

Gardenias sometimes look yellowish at this time of year. If they are chlorotic, give them a drink of a solution made up of one ounce of iron sulphate dissolved in two gallons of water.

Cuttings root rapidly in the spring. Make some Chrysanthemum cuttings not only for the greenhouse, but also for garden planting. Hydrangea cuttings rooted now will blossom next spring.

It is not too late to start Tuberous-rooted Begonias, Caladiums, and Cannas. Tuberoses started now will blossom in July and Gloriosa-lilies will flower in the autumn.

Keep your spray schedule operating, for bugs multiply fast at this time of year.

March is an ideal time to increase your stock of prize Dahlias. Single tubers planted in light soil now will give a great many cuttings over the next month or two that can be rooted for garden planting. Such cuttings will flower well the first year.

Cut back old plants of *Buddleia asiatica* and *B. farquhari* after they have finished flowering. Repot if necessary and start them into a new growth cycle. Pinch them back occasionally so that their growth will be compact.

Seeds to Sow in March for Greenhouse Flowering

Plants	*Time for Flowering*
Baby's-breath, Annual	June
Bellflower, Italian (seeds or cuttings)	Late summer and fall
Candytuft, Hyacinth-flowered	June
Cherry, Jerusalem	Fruit in December
Freesia	October, November
Kalanchoe	January, February
Snapdragon	July, August

Now is surely the time to read carefully Section 11, Chapter VIII, entitled Bedding Plants. Note the various groups of plants and plan your own seeding schedule so that your young plants will be of the correct size when you want them for outdoor planting.

APRIL

Now it is that those home-greenhouse gardeners who have cold frames appreciate these outdoor structures more than ever, for not only do they take care of the overflow from the greenhouse, but they serve as early seedbeds for many garden plants. An average of a month can be gained in growing annuals simply by using a sash-covered, sun-heated cold frame.

Miscellaneous Greenhouse Duties for April

April sun is hot, and one must be careful to add additional shading to greenhouses to protect tender plants. Many plants other than shade-loving ones can stand a very light protection from now through the summer months. This may take the form of a shading compound applied to the glass or of Saran or muslin stretched inside the greenhouse.

April is a good time to buy in single tubers of new varieties of

Dahlias, for each tuber planted in a greenhouse will soon yield a fine group of cuttings which can be quickly rooted, thus increasing one's supply of plants manyfold. These rooted cuttings will produce fine flowering plants during the summer gardening season.

Young Carnation plants grown from cuttings rooted in February and March should now be in a cold frame, and they should be pinched back regularly to induce branching.

Runners of greenhouse Violets can be rooted this month and planted in benches in May and June for flowering next winter.

Caladiums started now will stay attractive much later in the fall than plants forced into growth earlier in the spring.

Hymenocallis (*Ismene*) and Tuberose bulbs planted now will blossom in August and September.

Make cuttings of *Buddleia asiatica* and *B. farquhari* now. They will blossom in January and February.

This is an excellent time to make cuttings of Chrysanthemums. Even though your greenhouse is small, take a bit of bench space and try a few of the large Mums. The smaller-flowered Pompons give more flowers per square foot of bench space than any other flowers.

Calanthes start new growth in late March or early April. Be sure that this tender growth is protected from the sun. Red-spider mites can be troublesome on Calanthes; so keep after them with a regular spray program.

Watering is one of the most important jobs in a greenhouse, and the art of doing the work properly spells the difference between ordinary and extraordinary greenhouse growers. Watch your plants carefully. You will find that some require much more water than others though they may be growing side by side. Strive to keep the soil in a mellow condition, neither wet nor dry, and remember that when a plant wilts, it suffers root damage that takes some time to mend. During this season when the sun is bright and the greenhouse is full of plants, it requires careful attention and good judgment to do a good job of watering.

Seeds to Sow in April for Greenhouse Flowering

Plants	Time of Flowering
Anemone	October to March
Baby's-breath, Annual	June
Aster	August, September
Celosia	Late summer, fall
Cineraria	February, March
Freesia	November, December
Kalanchoe	January, February
Pepper, Ornamental	Fruit in fall
Primrose, Fairy and Obconica	December to spring
Snapdragon (summer-flowering, single-stem)	July
Streptocarpus	Winter
Zinnia	May, June

MAY

In May the thoughts of most home gardeners turn to the out of doors and the host of flowers that fill their gardens at that season. Most of the flowering plants in greenhouses will have faded toward the end of May; so it is a good time to do some housecleaning. Set plants outdoors for the summer. Many of them, including such tub plants as Camellias, can go under the filtered shade of a tree to spend the summer. Other plants that enjoy some shade can be placed in a shaded cold frame. Such plants as Cyclamens, Azaleas, and Hydrangeas come in this category. You may easily make a lath shade for your cold frame, or use a piece of snow fencing. The moving pattern of light and shadow that this type of shade gives seems to serve plants very well.

Miscellaneous Greenhouse Duties for May

This is the month to bench your rooted cuttings of Chrysanthemums so that you will have flowers during the autumn season. Pompon Chrysanthemums give a tremendous return in flowers for the amount of bench space they occupy.

Next month it will be time to bench Carnations. Get the soil ready now so that you will not have that heavy job to do at the last minute. If you have not started your own Carnation cuttings, this is the time to find a florist friend who will sell you a few plants.

Watch the shading situation of your greenhouse carefully. Such plants as Ferns, Palms, Orchids, Caladiums, Tuberous-rooted Begonias, and Gloxinias all need protection from the sun.

Foliage plants of all kinds root and grow very rapidly during the warm days ahead. Give them shade and high humidity, and they will grow as luxuriantly as though they were back in the jungle.

Jerusalem Cherries may be planted out in the garden. Pinch them often until late June to induce branching. In late summer pot them up and bring them into your greenhouse. Their colorful berries will stay on the plants for months.

Bulbs of Tuberoses, Sprekelias, and Zephyr-lilies planted now will blossom in late summer.

Cuttings of Marguerites taken now will make nice flowering plants for next winter. Hydrangea cuttings will mature into fine plants for flowering next spring. Geranium cuttings taken now can be grown into large plants during the summer, and if all flower buds are removed, the plants will flower profusely in the greenhouse next winter.

This is the time to begin preparing your Poinsettias for next Christmas. Last year's plants can be brought out from under the bench, where you put them when they finished flowering during the winter. Cut them back hard; give the soil one good soaking; then keep it on the dry side until new growth starts. New buds will start quickly if you will syringe the tops of the plants several times a day. These plants may be left in the greenhouse for cutting production, or they may be planted in the garden for the same purpose. Cuttings may be taken from June until late summer.

Greenhouse Violets should be benched this month. Remember that they need a cool, shady greenhouse. Perhaps you can plant them in flats and keep the flats in a shaded cold frame during the summer rather than try to keep your greenhouse as cool as they would like it to be.

Seeds to Sow in May for Greenhouse Flowering

Plants	Time of Flowering
Anemone	October to April
Aster	September
Baby's-breath, Annual	July
Begonia, fibrous-rooted	Continuous, starting November
Cineraria	January, February
Forget-me-not	Winter
Freesia	January, February
Primrose, Fairy and Obconica	January to March
Snapdragon	August, September
Zinnia	June

JUNE

One of the nicest things about horticulture as a hobby is that there is a constant change within the over-all pattern. Plant life follows the circle of the year, unfolding new beauties with each passing season. When one has a greenhouse, there is no need to wait out the months when outdoor plants are dormant, for every season is a growing one under glass. In order to have flowers in the winter, however, it is necessary to make certain preparations many months ahead of time. Thus we find that June is a season in which to prepare for the following winter.

Miscellaneous Greenhouse Duties for June

If you want to have Carnations in your greenhouse next winter, this is the time to bench the plants. Try to choose a cloudy day and move them with as little shock to their root systems as possible.

Potted Chrysanthemums make attractive additions to a greenhouse and, of course, are fine to move into a house for decorative purposes when they are in flower. Some growers pot up three or four rooted cuttings in a pot and grow them together. Another fine idea, though, is to grow the individual plants in small pots, and when they have attained some size, transplant uniformly sized plants into larger pots. It is easy to get large, well-shaped plants in this way which will all flower at the same time.

If you will start this month to take cuttings from your Poinsettia stock plants, you will have plants of various sizes at Christmas time. Cuttings taken now will be tall, whereas later cuttings will develop into much shorter plants.

Cuttings of Stevia should be rooted early this month and planted in the open garden. Pinch them often to induce compact growth. They can be taken from the garden in late August or September and brought into the greenhouse for flowering.

Sow Pansies in your cold frame this month. They will make a fine growth during the summer and be ready to bench in the fall for winter flowering.

Divide Gerberia Daisies in June. They do well when grown in large deep pots.

Bougainvilleas should be through flowering by now. Cut them back hard and repot if necessary. New growth formed this summer will blossom next spring.

A shaded cold frame is an ideal place in which to keep many plants during the summer months, especially those that cannot stand much heat. Azaleas, Cinerarias, Calceolarias, Primroses, Cyclamens, and Hydrangeas do well in such a location.

Azaleas benefit by being fed every two weeks with ammonium sulphate at the rate of one ounce to two gallons of water. In order to keep the foliage a deep green, water them once a month with a solution of iron sulphate, one ounce to two gallons of water. It is a good idea to syringe Azalea foliage daily with a forceful spray of clear water.

In order to have shapely Genistas for next spring, prune the plants now so that they will develop a compact habit of growth.

Seeds to Sow in June for Greenhouse Flowering

Plants	*Time of Flowering*
Aster	November
Baby's-breath, Annual	August
Cineraria	January, February
Cyclamen	18 months after sowing
Forget-me-not	Winter

Plants	Time of Flowering
Freesia	February to April
Lupine	Early spring
Primrose, Fairy and Obconica	Late winter and spring
Snapdragon	September, October
Sweet Peas (winter-flowering)	September to December
Wallflower	January, February

JULY

The watchword for July is *water*. At this time of year the sun is hot, the air is dry, and the days are long. It is an easy matter to allow plants to dry out. Remember that whenever a plant wilts, it is a sure sign that its feeding roots have been damaged. Water your plants often and be sure to wet down greenhouse walks so as to increase the humidity. Syringing plants not only helps to maintain humidity, but also does much to control red-spider mites, which are especially troublesome during hot weather.

Miscellaneous Greenhouse Duties for July

Although this idea has no particular bearing on greenhouse management, you may be interested to know that this is a fine time of the year to propagate many kinds of woody plants, including evergreens. A closed case, kept warm and highly humid, will do a good job for you. In order to facilitate rooting, dip the ends of the cuttings in a rooting hormone.

July is the month in which commercial florists take most of their Poinsettia cuttings. Fresh cuttings must be misted often and shaded so that they will not wilt too much.

If you are growing Hydrangeas for next spring, do not pinch any stem tips out after the middle of July. From now on endeavor to foster the strongest kind of growth so that you will have large terminal buds, for they are the ones which will eventually produce flowers.

This is a good time to sow the seeds of Pansies. Those destined for flowering in the greenhouse should be brought indoors in the early fall. Plants for next spring should be left in the cold frame over winter.

Seeds to Sow in July for Greenhouse Flowering

Plants	Time of Flowering
Begonia, fibrous-rooted	December on
Browallia	Continuous, starting fall
Calceolaria	April, May
Calendula	November on
Cineraria	January, February
Forget-me-not	Winter
Kalanchoe	January, February
Lupine	Early spring
Mignonette	November
Nemesia	February
Primrose, Fairy and Obconica	February, March
Snapdragon	December, January
Stock, early varieties	Late December, January
Stock, late varieties	January, February
Sweet Peas (winter-flowering)	November to February
Wallflower	February

AUGUST

The tempo of activity in greenhouses must increase in August as preparations are made for the winter season ahead. You will notice that this month's list of seeds to be sown has many more varieties on it than last month's list. Certain of the early bulbs are now available and should be planted soon. The latter part of this month brings cooler nights, and you will see that cool-loving plants such as Cyclamens, Cinerarias, and Calceolarias begin to look more robust. An important point to remember about greenhouse management in early fall is this: When temperatures fall and greenhouses begin to feel cold and damp, it is time to turn on the heat even if only long enough to lower the humidity. Cool, damp conditions foster the spread of leaf diseases that can plague plants all winter long.

Miscellaneous Greenhouse Duties for August

Repot Cyclamens into their final-sized pots this month, and

when you do so, be sure that the top half of each tuber is above the soil level. Feed them every two weeks with a mild complete fertilizer and see that they are spaced far enough apart so that there is a good circulation of air around them.

Give your Poinsettias full sun and feed them biweekly with a complete fertilizer. Healthy dark-green foliage is a sign that they are doing well and will have large flowers in December.

The middle of August is the latest date to pinch back Stevias, Carnations, and Chrysanthemums. Let Stevias stay outdoors until nights become cool so that their growth will become hard; then bring them into a bright location in your greenhouse. Carnations should be nice bushy plants by this time of year and should begin to flower in October. Feed Chrysanthemums every two weeks until the buds show color.

Repot Martha Washington Geraniums, cutting the plants back if necessary. They will make a thrifty growth with the return of cool weather.

Azaleas in cold frames should have the shades removed now. Give them full sun and syringe them often, especially in hot weather. This will not only help plant growth, but will help to discourage red-spider mites.

Plant Freesia bulbs now to flower in December. Oxalis planted now will flower all winter and spring. Lachenalias should be potted up now and kept in a protected cold frame until November. Bring them into the greenhouse then and they will flower between late December and early February. Nerines started now will flower sometime during the period from September to December. Montbretias planted now will flower in early spring.

Pansies for outdoor flowering next spring can be planted now and kept over winter in a cold frame.

Seeds to Sow in August for Greenhouse Flowering

Plants	*Time of Flowering*
Begonia, fibrous-rooted	Continuous, starting January
Blue Lace Flower	February to April

Plants	Time of Flowering
Browallia	Continuous, starting fall
Calceolaria	May
Calendula	December to March
Cineraria	February, March
Forget-me-not	November on
Lupine	February, March
Marigold (winter-flowering)	November to January
Mignonette	December
Nasturtium	Winter and spring
Nemesia	February
Pansy (winter-flowering)	February through spring
Primrose, Fairy and Obconica	February, March
Schizanthus	March
Snapdragon (single-stem)	December
Snapdragon (pinched)	February to April
Statice	January, February
Stock	January, February
Sweet Peas (winter-flowering)	November to March
Thunbergia	Winter and spring
Wallflower	March

SEPTEMBER

The cool nights, bright days, and occasional gentle rains of September make the season seem like a second springtime to gardeners. To those who have their own greenhouse it is truly the beginning of another gardening year, a season when exotic flowers from far-off lands bring spring and summer back again despite the outdoor weather.

The autumn season is one in which automatic ventilation is a great labor saver, for though the days may be cold, the sun still is powerful enough to make closed greenhouses much too hot for healthy plant growth. If you do not have automatic ventilation, be sure to open the ventilators by hand. Too much ventilation is far preferable to not enough.

Miscellaneous Greenhouse Duties for September

All of a sudden your greenhouse will be filled to overflowing as you bring in tender plants of all kinds this month. Now is the time to be ruthless and discard all those which do not measure up to good health standards. Do not run a plant hospital all winter!

Early fall is the time to pot up perennials if you intend to force them this winter. Get them well established in pots in your cold frame during the next month or so.

Certain bulbous plants need to rest during part or all of the winter. They should be gradually dried off as their foliage matures or their flowers fade. Achimenes, Amaryllis, Tuberous-rooted Begonias, Caladiums, Gloriosa-lilies, and Gloxinias should be treated in this way.

Any flowers that need disbudding, such as Mums or Carnations, should have the job done as soon as the side buds are large enough to be removed easily. See that growing plants of this sort have proper support as they increase in size so that they will not lodge against one another.

A few plants of Chives and Parsley should be potted from the garden now to provide winter garnishes.

This is the season when you must bring under cover any soil that you plan to use in the greenhouse during the winter. It is embarrassing to try to dig it after the ground freezes.

Be sure to bring in Jerusalem Cherries and Ornamental Peppers before the first cold spell.

Space out your Cyclamens. They must have a free circulation of air about them to do their best. Most commercial growers set each pot of Cyclamens upon an inverted pot so that the plants will be high enough to be certain of having a good movement of air around them.

Genistas brought into a cool greenhouse now will flower in February.

Greenhouses may well need heat during some September nights not only to provide warmth, but also to lower excessive humidity that is so conducive to the spread of many diseases.

Start off your autumn season with a regular spray program so as to keep insects and diseases to a minimum.

Seeds to Sow in September for Greenhouse Flowering

Plants	Time of Flowering
Calceolaria	April
Calendula	December to February
Cineraria	February, March
Clarkia	Early spring
Chinese Forget-me-not	March, April
Godetia	Late winter, spring
Larkspur	February, March
Lupine	April
Mignonette	January
Primrose, Fairy and Obconica	February, March
Salpiglossis	April
Schizanthus	March
Snapdragon (single-stem)	March
Snapdragon (pinched)	Late March to May
Stock	March
Sweet Peas (winter-flowering)	December to March
Wallflower	April, May

Bulbs to Plant in September for Greenhouse Flowering

Bulbs	Time of Flowering
Alstroemeria	March to May
Anemone	January to March
Brodiaea	March, April
Calla-lily	Continuous, starting January
Calla-lily, Black	February
Calochortus	February, March
Freesia	January, February
Hyacinth (precooled)	December
Iris, Wedgwood (precooled)	December
Ixia	February, March
Leucocoryne	February, March
Montbretia	Early spring

Plants	*Time of Flowering*
Narcissus (precooled)	December
Narcissus (hardy types to cold frame)	Winter forcing
Narcissus, Paper-white and Soleil d'Or	4 to 6 weeks
Ornithogalum	Winter forcing
Oxalis	Fall, winter, and spring
Ranunculus	January to March
St. Bernard's-lily	March, April
Sparaxis	February, March

OCTOBER

All cool-loving plants make good growth in October, for the hot days and nights of summer are definitely over. Cyclamens will begin to flower this month, and, if they are kept cool, will continue to have blossoms until March or April.

Be careful of watering this month and next. Try not to splash water on the foliage. See that your greenhouses are warm enough so that moisture does not condense on the leaves. It is false economy to withhold heat now, for unless dampness is eliminated, your plants may develop leaf diseases.

Miscellaneous Greenhouse Duties for October

Toward the latter part of October there are apt to be dull cloudy days; for that reason shading compounds on greenhouse roofs must be removed. Do the job gradually so that the plants can become adjusted to the increased light.

This would be a good time to read over Section 3, Chapter VIII, pertaining to bulbs, for October is the month in which hardy bulbs should be potted and placed in a cold frame to develop roots before winter forcing. In addition to such large hardy bulbs as Narcissus, Hyacinths, and Tulips you will find that Crocuses, Chionodoxas, Squills, Snowdrops, and Grape Hyacinths force very easily and give you a greater variety of plants than most commercial florists try to grow.

It is not too late to pot up some perennials for winter forcing. Why not include some hardy Lilies among them? You will find that they are especially satisfactory. Set all the plants in the cold frame until after the first of the new year.

If you want to be sure that your Christmas Cactus blossoms this year, see that it is kept cool this month. Temperatures close to 50 degrees will enable it to initiate flower buds.

Garden Chrysanthemums that are in danger of being nipped by frost can be lifted and brought into the greenhouse for flowering, then placed in a cold frame for protection over winter.

Among the plants to put in the cold frame now should surely be one or two Rose Daphnes (*Daphne cneorum*). Bring them into the cool greenhouse after the first of the year.

Genistas kept in a cool greenhouse will flower in March and April.

Seeds to Sow in October for Greenhouse Flowering

Plants	*Time of Flowering*
Ageratum (tall-growing)	Early spring
Blue Lace Flower	March, April
Calceolaria	May
Calendula	April, May
Candytuft, Hyacinth-flowered	February
Chrysanthemum, Annual	April to June
Cineraria	March, April
Cyclamen	14 to 15 months
Feverfew	May
Larkspur	April
Mignonette	February
Schizanthus	May
Snapdragon	April, May
Statice	February to May
Stock	April, May
Sweet Peas (winter-flowering)	February to May
Sweet Peas (spring-flowering)	April to June

Bulbs to Plant in October for Greenhouse Flowering

Bulbs	Time of Flowering
Amaryllis	January, February
Anemone	January to March
Chionodoxa	Winter forcing
Crocus	Winter forcing
Freesia	February, March
Gladiolus (Baby Glads)	February, March
Grape Hyacinth	Winter forcing
Hyacinth	Winter forcing
Iris, Wedgwood (precooled)	January, February
Leucocoryne	March
Lily, Easter (not prepared)	April
Lily, hardy types	Winter forcing
Montbretia	Early spring
Narcissus (hardy types)	Winter forcing
Narcissus, Paper-white and Soleil d'Or	4 to 6 weeks
Ranunculus	February to April
Snowdrop	Winter forcing
Squill	Winter forcing
Tulip	Winter forcing
Veltheimia	Early spring

NOVEMBER

Greenhouse work slows down in November, and a home gardener begins to reap the rewards of his past diligence. Outside gardening in northern areas comes to a standstill at this time of year, and a greenhouse really comes into its own.

There is usually more cloudy weather in November than during any other month. Be careful to keep plants on the dry side and the relative humidity low. Most plants can do very well without feeding from now until January, for growth forced under poor light conditions tends to be too succulent for good flower production.

Miscellaneous Greenhouse Duties for November

The last of the greenhouse shade should come off during November. Even shade-loving plants need little or no protection from the sun during the next two months.

Cold frames should be closed with the arrival of cold weather. Mulch them with straw, salt hay, or excelsior. Sash should be opened on warm days so that plants will not make premature growth.

Make leaf cuttings of Christmas Begonias now for next year.

Cinerarias must not be allowed to become pot-bound. Move them to larger pots as they increase in size.

Bring Lachenalias in from the cold frame early this month. They will blossom irregularly from December to February.

Precooled Hyacinths and Narcissus brought in from cold frames this month will flower in December. Keep Hyacinths in a dark place until the growth is three to four inches tall.

Poinsettias should be kept somewhat on the dry side from now until Christmas so as to harden their growth. A last feeding early this month should carry them through to the blossoming season. Be sure to stake any tall Poinsettias, for as the heavy flower bracts develop, the stems will bend over unless they are given support.

Seeds to Sow in November for Greenhouse Flowering

Plants	Time of Flowering
Begonia, fibrous-rooted	Continuous, starting April
Candytuft, Hyacinth-flowered	March
Candytuft, Umbellata-type	March
Cornflower	Early spring
Cyclamen	14 to 15 months
Feverfew	May, June
Larkspur	April, May
Lupine	April, May
Mignonette	March
Snapdragon	April to June
Stock	April, May
Sweet Peas (spring-flowering)	April to June

Bulbs to Plant in November for Greenhouse Flowering

Bulbs	Time of Flowering
Amaryllis	February, March
Freesia	March
Gladiolus (Baby Glads)	March
Hyacinth	Winter forcing
Iris	March, April
Lily, Easter (not prepared)	April, May
Lily (hardy types)	Winter forcing
Lily-of-the-valley	3 to 4 weeks
Narcissus (hardy types)	Winter forcing
Narcissus, Paper-white and Soleil d'Or	4 to 6 weeks
Tulip	Winter forcing

DECEMBER

When the weather is inclement out of doors, a warm greenhouse full of flowering plants takes on the aspect of a sanctuary. This seems to be especially true during the Christmas season. Your holiday guests will all want to peek into the greenhouse. If you have a few Orchids in blossom, the setting will be idyllic. They are easy to grow, and, no doubt, you will be so pleased with your first flowers that you will send for more Orchid catalogues.

Miscellaneous Greenhouse Duties for December

Late in December you will be able to cut the first branches of flowering plants for forcing. Pussy Willow, Japanese Quince, Cherry, Spirea, Forsythia, and Flowering Almond all force easily. Cut them on a mild day and set them in deep water in a warm greenhouse. Cover them with plastic or wet burlap to keep them from drying out until the buds are well formed.

Keep Cacti and other succulent plants very dry at this time of year and give them as much light as possible.

Take leaf cuttings of Christmas Begonias if you did not do so last month. They will flower in twelve months.

During all the year, but particularly when days are cloudy and dull, it is important not to have your plants crowded together. Space them out and restrict the number of plants you grow if necessary, for plants that must compete with each other for light will never look their best.

Seeds to Sow in December for Greenhouse Flowering

Plants	Time of Flowering
Baby's-breath, Annual	March
Begonia, fibrous-rooted	Continuous, starting May
Begonia, Tuberous-rooted	May until frost, outdoors
Calendula	April, May
Candytuft, Hyacinth-flowered	May, June
Candytuft, Umbellata-type	May, June
Chrysanthemum, Annual	May to July
Cornflower	Early spring
Feverfew	May, June
Godetia	March, April
Larkspur	May
Lupine	May
Nemesia	May, June
Petunias (ruffled, fringed, double)	May until frost, outdoors
Salpiglossis	May, June
Scabiosa	June
Stock	May
Sweet Peas (winter-flowering)	April, May
Sweet Peas (spring-flowering)	May, June

SUGGESTED REFERENCE LIST

Bailey, L. H., *The Standard Cyclopedia of Horticulture,* 3 vol., The Macmillan Company, New York.

Graf, Alfred B., *Exotica 2,* Roehrs Company, Rutherford, New Jersey.

Laurie, Alex, and D. C. Kiplinger, *Commercial Flower Forcing,* The Blakiston Company, Philadelphia.

New Illustrated Encyclopedia of Gardening, edited by T. H. Everett, Greystone Press, New York.

Post, Kenneth, *Florist Crop Production and Marketing,* Orange Judd Publishing Company, Inc., New York.

Taylor's Encyclopedia of Gardening, edited by Norman Taylor, Houghton Mifflin Company, Boston.

SOURCE LISTS FOR UNUSUAL PLANTS

Graf, Alfred B., *Exotica 2,* Roehrs Company, Rutherford, New Jersey.

Plant Buyers Guide, Sixth Edition and Supplements, Massachusetts Horticultural Society, Boston.

PERIODICALS

African Violet Magazine, Box 1326, Knoxville, Tennessee (Gesneriads, particularly African Violets)

American Orchid Society Bulletin, Botanical Museum of Harvard University, Cambridge 38, Massachusetts.

The Begonian, 6525 West Eighty-ninth Street, Los Angeles 45, California.

The Bromeliad Society Bulletin, 752 Twenty-sixth Street, Santa Monica, California.

Cactus and Succulent Journal, 134 West Union Street, Pasadena, California.

Camellias, The American Camellia Society, P. O. Box 2398, University Station, Gainesville, Florida.

The Gloxinian, American Gloxinia Society, Inc., 26 Eve Lane, Levittown, Long Island, New York. (All types of Gesneriads.)

National Chrysanthemum Society Bulletin, 65 Elizabeth Street, Keyport, New Jersey.

INDEX